THE AESTHETIC CODE OF
DON RAMÓN DEL VALLE-INCLÁN

by

Gerard Flynn

74851

FIRST EDITION

Copyright 1994, by Gerard Flynn
Library of Congress Catalog Card No: 94-90113
ISBN: 1-56002-445-3

UNIVERSITY EDITIONS, Inc.
59 Oak Lane, Spring Valley
Huntington, West Virginia 25704

Cover by Bob Burchett

ACKNOWLEDGEMENTS

Excerpts from my book, *Luis Coloma* (Copyright, 1987 by G.K. Hall & Co.) are reprinted with permission of Twayne Publishers, an imprint of Macmillan Publishing Company. I am grateful for this generosity.

My article "Sor Juana Inés de la Cruz: Las Trampas de la Crítica" is reprinted in its entirety with permission of Luis Cortest, who is the copyright holder of *Sor Juana Inés de la Cruz: Selected Studies* (Asunción: *Cedes*, 1989). I want to thank Professor Cortest for his kindness.

Gerard Flynn
University of Wisconsin-Milwaukee

This book is dedicated to the memory
Of
Professor Otis H. Green
And
Professor William L. Fichter,
who were very kind

TABLE OF CONTENTS

"This is the night when the veil between the two worlds thins . . ."

Said of Halloween in Irish
Celtic Mythology

PROLOGUE

The present study will differ from other works of literary criticism in several respects. It will read not so much like a monograph as a series of essays, some of them longer some of them brief, composed in my mind over the years but written down in a few comparatively short periods. Perhaps, *toute proportion gardée*, I can compare them to the *pensées* of Blaise Pascal, thoughts written on a slip of paper and placed in the end table over night.

In the present tome I have set forth some finished ideas but also offer some that are inchoate. I have a hunch the latter are right. One cannot do this when writing an article for *BHS* or *HR*, but in the freedom of my *pensées*, why not? My hope is that my hunches (I am fond of calling them intuitions) will serve as a dissertation for future students, whom I shall not see but can nevertheless look upon as mine. The present volume, then, is a source book for students as well as a finished criticism.

Many years ago I was impressed by a chapter in E.C. Riley's study of Cervantes, where he introduces Horace's idea of poetry, the *dulce et utile*. This Horatian insight became the *deleitar enseñando* of the Golden Age of Spain, with emphasis on the joy induced by literature. One can thus account for Cervantes's exemplary novel; in *La gitanilla*, for example, the reader should enjoy Preciosa's history above all for its wonderful tale, but later, by an interior illumination, his soul will profit amidst the joy. Preciosa: What a fine example of love! I hope that my essays, my *pensées*, will be a bit like that.

In modern times Desmond MacCarthy has said this better than anyone:

> The first step to culture is to learn to enjoy, not to know what is best.[1]

Perhaps, dear reader, you will not know what is best, but I hope you have an enjoyable experience.

There will be a great deal of repetition in this volume, which may enhance the study because repetition, a constant musical beat, over and over again, is Valle's own method. I can only hope my recital is as effective, or delightful, as his.

Another reason for this book's style of thoughts-essays-repetition, is the question of time. Were I able, I do not have enough time to write another *Erasme et l'Espagne* or *Lengua poética de Góngora*[2], so I shall settle for a catena of *pensées*, attempts. Again, I hope they will be found delightful and a source of illumination.

Post Script: Unamuno once said that every prologue is really an epilogue. You write a novel or history and after it's over you write the Prologue! The sequence is logical although the chronology of *pro* and *epi* is confused. And so it is with *The Aesthetic Code of Don Ramón María del Valle-Inclán*. As I was writing parts of the book over the years, I also wrote three or four proems, then, finally, the last chapter, and only after that the prologue. So here, dear reader, you have it, *pensées*, proems, essays, prologue, though not in that order. I hope you enjoy them.

Gerard Flynn
February 7, 1993

PROEM I

The Gnostic and the <u>Garbancero</u>

In 1956 I began teaching at Rutgers University and in an intermediate class had to prepare the *Sonatas* of Ramón del Valle-Inclán. I spent several hours a week on them, and over the next few years read them carefully, slowly, some eleven times, such was their profundity. I never took the *Sonatas* other than seriously although one instructor used the Niña Chole episode to hold his students' attention by scandalizing them, and one European Hispanist advised me in a letter that you can't always take Valle seriously. I didn't agree with this alleged levity then and I don't agree with it now; in any case I began sending my written thoughts to *Hispanic Review*, which published two or three of my articles. I received warm encouragement from Professor Otis Green of that journal and through him from Professor William Fichter of Brown. They seemed to think I had caught on to something and urged me to continue my Valle studies.

If I had glimpsed a literary truth it was a very simple one, so simple I can state it in nine words, or in seventeen if I choose to explicate one philosophical word. And this leads me to an observation concerning metaphysics: In our flesh and blood world complication and intricacy seem to bring a higher dignity, as in an advanced computer, which commands more respect than an abacus or finger count, or a modern racing machine, which draws more attention than a bike. But in metaphysics the opposite truth obtains. The more simple being holds a higher state, until one arrives at the Uncaused Cause or Abentofail's Agent, which is Pure Act. Even the Bible suggests Absolute Simplicity, calling the author of creation, the Almighty, *I AM*, with no predicate whatsoever.

And so perhaps, if simplicity be considered not a loss but a gain, there may be some hope for the literary truth that Professors Green and Fichter thought I had descried. I hope so, for I have always been of the opinion that Valle-Inclán holds the central position in the Generation of 1898 and in Modern Spanish literature; indeed, I see him as the key to Spanish literature from Moratín's day to the present. To my way of thinking, he also holds the key to other literatures as well. I repeat: Valle's key is very simple.

After 1963 I stopped intensive work on Valle-Inclán, for reasons I shall leave in the inkwell, and started studying authors who were his opposite, namely, Fernán Caballero, Manuel Tamayo y Baus, Benito Pérez Galdós, Padre Luis Coloma and Pío Baroja, although, Tamayo excepted, they were not quite as much the opposite as Valle himself would have imagined. One of these

7

authors is the giant, Galdós, whom Valle or at least his creation, Max Estrella, called Don Benito El Garbancero, correctly I think, given that author's metaphysical preference. Consequently I have given this book about the one-armed, goat-bearded, caftan-wearing, abracadabra vatical poet from Priscilianus's Galicia, the subtitle of *The Gnostic and the Garbancero*, for that's what the book is about, aesthetic gnosis and Spain, the incorrigible land of chickpeas.

Written during the 1980's
Gerard Flynn

PROEM II

The Code of Don Ramón del Valle-Inclán

Several years ago at a language conference I attended a session on Valle-Inclán. One of the speakers made an extraordinary statement; she said there was a code in Valle's literature, and when I asked her what that code might be she said she didn't know but she was convinced there was a code. She did not elaborate. It had never occurred to me to call it a code[1], but surely that's what it is, in Webster's definition:

> . . . a system of symbols (as letters, numbers or words) used to represent assigned and often secret meanings.

Valle's letters, numbers and words are used to represent assigned meanings, and those meanings are indeed secret; and (according to Valle) not by chance or the whim of Valle but by the *nature of things*, or if you will, by Ontology. The artist is the priest who penetrates the mystery of being, wherein lies the Truth, and so his art becomes a clandestine epistemology. A gnosis. ¡Abracadabra!

One of the beauties of deciphering the code lies in the light it throws on so many other events[2] of nineteenth century art: the blue flower of Novalis and Romanticism, the *garbanceroísmo* of Galdós and Realism, the *intrahistoria* of Unamuno, Azorín's ideal horizon (*lejanía ideal*: ¿Adónde irá ese caminito?[3]), Darío's *azul* and Symbolism, Baroja's rhetoric in *tono menor*, and the extreme formalism of a twentieth century critic like Pedro Salinas. For these reasons I should place Valle-Inclán at the center of modern Spanish literature. This is my bias.

I should like here to make an observation not usually found in literary criticism. When I was younger (1956-1960) I found that Valle's literature made a profound sexual impression on me even though it contains none of those anatomical descriptions and bedroom exercises associated with provocative poems and novels. I believe this sexuality is significant because it is an integral part of the code and is designed to be that way. Valle would, so to speak, ally sex with the blue flower. A most memorable example of this erotism is found in the *Sonata de estío*, not so much in the extravagant Niña Chole,[4] who is meant to shock a traditional Castilla, as in Nature's being a *gran fiera fecundada*, a panting pregnant panther. Nature is pointing to something, or to somewhere, which is also suggested in the novel's subtitle, *Tierra Caliente*.

I speak of Nature, as Valle does, and here the reader might

9

turn to the Greeks for guidance. Owing to a rampant idealism, twentieth century critics have gotten away from Nature and its forms, away from metaphysics, and away from a reverence for the universals. They like to engage in critical trends, such as reader's response[5], which shows little respect for invariable truth; but in studying Valle at least, I believe we must return to form, I should say to the *fondo y forma* of the nineteenth century that created him. Let me simply say at this stage of my thesis that Valle's code is a search for form, or better said, Form.

There are forms, agents of activity everywhere, expressing themselves in various ways, and I should define Nature as the sum of all the forms. Nature is constantly pointing, and, according to Valle, only the artist can descry her direction. But what is she pointing to? The hope of my essay is to answer this question.[6]

PROEM III

Thoughts Concerning the Literary Code of
Don Ramón del Valle-Inclán

Professor Mary Flynn Fleming
Mount Senario College
Ladsysmith, Wisconsin

Dear Mary,

These thoughts are for you, who have taught Spanish faithfully for so many years. I only hope their quality comes to a fraction of the love I write them with, for then they shall be a very fine collection indeed.

If the word thoughts *reminds you of Pascal's* pensées, *you should know that the similarity is deliberate. He was writing an apology of his religion and so he had to pull out all the stops, resorting now to his scientific and quasi-scientific proofs (*géométrie*), and now to poetry and intuition (*finesse*). Although he was capable of poking fun, as he did in his* Provincial Letters, *you will find none of that spirit in his* thoughts, *where his manner is always serious. Pascal's thoughts are really an essay, an attempt to combine belief, science and poetry into a compelling argument, a cynosure that will attract his libertine friends to God, and yet he excoriates the typical essayist, Montaigne. The latter too attempted to express his ideas, but for Pascal he was too vague, too vacillating and wanting in the certitude of belief. Perhaps we can call Pascal's thoughts an essay unique in its kind.*

In the present volume I hope to follow Pascal's example. Unlike him, I have not discovered a basic law of Physics, nor am I Master of my nation's prose, but I do have a vision of sorts. I want to finesse a little, and to prove a little, so that my readers, my libertines, will move into my magnetic field and receive it. I am not the peer of Pascal, and Valle-Inclán is hardly the Supreme Being, although he is a high literary priest of sorts, a strange sage, a prophet, a keeper of the seals, a bearer of the Word. What is that Word? If I can find out, my revelation will account for Valle's caftan and ring, the abracadabra, and the religious respect he is often held in, for example, in Gómez de la Serna's musical biography; which is not so much a biography as a cantata and sonata.[1]

I believe that Valle-Inclán holds the central position in modern Spanish literature, and I want to share this belief with you, my libertine. If you understand the sonatas *and* esperpentos *you will understand the literary role of Unamuno, Baroja, Azorín, Galdós and others, and trans-Pyrenean authors also, for example,*

11

the Symbolists. But lest I be culpable of a rhetoric of assertion, let the thoughts begin.

> *Love,*
> *Dad*
> *December 26, 1984*

P.S. I am looking for certitude and the reader's ultimate conversion.

CANTO I

Pensées

1. Unlike Pascal, I have entered old age and have not left my thoughts scratched on slips of paper, to be ordered by those who might find them. I myself am the orderer. Similarly, Valle-Inclán ordered his works, giving *La lámpara maravillosa* a special position. Defying chronology, he ranked it in first place, whereas it appeared in 1916, and with it he might have ranked *Claves líricas*, Chapter Six of the Third Estancia of *Flor de santidad*, and the prologue to *Visión estelar de un momento de guerra*, which is called *Breve noticia*. All of Valle's works are stellar visions, millenary histories, lyrical keys and prodigious lamps pointing to something, or revealing something. That something is the subject of these *pensées*.

2. Just as logic and poetry do not always coincide, so Valle's works do not coincide with conventional criticism. This distinction may be summed up in his favorite word, *abracadabra*, ¡Abracadabra! The sonatas are not unlike glossolalia. They can, however, be deciphered.

Remember what Philip Carey said to the poet Cronshaw in *Of Human Bondage*, and what Cronshaw said in reply. Philip, who was always seeking a meaning in life, asked what that meaning might be, and Cronshaw said it would do no good to tell him, he had to find out for himself, otherwise he wouldn't understand. At last, Cronshaw, pointing to a Persian rug, said that it holds the meaning of life, there, you must decipher the rug. At novel's end, after many tribulations, Philip decides the rug is undecipherable. Life has no discernible meaning.

But Valle's oriental rug can be deciphered, or if you will, decoded. After all, he has left the marvelous lamp.

3. Professor Otis Green once wrote that scholars should exercise "textual control of the imagination." Textual control is proof, Pascal's *esprit de géométrie*, and imagination is intuition, his *esprit de finesse*. Thus literary criticism is not exactly scientific proof on the one hand nor poetical intuition on the other, but a union of the two, a peculiar hybrid; which like all hybrids may be beautiful and luscious and at the same time sterile. But it need not be sterile. My heart tells me that Valle-Inclán would scorn such distinctions, and scorn literary criticism itself, by transforming it into a series of gargoyles, a new poetry called *esperpentos*. Were he to criticize the books of criticism as Cervantes did the books of chivalry, he would simply create a tyrannical criticaster (*Tirano Criticón*) drooling amidst his golden coin, with a facial tic, reciting platitudes. Valle might accept the finesse of criticism, because finesse is poetry, but never the *géométrie*, which demands discursive reasoning. We said before

that Valle's works are stellar visions revealing something; well, such a revelation is never scientific. It demands belief. (Read *La lámpara maravillosa*).

4. Valle's grotesques bring to mind Quevedo and Baudelaire. One must study the Quevedo of spittle and ordure, Don Pablos, to understand Valle, and one must also study the significantly comic and absolutely comic of the French poet's essay on laughter. Although Valle's esperpentos, *El ruedo ibérico, Tirano Banderas* and others are significantly comic, and no ordinary writer of comedies can match their profound meaning, this significance in a way is a fringe benefit, one of the perks as they call them nowadays; for the true art is in the grotesque, the absolutely comic, the poetic delight of aesthetic deformation, the gnostic know-how, the creation of something that never existed before. "That never existed before": The orthodox would say the creation as if out of nothing, whereas the heterodox would drop the *as if* and say the creation of something out of nothing. This truth accounts for the modern Spanish dichotomy, the spiritual civil war with the authors of 1898 at the center.

5. In spite of his many harsh critics, Menéndez Pelayo was right to call his book *Los heterodoxos*. Young and impetuous, he was accused of intolerance, especially of the *krausistas*, but a man of his genius, who knew Greek, Latin and European literature, could see the entire structure and the cracks in the wall:

> Miré los muros de la patria mia,
> si un tiempo fuertes, ya desmoronados[1]
> I looked at the walls of my fatherland,
> if formerly strong, now crumbling.

And Valle could see the crumbling structure too, not with don Marcelino's orthodox erudition and proofs but through the poet's finesse. And he chose to be heterodox, indeed, to be a heresiarch. That is the meaning of the cabala, the numerology, the caftan, the turban, the ring, *ceceo*, the pose, the *poética manquedad*, the abracadabra and total scorn. The Arch-Poet, Arch-Priest don Ramón del Valle-Inclán y Montenegro, the strange Galician for whom the path was opened by that other strange Galician, Priscilianus.

6. These thoughts do not divagate. If they seem to wander, they are only destined to go here and there in order to throw some light on the poetic creation and gnosis of Valle-Inclán, the central figure of modern Spanish literature. . . . But, you will say, that is an arbitrary statement. *You* say he is central: It's a question of apples, oranges, pears and plums. *You* are merely saying that apples are the best; you exercise your rhetoric of assertion and then say that your assertion proves what is to be

14

proved, that Valle is central . . . To which I reply: "No, not at all, Apples are better for some things, apple pie for example, and oranges are better for others, an orange drink. I am not arguing that Valle is the greatest of modern poets (although I do believe he is); I am saying that he above all others will lead us to an understanding of modern Spanish literature: for example, if you understand him, you will understand the *garbancero* Galdós, although the converse proposition will not hold." (I am not derogating Galdós, who was more than a *garbancero*. But he was that too.)

7. The reader of William Fichter's collection of Valle's early writings will learn that Valle had great admiration for Galdós, but even so in *Luces de Bohemia* Galdós is called Don Benito el Garbancero, the chickpea man. *Garbancero* is a true *clave lírica*.

8. The late Dr. Félix Martí-Ibáñez once wrote me to say he had a beautiful edition of the *Sonatas*, in leather covers, vellum and silk tassel, bound as if they were prayer books. I find this religious edition of Valle's musical sacrileges to be fascinating. And strange. In the *Sonata de Primavera* the Marqués de Bradomín, "tweaking his moustache," makes fun of virtues associated with the Virgin Mary; in *Estío*, the Niña Chole performs an extremely indecent action before a statue of the Child Jesus; in *Otoño*, a would-be Mary Magdalene is mocked and made to sin on her death bed; and in *Invierno* Bradomín scornfully and incestuously scandalizes his own daughter. And yet these scenes, these parables, these *exempla* are bound as if they were a Missal or breviary. How does one account for this incongruity? What would Pedro Salinas say of such an edition, he with his extreme formalism?[2] What would Dámaso Alonso say, who in his book on San Juan held all art to be religious? How does the reader himself account for this attitude? These questions are profound and not to be glided over, as some critics would have it. They must be addressed, and answered. No matter what the answer, one thing is certain: No one but an ostrich, a Tertullian perhaps, will deny the great artistry of Don Ramón María del Valle-Inclán.

9. Valle-Inclán is one of those authors who becomes part of one's own biography, not that everyone will select the same authors. Raymond Lull is like that, Pascal, Montaigne certainly, Voltaire, the cynics, perhaps an H.H. Munro, or a Kierkegaard. Not that the relationship is always amicable. I myself first came to Valle-Inclán in my late twenties, midst the springtime and summer of my life, *primavera-estío* you might say, and I found his literature to be extremely erotic. Purposely, I thought. This is a fact requiring no proof: I assent to it with the same certitude I have when I say a boulder is heavy or a frozen lake cold. I sometimes wonder if it is valid to divide the critics into male and female. Do male readers share my experience? I don't see how

not. Do female readers share it? I don't know and I am not one to take polls (you know, 57% of women say &c.). I shall have to assume that all readers know whereof I speak. This judgment of erotism is interesting because I recall no lurid scenes in Valle-Inclán, no bedroom activities, no contrivances such as those found in best-selling novels, no detailed anatomical descriptions. But I do remember the music, the rhythm, the beat and the image of Nature as a "gran fiera fecunda," *tierra caliente*, and I remember Joan Maragall's[3] likening the supreme act of a man and woman together to the dance, and Valle's saying that the dance is the highest form of art.[4] Eros is a rhythm, unquestionably, and the sonatas are a rhythm.[5] Can we call the esperpentos an arhythmic rhythm, a gnostic delight?[6] The question arises: Are Eros and the sonatas the same rhythm, or merely similar; or, if they are similar, do they proceed from the same source, and if so, what is that source?

10. I remember a scene in Valle in which a pack of hunting dogs strips a woman of her clothing (*Aguila de blasón*, Jornada 2a., Escena 4a.). There is no description of the flesh, no lusting, no canine sodomites, just the grotesque action. One might call this Valle's gargoyle, something like Baudelaire's absolute comic, something that did not exist before, a newly created action, and there is no doubt it has a strange beauty or at least a strange allure. What does all this mean? Is there an ethical consideration here, or can one simply employ Salinas's formalism and say the beauty is in the creative act? Valle himself would agree with Salinas:

> Para los gnósticos la belleza de las imágenes no está en ellas, sino en el acto creador, del cual no se desprenden jamás, y así todas las cosas son una misma para ser amadas, porque todas brotan de la eterna entraña en el eterno acto, quieto, absoluto y uno. (*Lámpara*, p. 71)

> For the gnostics the beauty of images is not in the images themselves, but in the creative act, from which they are never detached. Thus all things are one thing alone in their capacity to be loved, because they all spring forth from the eternal will, in the eternal act, which is quiet, absolute and one.[7]

By this reasoning a young girl's love for her sea captain, a boy's obedience to his mother, the abuses of a nymphomaniac, and sacrilege are all the same in art because they issue from an eternal, quietist will.

11. I may be asking too many questions. Perhaps I should

16

change my mode of persuasion and make more assertions. But in answer to this suggestion of indecision, I shall say that my interrogations are, so to speak, my wager theory. Just as Pascal asked his libertines to consider the odds before them and vote for the religious life by purity of action, so I ask my reader libertines to answer my questions in the affirmative; they are rhetorical questions, to be answered affirmatively. Yes, there is an ethical consideration. Yes, Baudelaire's absolutely comic does apply. Yes, the readers share my experience, and so forth.

12. The case of Valle-Inclán resembles that of Góngora, who lay in waiting almost three hundred years to the day (1627-1927) to be interpreted properly; when Dámaso Alonso, and after him Pedro Salinas and others, opened the door. Góngora, the Prince of Darkness, and Valle-Inclán, the Prince of Clowns, Prince of one-armed, lisping, scorning, fooling, turban-hatted insolent magicians in the sideshow. A sideshow clown must be deciphered for our enjoyment. But the truth runs much deeper. Our enjoyment, yes; our enjoyment is consequential because man is the *homo ludens*, the playing animal, and this particular window must be opened on his soul.[8] So let us decipher Valle-Inclán for our enjoyment. But man also seeks to understand; he is also the rational animal who wants to know why and wherefore, what this world is all about, just what is going on in the Generation of 1898 and this twentieth century. The dianoia. More than any other Spanish author, Valle holds the answer. He is the keeper of the keys, *claves líricas*, unlocking the dream of modern literature. So let us decipher Valle-Inclán on this score also.

13. It is nice to know one is not alone. I speak of deciphering, which suggests a cipher, but I heard it differently in the spring of 1984, when a young lady gave a talk on Valle in which she spoke of a code. During the discussion I asked her about that code, what it might be, and she said she didn't know. A code's existence was obvious to her, but its quiddity was not. Thus we are seeking a Rosetta stone to decipher the hieroglyphs of the incorrigible hierophant, the heresiarch, Don Ramón María del Valle-Inclán, the *ceceoso*, the glossolalia man who does not speak our common language. Where does one find it?

14. The code is to be found in *La lampara maravillosa*, which Valle has listed as the first of his works, before *Flor de santidad* and *Jardín umbrío*, although he wrote it later in his career (1916). The code can also be found in his sonatic[9] style, and in the works of Unamuno, Antonio Machado and Azorín; and the reverse code is there in Baroja's masterpiece, *Camino de perfección*. Baroja's *Bah humbug!* and Valle's *sonata* are two sides of the same coin, or at least two manifestations of it.

15. The code lies hidden in German metaphysics.

16. The most discerning of modern epistemologies is John Henry Newman's *Grammar of Assent*, in which he says we do

not prove the most important things of our life but assent to them. This grammar of assent explains the plight of Cervantes's *curioso impertinente*, the man who was too curious for his own good; he attempted to prove the unprovable and thus became his own wife's satan. I assent to Valle's central position and to his using a code; and I shall give evidence, employing I hope textual control of the imagination. There will be science and poetical insight: Nevertheless, at the end of the thoughts in this present book, one must make the assent or withhold it.

17. I have mentioned German metaphysics. One can imagine a *valleinclanista* mocking a rigid Teutonic schoolmaster, or one may recall Baroja's scorn of Wagnerian sentimentality, which is a sort of wholesale metaphysics. German philosophy, however, runs extremely deep in Spanish literature, providing several codes, especially *the* code, that of Valle-Inclán. And here I do not refer to Nietzsche.

18. It is strange how an author so unlike his critic can have such an effect on him: Valle, the libertine gnostic, the irreverent ascetic from Galicia, the great artist who has described his pantheistic vision from a mountain, and I, the traditionalist, who favors the intellect and plodding ways of discursive reasoning. And yet I relate everything I read nowadays in Spanish literature to Valle's central position. I have just completed a book on Padre Luis Coloma, S.J., author of the thesis novel, *Pequeñeces* (1891), and it is difficult to think of any writer more unlike Valle: Coloma, the fire and brimstone Jesuit, heaping hell's scorn on atheists and heretics. Nevertheless, I found in Coloma's favorite work, his novel *Boy*, a passage resembling Valle-Inclán's *sonatas* and *esperpentos* (with less lyricism to be sure, for Coloma was wont to preach rather than sing); so much so, that I call this Jesuit a distant cousin of the anti-Jesuit, Valle-Inclán. And when I read Somerset Maugham's *Of Human Bondage*, where Philip Carey seeks a faith, I immediately think of Pio Baroja's *Arbol de la ciencia* and *Camino de perfección*, and through Baroja of Valle.

19. This fall of 1984 I have read two milestones, Robert Pirsig's *Zen And The Art Of Motorcycle Maintenance* and Umberto Eco's *The Name Of The Rose*. Pirsig wants to transcend the objective (classical) and subjective (romantic) to arrive at something he calls *quality*, which I interpret ontologically as a ground of being. This seems to be a cognate of Valle's *code*; let us use this word as both a system of communication and the thing communicated, as both Valle's unique Spanish prose and the message he is anxious to convey.[10]

20. It may even be that I owe the prosaic title of my thoughts, "Thoughts Concerning The Central Literary Position Of Ramón del Valle-Inclán," to Pirsig's unusual title *Zen And The Art Of Motorcycle Maintenance*. Zen of course will catch the eye,

whereas the rest of the words, though not the concept, are prosaic. Pirsig puts Zen and Motorcycle Maintenance together, as if their connection were to be taken for granted, and I assign Valle a central position as if that were an undoubted truth also. But I am prepared to write a long essay in its defense.

21. As for Umberto Eco, I relate him to Valle on a *corazonada*, a hunch. His rational investigator, William of Baskerville, frequently alludes to his colleague, William of Occam, and I have wondered if Occam's nominalism has something to do with it, the code I mean, or rather opposition to it. Valle-Inclán was not a nominalist, anything but, for he does hold to universals, the *terminus ad quem* of his code.

We are on formidable ground, German metaphysics, Valle's code and fourteenth century philosophy. I shall have to do some research into nominalism, conceptualism and realism. At this stage I had hoped to avoid this sort of research, relying on the equipment I already possess, but I may be able to point out a truth here. Scholasticism has been so generally shunned since Erasmus's scorn, the Cartesian reception, and Voltaire's subsequent scorn, that it may be time to return to medieval studies if we are to interpret modern thought.

I should say that Valle is a realist, in the fourteenth century sense of the word: Plato's Forms are real to him. They are also accessible.

Valle is not a nominalist, nor a conceptualist.

22. Ten or twenty years ago I read a book by a man named Griffin called *Black Like Me*, and I must now write about the hate stare, which some of my readers, my libertines, will have experienced. Griffin was a white man who by means of unguents and herbs made himself look black. Traveling around the country to see what it was like to be "black like me," he learned he often had trouble reaching toilet facilities on time, and sometimes he had an alleged sexual prowess thrown up to him. But his most memorable experience took place in Louisiana, near the Mississippi border, when a white man on a train gave him a stare penetrating his whole being. Perhaps it was the first time Griffin had ever seen hatred, incarnate so to speak.

I myself have seen such a stare, at a Jesuit university in the 1950's, where I attended a scholarly convention. I was talking to an eminent Hispanist, a scholarly gentleman who was universally admired, when a young Spanish Jesuit walked up and was introduced by another party. This Jesuit, a tall, thin handsome man in his thirties had the sweetest disposition and friendly smile; nevertheless, as we spoke, the Spanish scholar gave him the hate stare, and I have since often thought: What a terrible circumstance! The ages between the two were exactly right, they could have been father and son. They even had that peculiar cranial configuration you see in some Spaniards, descendants perhaps of the Visigoths. Nevertheless, one could see the hate stare.

Perhaps this was what Unamuno was trying to tell us in *Abel Sánchez*, Machado in *Alvargonzález* or Valle in his *Guerra carlista*, namely, the theme of Cain and Abel. In any case, I don't want the hate stare to be a part of the deciphering of Valle-Inclán. When I call him a heresiarch (or Unamuno), I mean just that, he is a heresiarch, a leader in heresy, a man consciously creating a doctrine at variance with orthodoxy; and I can prove this to my satisfaction, and, I hope, the reader's. Within the pages of these thoughts no term is meant to be pejorative, nor is any term meant to be amelioratory. And I hope this criterion will obtain for other figures in this book, from Bradomín and Baudelaire to the tyrant Banderas, Schopenhauer and Wagner. Even so, my thoughts are not without bias.

Put it this way: I am fond of Fernando de Castro and Gumersindo Azcárate, and also of Marcelino Menéndez Pelayo and José María de Pereda. I prefer Castro's kindness and don Marcelino's erudition. I have written favorably of Azcárate, and I don't think Pereda's novels are as poor as his detractors would have them.

23. Where was I? Oh yes, it is time to review. These *pensées* have spoken of the two *esprits* of Blaise Pascal, textual control of the imagination, Galdós, sacrilege, erotism, the code, the grammar of assent, metaphysics, fourteenth century realism, hate stares, Cain and other events. And they do not divagate. There is a prologue, three proems, these thoughts, which are a fourth proem, and then Canto II, *La lámpara maravillosa*, which I am anxious to get to, and after that, stellar vision.

24. Is there a code? A code to this universe? Somerset Maugham suggests that there is, and then, that there isn't. Do you recall Philip Carey in *Of Human Bondage*, when in a Parisian cafe he asks Cronshaw the poet for the meaning of the universe? Cronshaw points to a Levantine carrying a Persian rug and says, there, there in the design of the rug lies the code, the cipher, the secret meaning. Philip doesn't understand and asks Cronshaw to reveal it to him. Cronshaw says "if I did you wouldn't understand, you must find it out for yourself." Philip says "you are cryptic." Cronshaw replies "No, I am drunk." Philip continues his search for the cipher throughout the novel and at the end comes to a pessimistic conclusion.

I am holding back the code, which is Valle's *camino de perfección*, way of perfection. Why not state it right now, get it over with and proceed to Valle's novels and plays and lyrical keys one by one (every one of his works is a *clave lírica*!). It doesn't work that way. The code must be approached gradually, it must be worked up to, and the critic, like Valle before him, must hammer and hammer and strike and strike the anvil until a magnetic field is created in which the reader will easily find his place. That's the way Valle has done it, and if the critic doesn't follow suit his cold logic may hamper comprehension. Perhaps that is what Cronshaw meant when he said "if I explained it to you you wouldn't understand." And this reminds me of a review article by Edward Sarmiento (BHS, 1957).

25. In 1957, Sarmiento wrote a favorable review of François Meyer's *L'ontologie de Miguel de Unamuno* in which he, Sarmiento, clearly admired Unamuno's prose but not his philosophy. Of the philosophy, the "Unamuno potion" as Sarmiento calls it, he wrote:

> *Querer serlo todo* is an absurdity; it is indeed a tragic absurdity. The human spirit may be simple or empty. There is no alternative. Unamuno was not simple. This is not to call in question his immense poetic power, and he will remain a great name in Spanish literature but a mere curiosity in the history of philosophy. *(Bulletin of Hispanic Studies*, 1957 (vol. XXXIV), 54-56).

In metaphysics the more simple the being, the greater the perfection: the Simple Being is the First Cause (God Himself). Given Sarmiento's humoristic dichotomy, since Unamuno is not simple (he is not God) then he must be empty. Sarmiento scorns Unamuno's philosophy but praises his "immense poetic power." He is surely a great name in Spanish literature.

Similarly, it may be unfair not to distinguish between Valle's gnostic philosophy in the *Lámpara* and the art of his novels, plays and poetry. I for one find his *Lámpara* to be a philosophical curiosity whereas I would never question his immense poetical power. He is to me the first name in modern Spanish literature.

26. Just before 1901 Unamuno wrote a letter to Clarín describing his religious plight and novelistic style, in which he says he writes "sin maroma lógica," without a logical thread. Unamuno would go to the very essence of things, to the Quintessence, to the marrow of their bones so to speak, to the *tuétano*, and *médula*, and then, angelically (according to him), write it hastily down without the major and minor premises of logic, with only the CONCLUSION.

Although that may have been Unamuno's highest aspiration, his works are rigorously and repetitiously logical. Given his major premise, namely, the intrinsic contradiction within being, everything in his literature sequentially follows: a man envies his best friend (*Abel Sánchez*); a spinster aunt keeps insisting "I am the mother, the mother, the mother" (*Tía Tula*); a saintly candidate for canonization has lost his faith (*San Manuel Bueno*);

a man torments his wife into insanity, insisting "I love you, I love you, I love you" (*Nada menos que todo un hombre*). These are all the plots of exemplary novels, logical models, and manifestations of Unamuno's major premise. The thought is logical, the style paradoxical and apparently free of logic, a sort of neo-baroque illogical logic, which is designed to amaze the reader (*admiratio*). There is a rigorous order within apparent disorder.

The same may be said of Valle's method. Like the baroque poet Góngora, he would never call a spade a spade, or bread bread and wine wine (see Pedro Salinas's essay on Góngora in *Reality and the Poet*). Valle must take the spade and wrap it in Celtic myth, in decadence, in sacrilege, in *contes cruelles*, in the *niebla* of a twilight zone (*crepúsculo* is his favorite word), in grotesques, in the excessive actions of a clown; but the spade remains a spade nevertheless. The spade is enveloped in a logical, linguistic code. There is a serious order, at times within apparent buffoonery: Logic in an author who if you called him logical would snap back: "Uzted ez un zopenco." Preciosa, the little gypsy, deliberately spoke with a *ceceo*, and so did the Galician gypsy, who uttered abracadabra *caló*, don Ramón María del Valle-Inclán.

27. To return to *Pensée* 24, why do I hold back the code? In his *Arte nuevo de hacer comedias* Lope says the playwright must not untie the plot until nearing the end of Act III, otherwise the audience will desert the theater. Withhold the denouement until verse 700 or so of Act III, bring in the *rey justiciero*, set things right, and then, a chiliastic ending. Verse 1000: The Chiliad. Valle would approve and liken his own art to *cipreses milenarios*.

So I shall retain the code. Valle put it all down in *Claves líricas* and *La lámpara maravillosa* and then wrote thirty exemplary plays and novels. There may be a paradox here: Read the novels and other works and you will find the key, but read the keys, *claves líricas*, and their strangeness may mislead you. Remember, moreover, it is always spoofing and then some. I cannot accept the dictum of a Hispanist who once wrote to me to say: "You cannot always take Valle seriously." The opposite is true. You must always take him seriously.

28. I have often thought that Valle could make millions on television today, writing what one observer has called "the hidden persuaders." When you buy a convertible you are not buying a car but a mistress, or at least a vehicle for a mistress. When you buy a cigarette you are a manly cowboy punching cattle in the wild wild West, Arcadia. And when you buy whiskey you are a man of distinction, with those striped pants and aristocratic suit. Then there are the seven capital sins: Pride, buy a Cadillac; Avarice, win the lottery; Lust, the convertible; Envy, again the Cadillac; Gluttony, drink like a man of

distinction, or Pepto Bismol; Anger, thrash those clothes with Soapso; Sloth, buy a CD, retire young. Valle's art is similar though on a much higher plane. His art is an art of gnostic, ethereal hidden persuaders: *crepúsculo, a lo lejos, manos pálidas, cipreses centenarios, ráfagas, un no sé qué quimérica ilusión.* His lexicon, his syntax, his images are part of a carefully elaborated system designed to lead the reader to gnosis. Thus they are an intelligible series of ciphers, a code.

29. Valle could make a fortune on the television tube, but were he here he would not. He *would* not sell his art. Valle-Inclán is a living example of free will. If you presented him with this hoary Scholastic doctrine of free will, he would most likely scoff and scorn: *Uzted ez un fraile zopenco.* But the action of this great ascetic would belie his words, and actions speak louder than words. He *would* never sell his art to commerce. Free will. Ironically, with respect to *libre albedrío*, his actions are *castizo*, (how he would hate that word!) His actions, not his words, are *castizo.*

30. In metaphysics, the more simple a being is, the greater its dignity, the Almighty being Pure Act. Metaphysicians should study the style of Valle-Inclán and *La lámpara*, because they will understand them better than the literary critics with their trendy schools today. The critics are ergotists, complicated beings, divagators, introducing all sorts of premises, voices, signifiers, unreliable authors, implied authors, reader response, signs and structures. They are overly scientific, too much given to *géométrie* and insufficiently to *finesse*. They want literature to confirm to their pigeon holes, whereas their partitions should be shaped by literature. Their sabbath should be made for literature, not literature for their sabbath. Their readership wanders from simple textual control of the imagination.

But Valle's works will not suffer all sorts of criticism. Proximately he has created a ruthless synthesis—let us call it *écrasez l'infâme*—whereas ultimately his message is simple. He is close to theology. His code is simple and so acquires a certain dignity. *Écrasez l'infâme*, which is only proximate, should not be allowed to obscure the code.

31. Both Valle and Unamuno spoke of their *Verbo* and its eucharistic grace. The imitation of Christian doctrine, the *Logos* of St. John, and perhaps a parody, is obvious. Let us interpret the phrase benignly: The poet's *Verbo* is a creative act bringing a sort of grace. What does it do? Just what is the *Verbo*? That is all in the code.

32. This critic is not without bias. I accept Valle's criticism of hypocritical clergymen with the *ojos entornados*, but I do not accept his playing with sacrilege in the various sonatas. Nor would I accept a parody of the Logos if that were his design. It doesn't seem that way, however; his *Verbo* belongs to the code

rather than to *écrasez l'infâme*.

In any case, I shall interpret his Logos, the poet's Word, benignly. I feel that Valle is trying to mesmerize me, magnetize me with his Word (poetry), and that is part of the code.

33. Northrop Frye has said that censorship is to literature what lynching is to justice—surely an apt statement. Professor Frank Tannenbaum once told me at Columbia that there is always censorship, the real argument is not the existence of censorship but whether it will be your censorship or mine: Here is another apt statement, but it requires explanation. In speaking of censorship, I am not concerned with the good of a doctrine or its evil, but simply with the exercise of coercive power.

Could someone stage a play today, on television, lauding Gobineau's inequality of the races? Obviously not. Some agency would censor his thought, the United States government, or the beer companies sponsoring the program, or ethnic lobbies; or the workers would simply down tools. Gobineau's theme is now illegal as well as immoral, and even if it weren't it is bad economics. So there will always be censorship, yours being good and mine bad if you are the arbiter.

Is there a non-lynching censorship? Perhaps, although it is self-punitive. After Evelyn Waugh wrote *Brideshead Revisited* he felt remorse over some aspects of Julia's adultery and so he altered the words of his second edition of *Brideshead*. Although this coercive power was self-imposed it was nevertheless censorship; here, the deliberate suppression of language so as to alter an image. Did Waugh do the right thing? It's hard to say. He thought so. Can one be said to lynch oneself or one's own creation? If Goethe knew that the *Sorrows of Young Werther* would lead to suicides (Larra's perhaps?), should he have kept it *in petto*? Suppressed it? If Schopenhauer knew that his essay on suicide might have the same effect, or if a professor teaching Seneca knew that a student would on that account take his own life, should the one not publish his essay and the other not teach certain writings of the great Stoic? Change his class? No matter how you answer these questions you cannot separate ethics from aesthetics, for works of art have ethical effects. One might as well try to separate the taste of food from its effect on the stomach, the taste causing the food to be devoured in the first place.

Do Valle-Inclán's writings have an unwholesome effect on some readers? I believe they may; I don't see how one can play decadently with the world of archaic imagery, with myth and sacrilege, without having some effect on many and perhaps all of the readers: Swinburne at the flogging block, lots of leather, Our Lady Of Pain, and that sort of thing. Then how should one respond? With censorship? No. One should respond by writing another *Don Quixote*, as Cervantes did when he clearly saw "the

24

problem of the book" (consult the criticism of Leo Spitzer). The best solution, the best censor, is laughter: "Don Ramón, el zopenco ez uzted, Gómez de la Zerna, y todoz loz zuyoz." It is time to hint at the code. Valle-Inclán deplored the phenomenal world and its manifestations, such as hypocritical clergy and corrupt politicians. In his zeal to ridicule this world he engaged in sacrilege and indiscreet decadence. He was clearly at fault, BUT, this social judgment should not be cast on his art. He was truly a great poet.

Although Valle deplores the phenomenal world, it has a saving grace of sorts, it is pabulum for the *esperpento*. A word of explanation is in order here: No Galician field at sunset, observed with stellar vision, from a hill, in an eternal moment, can be an *esperpento*. Lest you doubt this, read *La lámpara maravillosa*. We professors might call such a field a phenomenon, but then we professors are hylics. *Zopencos*. Doomed to the sterile categories of Time, without the *Verbo*.

34. Repetition is desirable. I have a bias. I do not think that in living beings you can separate ethics from aesthetics, although (1) you may do so hypothetically, and (2) you may be forced to try to do so as a social *modus operandi*. After all, who will make the ethical decision about a book's unwholesomeness, and, more than that, who will execute this decision? We do not want to turn *Amadis* and *Tirant* over to the secular arm of the housekeeper.

Yes, repetition is desirable. After all, Valle repeats and repeats and repeats, one clear simple message, and he repeats it again, and that is part of the code. A simple code indeed, recited over and over again, in the *Lámpara, Claves líricas* and thirty-odd abracadabra volumes.

35. I had hoped to get past these *pensées* by now, to the *Lámpara*, but I have two more thoughts at least. Valle-Inclán is like that: As I write these lines in my notebook, I keep scribbling the germ of ideas in the top margin, so that now I am up to numbers thirty-six and thirty-seven. If an author can do that to you, then you must have a deep well to draw from.

The intentional fallacy, the autobiographical fallacy: One should not heed them when interpreting the men of 1898. Pío Baroja says that Andrés Hurtado of *El árbol de la ciencia* is his counterpart, discounting a few fictitious details:

> En mi novela *El árbol de la ciencia* he pintado
> una contrafigura mía, dejando la parte psicológica
> y cambiando el medio ambiente del protagonista,
> la familia y alguna que otra cosa. (Chapter IX)

Andrés's pessimism is Baroja's pessimism, and his uncle Iturrioz's estimate of the two lions of the North, Kant and Schopenhauer, is Baroja's.

When Unamuno writes to Clarín, describing his spiritual crisis of 1886, one might as well be reading one of his exemplary novels, where a character agonizes over consciousness, reality, the dicta of the head and promptings of the heart. *All* of Unamuno's works (novels, plays, poems, essays, letters) are exemplary, and, in his own words, cardiac. They come from the heart. His characters like he himself are cardiac cases. Unamuno is truly *El condenado por desconfiado*, the diffidence coming from the heart.

As for Valle-Inclán, I am first concerned with the alleged intentional fallacy. An author does not write a thousand lyrical keys, both within the book of that title (*Claves líricas*) and without, unless he has some specific goal in mind, something he intends to plant in the reader's thoughts. Valle is the master of recital who does not capriciously engage in amassing words like: *crepúsculo, inmóviles, misterioso, azul, penumbra del jardín, estremecimientos, temblaba, lejana, lejanía, balbucear, ritmo eterno, estela, ensueño, ilusión, sueño, deshoja, eco milenario, místico vuelo, quimeras, rosas, rosales, secreto, ansia ideal, párpados pálidos, ojos entornados.* . . . he does not write out of caprice, nor does he vainly write sentences about *tierra caliente* like this:

> Un vaho pesado calor y catinga anunciaba la proximidad de la manigua y el crepúsculo enciende con las estrellas los ojos de los jaguares.
> (*Tirano Banderas*)

He does not write such words and phrases out of mere linguistic play, although linguistic play is certainly part of his delight. When Valle writes he is, to be sure, the *homo ludens*[12], the one-armed bandit from Galicia playing Robin Hood, but he is also the hierophantic don Ramón del Valle-Inclán y Montenegro, Marqués de Bradomín y Cara de Plata, keeper of the keys, the lyrical celestial keys (*sueños celestes*) rivalling those of San Pedro. *Crepúsculo, penumbra del jardín, inmóviles, misterioso* &c.: They are part of the code, one is tempted to say they are the code. The gnosis.

36. I remember harboring suspicions when I first read Valle-Inclán, and I will readily confess I was confused. The sonatas were obviously the work of a genius, and I guess at that time (1956-1960) my favorite Valle pieces were the Carlist trilogy and *Tirano Banderas*. Perhaps they still are; in any case, no where else can one capture so readily, so easily, the quintessence of the Carlist Crusade and Latin American polity. Quintessence, the constituent matter of heavenly bodies, the fifth element beyond the mundane four: A word like *quintessence* approaches the code. Essences will not suffice. They will not do. They smack of

26

rationalism. Let them be anathema. We must look for something beyond the stodgy old Greeks, torpid friars *con los ojos entornados*, frigid Frenchmen (I think, therefore I am) and ludicrous German metaphysicians, but not all the Germans, certainly not Kant. We must go beyond essences to . . . the evocations of ancestral memory.

Be that as it may, I was confused. Here amidst the alpine heights of *La guerra carlista* I came across the *Lámpara maravillosa* with all that theosophical, pantheistic, Pythagorean, Manichaean, karma memory, Madame Blavatsky, abracadabra, quietist balderdash, with the engraving on the frontispiece of a one-armed, goat bearded, turban-hatted melancholy clown. And a famous Hispanist wrote me to say: "You can't always take Valle seriously," although another told me "Valle-Inclán is the author of a ruthless synthesis." (These sentences are engraved in my memory). What was I to think? And then, as I read Valle over many many times it began to dawn on me . . . This dawn is a twilight, a *crepúsculo*, a result of the code. Remember there are in Nature two *crepúsculos*, two twilights, one after sunset, one before sunrise, and they are undistinguishable. They resemble in a vague way, at least literally, San Juan de la Cruz's dark night of the soul, and to be sure, Valle introduces San Juan in the garden scene of *Primavera*, which is I believe the central and most unforgettable scene of all Valle's literature. Were I to select one word to describe the code it would be *crepúsculo*, a twilight code, a penumbra:

This is the night when the veil between the two worlds thins . . .

Just as Salinas has characterized Góngora's poetry as "the exaltation of Nature"[13], so I should characterize Valle's as "Nature's dawn," Nature being metaphysical as well as physical or phenomenal, and dawn existing beyond that glow you see on the horizon at five o'clock in the morning. You must go beyond the horizon. Libertine reader, Brother Pilgrim, you must venture beyond the horizon.

Curious, how in speaking of Valle I invariably invoke the mystics. Santa Teresa spoke of a *luz luz* and *nada nada*. I have seen the *luz luz* (unfortunately not hers); I have seen Valle's *luz luz* and *nada nada*. Repetitious stammerings such as these pertain to the *balbuceo* of San Juan:

un no sé qué quedan balbuciendo

and one will find a similar *balbuceo* in Valle:

¡Qué mezquino, qué torpe, qué difícil balbuceo el

27

nuestro para expresar este deleite de lo inefable que reposa en todas las cosas con la gracia de un niño dormido!

What a wretched, what a dull, what a difficult stammer we have for expressing this delight of the ineffable, which lies concealed in things like a sleeping child! (*Lámpara maravillosa*, p. 16.)

Apenas sabemos balbucear el secreto sentimental que nos hace distintos, porque cuando creemos vivir para nosotros, vivimos para la especie.

We scarcely know how to stammer out the emotional secret that makes us distinct, because when we think we are living for ourselves, we are really living for the species. (*Lámpara maravillosa*, p. 82)

This stammer will account for the abracadabra and apparent balderdash of the *Lámpara*. Let us follow the advice of Valle: Don't pay attention to the immediate evidence of the senses, the immediate appearance of what you read, but to the impression beyond it, beyond the horizon (*lejanía*), the impression you will ultimately receive if you read the sonatas time and again, listening above all to the music. The code is there. Just listen! Feel the rhythm! The code is music.

37. Holy smokes! ¡Porra! ¡Reporra! ¡Cáspita! ¡Recáspita! But away with such expletives, which belong to the *garbancero*, Benito Pérez Galdós rather than the sage of Galicia. We must return to more elegant, less phenomenal language, elegant because it pierces the veil of reality, nay, Reality.

I must speak of clowns, comic performers, who wear outlandish costumes and say outlandish things and entertain by tumbling. *Les funambules*. In society there are two types of clowns, those who draw attention to themselves and those who draw attention to an important issue. During the Vietnam War we Americans frequently saw these two types of clowns. Hundreds of buffoons drew attention to themselves by startling the bourgeoisie, a French invention, *épater la bourgeoisie*. I remember one such clown who the day the students closed down our campus said to me: "Boy, this is fun!"

But there were a few who drew attention to the serious issue, The War, by pouring lamb's blood over draft records; they acted like asses, they were tumblers and jugglers who welcomed arrest. And some wore clerical garments, caftans. They helped stop the war.

To the superficial, egotistic, Time-burdened phenomenal eye,

Valle-Inclán drew attention to himself; he was the extravagant, one-armed, goat-bearded *farsante* etcetera clown. But his art was far too profound to admit such judgment. Valle was not concerned with surfaces, superficies, phenomena, but with the issue, or I should say ISSUE, out there beyond Plato's cave. Although there are of course many visible benefits to his literature—his satire of American and Peninsular hypocrites, clerical puppets, fanatics and other breakers of decency—these corrective goods are fringe benefits, corollaries, perks you might say. Let us put the scene in Valle's gnostic way: If you are a spiritual man, or at least a psychic who can attune yourself to the artist's harmonious code, you may also enjoy Valle's satire of hylic men. But this satire is only proximate, whereas the issue is ultimate.

Don Ramón María del Valle-Inclán y Montenegro was a clown, a hierophantic ass, priest of the Eleusinian mysteries, a bellicose beard in a caftan, who made noises but also MUSIC, which is still heard today. And it will be heard.

38. Now let us return to *pensée* #36, where a young reader of Valle-Inclán spoke of his own confusion. How could the author of the eminent *guerra carlista* engage in theosophical caricature? But the statement is pleonastic, for theosophy itself is religious caricature, the musings of Rudolph Steiner. Pondering this, I came across the nonsense of another Celt, the Irish *gallego*, William Butler Yeats, whose position seems as central as Valle's: Yeats, the disciple of Madame Helena Petrona Blavatsky (1831-1891), and Valle, born in 1866, a probable disciple also. Is Theosophy more estimable than it seems? Perhaps. There is enough evidence here for a doctoral study in Comparative Literature. I say this ingenuously, with no thought of humor, but I can imagine Valle's reaction to my suggestion; he would write a story about an enamored doctoral student reading *The Celtic Twilight*, his head swathed in bandages, and about a cat with amputated ears.

A PhD is the stuff of an esperpento!

39. While I am on the subject of the crepuscular, let me say something about the Twilight Zone, which has become the title of a popular television series. It is probable that these adventures into the beyond, the *Más Allá* as they say in Spanish, are a very very pale reflection of the doctrine of Valle-Inclán. They hold the same relation to Valle's art as a penny dreadful does to *David Copperfield*, but even so they may help us understand the meaning of the code. And they may also be the spawn of nineteenth century French literature rather than the penumbral garden of Ramón del Valle-Inclán. Villiers de L'Isle Adam, Barbey D'Aurevilly, *contes cruelles*: TV's Twilight Zone.

Pensée thirty-nine is a good place to stop. I wish it were forty, a good round number, valleinclanesque, the Deluge,

Christ's fast in the desert, ten get you forty, a Pythagorean four by ten. Let us terminate this proem. On to the Second Canto!

CANTO II

La Lámpara Maravillosa

1. Now that I think of it, I am loathe to discuss the *Lámpara* fully here, for if I do I shall be eminently logical rather than poetical. (Valle would agree with this statement.) The *Lámpara* should be looked upon as the first of all Valle's books because it is an *abecedario*, an ABC, a grammar, a primer for the reader, musically suggesting the system of its author. The *Lámpara* is also one of Valle's many sonatas, and in this sense suggests rather than explains.

It would be unpleasant merely to explain the works of such a marvelous poet, to show a logical development of relationships; for example, "Page 1 of the *Lámpara* reads thus and so, and you will find evidence of this doctrine in *Luces de Bohemia*, page *equis*, edition of 1932; or, "Page 7 of the *Lámpara* reads thus, and evidence will be found in the *Marquesa Rosalinda* page *b*". This method displays too much textual control and insufficient imagination—more finesse is desirable. No, that is not the procedure, the ABC must follow the poetry, not the poetry the ABC. Let us read the works as they meet the eye and then approach the grammar for an understanding.

2. Even so, I shall say a few words about the *Lámpara*, which is a beacon throwing light. At first it seems to cast shade and confusion, but it really does throw light. Both shade and light. That is one reason it is marvelous.

3. *La lámpara maravillosa*, the prodigious lamp will throw light on the position of Valle-Inclán, but what sort of light? A partial answer to this question will be found in the subtitle, EJERCICIOS ESPIRITUALES, written in block letters so that no reader will miss the emphasis. These words ring a bell and flash a light (sound and vision) that cannot escape the attention of the Spanish reader. *Spiritual Exercises* comes from the pen of St. Ignatius Loyola, S.J., so it is significant that the terrible anti-Jesuit, Valle-Inclán, should invoke them. His usage of Loyola's title suggests that in everything Valle writes in the *Lámpara* we should look for ambiguity and philosophical duality. Irony. Although the phrase *spiritual exercises* is not exactly the code we are seeking, it is a sub-code pointing us to the rightful way.

On the one hand, *Spiritual Exercises* is a spoof, an attempt to ridicule in their most heinous form the Jesuits, that is to say, most heinous for Valle-Inclán. Valle is not alone in this disdain; one need only read *La araña negra* of Blasco Ibáñez and *AMDG* of Pérez de Ayala to see the utter contempt reaching back at least to 1767. Anti-Jesuitism for some was an obsession. On a much more moderate scale, one can see criticism of the Jesuits in the *apologia pro vita sua* of Cejador y Frauca, the history of the brothers Mir, one of whom abandoned the Jesuit order, and the defenses of Father Luis Coloma, S.J., whose fiction was disturbed by external criticism. In 1891 Coloma's thesis novel, *Pequeñeces*, rather like a small Dreyfuss Affair, caused a division in Spain splitting Madrid into two hostile camps.

Valle's criticism of the Jesuits in his subtitle arises then from a long background. His book could not be more heterodox; were a heretic to take the articles of faith in the Apostles' and Nicene Creed one by one, and deny each one in turn with a resounding NO!, he could not write a more heterodox book than the *Lámpara*. Nevertheless Valle takes the most Spanish and Catholic of saints and uses his words as an imprimatur for heresy! The waters of this joke run deep, especially in sonatas like *Primavera* and *Flor de santidad*. Consequently in Valle we must always look for a kind of religious perversion from orthodoxy (he says as much in his subtitle). The perversion is deliberate, from an ascetic who might go without eating and might despise fleshly needs in order to write his poetry: The creator of an ascetic *Umwertung aller Werte*.

The historical precedent for Valle's perverse action reaches back to ancient Gnosticism, and to libertine gnostics and *alumbrados*, who also professed to see a light. This is why Valle gives his *Lámpara* such a strong gnostic, antinomian cast. Was he formally a Manichaean gnostic? I shall leave the answer to other scholars since I am not his biographer, but as a literary critic I know that gnosticism will lead us to the code, and Manichaeanism is particularly helpful for deciphering the *esperpentos*. It will also serve to decode the hithermost side of the sonatas, and of reality. We may safely call Valle a literary Manichaean, of the libertine stripe.

4. I notice that José Martínez Ruiz used to call himself *Ahrimán*, before adopting the name *Azorín*. Ahriman, the Angra Mainiju, the evil spirit of Zoroastrianism contending against the good, creative spirit Spenta Mainiju.[1] Why did Martínez Ruiz assume this Zoroastrian posture, so similar to Valle's Manichaeanism? And why did he change his pen name for an *Azor-Azorín*, a small goshawk, a bird of prey? Was he to be a new Socratic gadfly perhaps? And how about Unamuno's *tábano*, his gadfly criticism of Europe and Spain? But Valle is more than a gadfly or hawk. He is a GADFLY, yes, beyond peradventure, but much more than that. If you doubt my words, read his twenty-odd sonatas in the *lámpara's* light.

Here is evidence for another doctoral study, but again Valle would excoriate such scholarly phenomena and discursive reasoning. He would write a story about a mummified esperpentic pedant, his belly inflated, drooling over dusty tomes, or he might compose a musical piece with an ardent female, a tome in her fluttering fingers, languishing in a garden and

drowning in a dark pool at twilight. Down with discursive reasoning! We must start with the chtonic.
5. Valle-Inclán gave the following order to his collected works:

I. *La lámpara maravillosa*
II. *Flor de santidad*
III. *Jardín umbrío*
IV. *El yermo de las almas*
V. *Sonata de primavera*
VI. *Sonata de estío*
VII. *Sonata de otoño*
VIII. *Sonata de invierno*
IX. *Corte de amor*
X. *Los cruzados de la causa*   X, XI, XII: This
XI. *El resplandor de la hoguera*   trilogy is called
XII. *Gerifaltes de antaño*   *La guerra carlista.*
XIII. *Coloquios románticos*
XIV. *Opera lírica: Cuento de abril. Voces de gesta.*
XV. *La marquesa Rosalinda*
XVI. *Claves líricas: Aromas de leyenda. El pasajero.*
      La pipa de Kif.
XVII. *Cara de Plata*
XVIII. *Aguila de blasón*
XIX. *Romance de lobos*
XX. *Visión estelar de un momento de guerra*
XXI. *Divinas palabras*
XXII. *Luces de Bohemia*
XXIII. *Retablo de la avaricia, la lujuria y la muerte. El*
      embrujado de Ligazón. La cabeza del Bautista. Sacrilegio.
XXIV. *Martes de Carnaval . . . Los cuernos de Don Friolera*
      La hija del capitán. El terno del difunto.
XXV. *Tablado de marionetas: Farsa de la reina castiza.*
      La cabeza del dragón. La enamorada del Rey.
XXVI. *Tirano Banderas*
XXVII. *La corte de los milagros*   XXVII, XXVIII, XXIX:
XXVIII. *Viva mi dueño*   This trilogy is called
XXIX. *Baza de espadas*   *El ruedo ibérico.*

To these we may add Professor William Fichter's collection of Valle's early pieces, which could be gathered under number III, *Jardín umbrío*.
    What are we to make of this list? The first nine entries may be called sonatas, and the fourteenth and sixteenth also. In a sonata one "annihilates the ideological meaning of words" ("aniquilando el significado ideológico de las palabras" —*Lámpara*, p. 29); one listens for the "musical miracle" ("el milagro musical de las palabras") and the undulations of music

33

("Adonde no llegan las palabras con sus significados, van las ondas de sus músicas"—*Lámpara*, 37); one penetrates the world of evocations, erotic evocations, through the religious words of the poet ("En este mundo de las evocaciones sólo penetran los poetas, porque para sus ojos todas las cosas tienen una significación religiosa, más próxima a la significación única"—*Lámpara*, 26); in our Dionysian life impregnated with mystical intuitions (*Lámpara*, 39), one experiences a "felicitous dissolving in the bosom of all things" ("un feliz desleimiento en el seno de todas las cosas,"—*Lámpara*, 73); one can listen to a prophet like Saint Bernard of Clairvaux who, "preaching in the old tongue of *oíl*, raised an army for the Crusade of Jerusalem, in foreign lands where he couldn't be understood"—*Lámpara*, 35. In other words a sonata is a musical miracle, a divine glossolalia, a gift of tongues, in which the brother pilgrim (*hermano peregrino*) intuitively transcends the veil of phenomena to arrive at eternal truths beyond. A sonata does not exclude the *esperpentic*, to coin a word from Valle-Inclán, the foolish, ugly and grotesque, which it frequently contains, but it resounds with the miracle transcending all deformation. Salvation through resonance. Lyrical transcendentalism.

The last seven entries on Valle's list, *Divinas palabras* to *Baza de espadas*, may be called *esperpentos*, aesthetic deformations of the frightful, ugly, foolish and absurd phenomenal world. This artistic procedure has been likened to the deforming mirrors in a sideshow, where a man is reflected now as tall and skinny, now squat and fat with bulging eyes and lips. Again, the *esperpento* does not exclude the sonata, since the reader encounters sonatic phrases amidst a bizarre, grotesque atmosphere, but the emphasis is on ugly fantasy. And, to be sure, the *Lámpara* spells this out for us:

> El espíritu de los gnósticos descubre una emoción
> estética en el absurdo de las formas, en la creación
> de monstruos, en el acabamiento de la vida. . . .
> Para los gnósticos la belleza de las imágenes no
> está en ellas, sino en el acto creador. (*Lámpara*,
> pp. 70-71)

> The spirit of the gnostics reveals an aesthetic
> emotion in the absurdity of forms, in the creation
> of monsters, in the termination of life. . . . For
> the gnostics the beauty of images is not in them
> themselves, but in the creative act.[3]

Whether one literally accepts Valle's gnosticism as Manichaeanism or Marcionism or the work of the man who kissed the ring of Giges and adored Hermes Trimegistus, or figuratively accepts it as a modern aesthetic gnosis overstating ancient symbols, the same truth obtains: Valle experiences aesthetic delight in creating the grotesque. In the scenes of a woman being stripped of her clothes by howling dogs, of a ne'er-do-well pushing his dear old aunt down the stairs, of a drooling dictator sending people to their deaths, of pigs eating a baby, of a man having his eyeballs roasted in a chimney fire—in all these absurd forms Valle, and his disciples who publish his works as breviaries, experience a movement of the soul. A movement of the soul toward—but that is the code, and I must follow Lope's dictum in his *New Art of Writing Plays*: wait until the last act for the denouement.

A pattern emerges. I will not insist on a strict mathematical formula, namely, that the first eight books are sonatas, the last seven esperpentos, and that there is a gradation in those in between, because such rigidity is not valleinclanesque. But let us say that dividing the thirty volumes into rough thirds, we have a passage from the musical world of the sonatas, through the here and now world of the Carlist civil war, to the mirror distortion of *El ruedo ibérico*; we have a passage from a penumbral, crepuscular world, the twilight, to the light of history (history, things as they happened, as Cervantes might say), to gargoyles. I want to repeat that the reader, the brother pilgrim, will find overlappings: The scorched eyeballs I spoke of before, these absurd forms, these monsters, appear in the historical *guerra carlista*.

In a nutshell, the music of the sonatas undulates towards the great beyond, beyond the horizon; the more historical works hold an eye on the horizon, their feet on the ground before them, and another eye on the grotesque; the *esperpentos* reveal beauty in monstrous images and so arrive at the horizon. Should this attempt to categorize the books seem nebulous, Valle might approve. For we have arrived at the *balbuceo*, the stammer, where categories are wanting:

Un día nuestros ojos y nuestros oídos destruirán las categorías, los géneros, las enumeraciones, herencia de las viejas filosofías . . . (*Lámpara*, p. 50)

One day our eyes and our ears will destroy the categories, the genres, the enumerations, legacy of old philosophies . . .

and

¡Qué mezquino, qué torpe, qué difícil balbuceo el nuestro para expresar este deleite de lo inefable que reposa en todas las cosas con la gracia de un niño dormido. (*Lámpara*, p. 16)

> What a miserable, what a clumsy, what a puzzling stammer we have for expressing this joy of the ineffable, which reposes in all things with the grace of a sleeping child.

Thus according to Valle, categories (even sonatas and *esperpentos* and history) are misleading because they fracture the ability to reach ultimate reality. There is only one real world, one meaning (to use a banal word), one Beauty, one gnosis, one Word (the thirty volumes, then, represent one Word); and to attempt to utter them is to stammer.

Only *garbanceros* attempt to categorize. I shall risk Valle's disdain and garbanticize: I shall divide his thirty volumes into roughly three parts. Alas, I fear I am one of the hylics.

6. You say Valle's *Guerra carlista* is historical. But compare it with Galdós's *Zumalacárregui* and his other *National Episodes*. How can you call them both historical?

I am tempted to say that Galdós's Carlists are essential whereas Valle's are quintessential. Galdós is less the chickpea vendor (*garbancero*) than Max Estrella, or Valle, seems to think he is, and Valle himself knows more about garbanzo beans than he himself will allow, but I shall discuss this later on. Suffice it to say that incorrigible gnostics like this abracadabra Galician, this Manichaean terror, are wont to see three groups in mankind: the hylics, the psychics and the spirituals or pneumatics. Jesuits and friars are obviously hylics although Loyola himself was not one (Loyola was not a Jesuit! Christ was not a Christian! And I suppose Aristotle was not an Aristotelian . . .) As for the psychics and spirituals, let us try to describe them. But first, let us rub the magic lamp. ¡Abracadabra, pata de cabra!

7. Just who are the hylics, the psychics, the pneumatics? How do we recognize them? What do they do? Do they leave a sign?

The pneumatics hold the celestial keys, the keys to the kingdom, the lyrical keys opening the door to the Holy Ghost, not the Third Person of the Christian Trinity (a category!) but the vital spirit, the soul, the breath of the heterodox, the *Alma Mundo*, which exists beyond phenomena and is merely veiled by them. The pneumatics used to be priests, ascetic mystics who had the gnosis, like Maní, but now they are sacerdotal artists, ascetics, mystics lighting the Lamp with their clusters of words, with their Verbo, not the *Verbum carum factum est* of the Nicene Creed (of that hylic Athanasius), which would *incarnate* the pneuma, phenomenalizing it, esperpentisizing it, but the *Verbo* of the pneumatologist, Don Ramón María del Valle-Inclán y Montenegro. This *Verbo* is pure form, devoid of matter. In the words of Pedro Salinas, the formalist who eulogized Valle-Inclán:

El que crea como yo, que la literatura, en su altísimo punto, es un procedimiento de objetivar, con ánimo de salvación perdurable, las experiencias humanas mediante un uso especial, o sea un arte, del lenguaje, de las palabras, verá la supremacía de una obra no derivada capitalmente del asunto o tema dado por la experiencia y sí del acierto de la operación subjetivante o poetizadora, fuente de la hermosura.[4]

I believe that literature at its highest point is a procedure of objectivizing human experiences, with a deep desire for everlasting salvation. I believe that this is done by a special use, or if you will an art of language, of words. He who believes this with me will see the supreme quality of a work as being derived not so much from the matter or theme as from the skill of the subjective or poetizing operation, which is the source of beauty.

The "operación subjetivante o poetizadora" of Salinas, which is idealist, comes from the same source as Valle's idealism. We are approaching the code, which will be discussed below.

Just as the Christ of orthodoxy is the Word who alone can bring us to Being, I Am That I Am, so in aesthetic gnostic heterodoxy the poet's *Verbo* can alone bring the brother pilgrim to the *Alma Mundo*.

And who might the other pneumatics be? They are those anonymous architects, creators of ancient musty millenary cathedrals, like the one in León, where catechumens can chant in the penumbra of the vestibules. They are ancient bards chanting the ballads of yore, the *romances*, in which princes hear the siren's song and go with the boatman in his strange barque, which never returns:

—Yo no digo mi canción
sino a quién conmigo va. (El Infante Arnaldos).

—I do not sing my song
but to him who goes with me.

—all this at dawn or eventide. Other pneumatics are centenarian blind beggars and pilgrims wending their way beyond the horizon, to Santiago de Compostela, the field vaguely lit by a star. And they are remote spiritual Carlists divesting themselves

37

of this world's riches to follow the path of nebulous glory, Bradomíns one and all. And Manrique, Per Vermúdoz (lengua sin manos, ¿cuómo osas fablar?), mío Cid, San Fernando, who all lived in the once-upon-a-time of nebulous deeds and plain simple language, when there were no such words as *thine* and *mine*, and young maidens could roam the fields at night without molestation; Santillana, he of archaic tone (Moça tan fermosa non vi en la carrera como una vaquera de la Finojosa), ascetic Luis de Granada, stammering San Juan de la Cruz. And all those strange beings and names of the karma memory, the dwellers of Plato's cave who somehow adumbrate the light, one day to go forth. These are the pneumatics, the aesthetic communion of saints, the spiritual fellows of Don Ramón María del Valle-Inclán y Montenegro. And who are the pneumatics today? Espronceda perhaps and Lorca. They are few and far between. Certainly not Quintana. Or Campoamor. Or Luis Coloma, friar-Jesuit of the *ojos entornados*. It is time for *carcajadas, risotadas, energúmenos, esperpentos*. The world of Comte the hylic. Better to use block letters: POSITIVISM, COMTE THE HYLIC.

8. And who are the psychics? The brother pilgrims who might make the grade if they heed the poet's Word. If they listen to the musical miracle.

Who are the psychics, denizens of the halfway house, with one foot in this phenomenal world and the other pointing toward, reaching for a horizon? It's hard to say, Moratín perhaps, but he was so prosaic, confining himself to time:

... yo lograba romper el enigma del Tiempo
(*Lámpara*, p. 29)

... I succeeded in breaking the enigma of Time

whereas Moratín, "el inmortal Inarco" (que no lo era) bound himself to the three unities, his plays taking place in ten, sterile, temporal hours:

Dios es la eterna quietud, y la belleza suprema está en Dios. Satán es el estéril que borra eternamente sus huellas sobre el camino del Tiempo. (*Lámpara*, p. 27)

God is eternal quietude, and supreme beauty is in God. Satan is the sterile one who eternally expunges God's traces on the road of Time.

Moratín, who could not break the fetters of his "cárcel de barro" (his "jail of clay", that is, his body) was glued to his senses. How different he is from the millenary balladeer of *El Infante*

38

Arnaldos. In Valle's lexicon *millenary* doesn't mean literally a thousand years but something so old and vague as to prescind from time.

Don Benito Pérez Galdós (1843-1920), professional *garbancero*, Benito the chickpea man: We are getting very close to the code; indeed the difference between Galdós and Valle is the code. We have in Galdós innumerable garbanzo beans (remember that Spain is "the land of the *garbanzo*"): Zaragoza and Numancia, what could be more essentially Spanish than they? Or Santiago Fernández, nicknamed The Great Captain—as great in his own way as Gonzalo de Córdova—who resisted Napoleon in Galdós's *Chamartín*? Or Sursum Corda? Or Juan Martín el Empecinado? Or Gabriel de Araceli, the enamored, when he hastens to Córdoba with Santorcaz and Marijuán, to see his beloved Inés? What could be more Spanish? This is Spain incarnate. And *that* is the trouble! Galdós's novels make Spain incarnate. Showing all the details, all the fleshly garments, all the arms, the traitors, the food, the wine, the rats, the houses, the rivers, the mountains, the trees, the money, the ships, the letters, the literature, the . . . ¡porra! ¡reporra! and ¡cáspita! ¡recáspita!, they are too phenomenal. Galdós's novels stop at nothing invoked by sterile time. They show the entire profile of things, all the details down the to the last grain of sand, so a Galdós novel is really a big garbanzo bean, weighing, one might say, three hundred pages, or, by multiplication (46 national episodes by 300 pages equals 13,800), thirteen thousand eight hundred pages. Millions of garbanzos! Ugh! So much realism is hard on the digestive tract; whereas a novel by the *alumbrado* Inclán may run a scant hundred pages with but a few, select significant details; significant and non-carnal, non-phenomenal and lyrical. Lyrical keys. Galdós devotes a whole novel to Alvarez Mendizábal (episode 2 of the third series of national episodes), but the Galician sage looks into his crystal ball and extracts a few lines:

La madre abadesa murmuró con los ojos brillantes:
—¡Como los hijos heredan el genio de los padres!
Y comentó el marqués de Bradomín:
—¡El genio del linaje! . . . Lo que nunca pudo comprender aquel desatentado ministro de doña Isabel.
—¡El destructor de los mayorazgos, y de los conventos!
—¡El destructor de toda la tradición española!

* * *

. . . pero los hidalgos, los secos hidalgos de gotera, eran la sangre más pura, destilada en un filtro de mil años y de cien guerras. ¡Y todo lo quebrantó el caballo de Atila! (*Cruzados de la causa*, p. 88)

The abbess murmured, her eyes shining:
—How children do inherit the spirit of their parents!
And then spoke up the Marquis of Bradomín:
—The spirit of their ancestry! . . . What that madcap minister of Queen Isabel never understood!
—The destroyer of primogeniture! And of the monasteries!
—The destroyer of the entire tradition of Spain!

* * *

. . . but the hidalgos, those lean, laconic hidalgos, were of the purest blood, distilled through a filter of a hundred wars and thousand years. And it was all shattered by the horse of Attila the Hun!

To understand Mendizábal, to see the quintessential light, we do not have to know his love life, his debts, his culinary habits, his actions in England, his house, his books, his physiognomy or even his politics and history. We only need know that for traditionalists he is the arch traitor, Vellido Dolfos, Conde Julián, don Oppas, Attila the Hun, the Spanish rat who sold out Spain. The destroyer of primogeniture and the Church.

The irony of the narrator's exclamation points will not be lost on the observant reader. Aesthetic Carlism, millenary tradition, legendary *cabecillas*, yes! These gnostic visions will lead to the code (See also the *Sonata de invierno*, which concerns the Carlist war.) But brutish fanaticism, egregious stupidity, bumbling venality, and hatred—in a word, hypocrisy, NO! These vices provide the stuff of puppets and *esperpentos*. Santos Banderas, ¡Chac! ¡Chac!

9. But Max Estrella's judgment (or perhaps Valle's) is too hard on Galdós. The latter is the greatest of *garbanceros*, whom we may define as "nineteenth century realist portrait artists of phenomena." Galdós, however, is also a poet, a man whose vision resembles Valle's. When Santorcaz crosses La Mancha and sees the two herds of sheep midst clouds of dust, he immediately hears trumpets, drums and clashing hooves and witnesses again

the Battle of Austerlitz. Nobody can beat the Emperor! Nobody! There, there is the Russian army, their guns, the frozen meadow of Pratzen! See the Emperor! Another Cid! How glorious! And Santorcaz carries his quixotic vision to the skies above, where, in the clouds, the battle breaks up in caricature. (Galdós, *Bailén*). Surely the Marquis of Bradomín kept vigil at Santorcaz's Austerlitz, and so did Cara de Plata, Montenegro, Santa Cruz and all the others. The Galician sage must have known that. Perhaps he was smoking his *pipa de Kif* and got carried away the day he had Max Estrella call his peer, Don Benito Pérez Galdós, a mere *garbancero*.[5]

10. I do not want to labor the point, but I love Gabriel Araceli too much to let him be called a *garbanzo*, a bean. Libertine reader, do you remember when Gabriel went to Cordoba in search of Inés and passed by a church where a gust of wind caught his attention and where the hand of the Virgin's statue seemed to move, beckoning him? The Mother of God was telling him "Here, Gabriel, here, she's in here." Phenomena don't act like that, that's not phenomenal. Galdós sensed the code, he was an artist. No, Max Estrella was wrong, don Benito was no mere *garbancero*, a chick pea man yes, but not merely.

11. *Libertine reader*: If Valle can call you and me *brother pilgrim*, perhaps I can address you as *dear reader* and give you my thoughts. My method is similar to Valle's: repeat, repeat, repeat, using a cipher of sorts until the reader understands, until his finds his place in the firmament. You may have perceived by now some light. According to Valle, realists interest themselves in phenomena, but impressionists want to transcend the phenomenal images of things. Unamuno called this *nivola*.

12. Very well, the pneumatics are the hierophant Don Ramón del Valle-Inclán, Priscilianus, hoary artists of yore, Molinos, and perhaps an Espronceda, Lorca, or Machado (Antonio), he who praises the legendary don Francisco Giner, a millenary figure, a reincarnation of San Francisco de Asís. The Machado of the coffin striking the ground would be a pneumatic if the scene is viewed as esperpentic.

The psychics are Benito Pérez Galdós; perhaps Moratín, although his unity of time tends to disqualify him; perhaps the Benavente of the *comedia de polichinelas*, but not the other Benavente, writer of phenomenal trash; most certainly not Ricardo León. As for Federico García Lorca,

Nana, niño, nana
del caballo grande
que no quiso el agua

who had the good sense to write his plays as poems, language of the spirit: Federico must be promoted to the ranks of the

41

pneumatics. He is far more than a psychic.

Well, then, who are the hylics? After the death of Calderón in 1681, everybody, well almost everybody. The eighteenth century writers were so poor they weren't even *garbanceros*, and those aesthetic pygmies even forbade the staging of *autos sacramentales*, which after all strive to pierce the veil of phenomena, to arrive at ultimate reality. That whole rationalist century was hylic. (I myself would spare Ramón de la Cruz from this general condemnation, and so, on reflection, might Valle). In the nineteenth century AUGUSTE COMTE is the COMPLEAT HYLIC WHO WORSENED THINGS, but a few authors escaped his satanic assault: Gil y Carrasco, he of the millenary *Bembibre*, Espronceda, Bécquer, Rosalía, it's hard to name any more, perhaps Larra. A lot of perhaps. But by and large, nobody. Then who were the hylics? Quintana, Balmes, Alarcón, Pereda, Juan Tenorio el ripioso, Doña Perfecta, Menéndez Pelayo, Tamayo, Cecilia Böhl de Faber, the Teutonic *jándala* with her "casticismo rancio y viejo." . . . Father Luis Coloma, S.J., is worse than she if that is possible. A colleague of Valle, don Pío Baroja, the bad man from Itzea, will supply the predicate nouns and adjectives for all these hylics; they are: *estúpido, eunuco, cretino, farsante, vejete ridículo, mala bestia* . . .

The hylics, grinding out platitudes and phenomenal rigidities, are *malas bestias*. And they all have *ojos entornados*, especially the priest Coloma and his friend the *beata*, Cecilia Böhl de Faber, who had the audacity to adopt the pen name *Caballero*.

Given Valle's extreme artistic bias, this list is accurate. There are very few pneumatics (an illiterate guitarist or dancer might be one, so their number is hard to determine), rather more psychics, and a host of hylics weeping and gnashing their teeth in the outer darkness.

Nevertheless, there may be some equivocation on Valle's part. Let us take the two worst names on the list, Cecilia Böhl de Faber (pen name, *Fernán Caballero*), who would Catholicize everything, even the air one breathes and the mountains, sky and fjords of Valle's native, pantheistic Galicia; and P. Luis Coloma, S.J., the humorless author of tendentious novels, who followed Fernán like a son. For Valle these would be the two worst hylics, and yet in them the reader can find an element pointing to Valle himself, to his code, his quest for the *Más Allá*, and also his *esperpento*. This is rather like saying that satan makes way for the Lord. Let us take the first satan, Cecilia Böhl de Faber.

13. Cecilia Böhl de Faber, *Fernán Caballero* (1796-1877). I have written a passage elsewhere on Fernán Caballero and should like to quote it here:

The Aesthetics of Fernán Caballero

Coloma modeled his *Recreational Readings* on
the literature of his elderly friend, Cecilia Böhl de
Faber (Fernán Caballero), who explains her
attitude toward art in chapter 7 of her novel, *La
gaviota* (The Seagull, 1849). Her explanation
accurately describes the aesthetics of Luis Coloma.
In *The Seagull* a young German doctor, Fritz
Stein, comes to Andalusia and lives in an
abandoned monastery with a Spanish family. On
All Saints' Day, this family discusses religious
customs and folklore, tells stories of a religious
bent, and sings songs and lullabies referring to
various plants and animals:

> There above, on Mount Calvary,
> little olive, fragrant bush,
> there sang the death of Christ
> four linnets and a nightingale.

The son Manuel introduces so many witty stories
into the conversation that his mother must explain:
"You can be sure, Don Federico, that there is no
event for which my son doesn't have a story, joke,
or witty anecdote, whether they come to the point
or not." The boy is *pueblo*, the Spanish people,
and after he comments on everything in his
sententious way, the narrator, who is Fernán
Caballero herself, enters the story to explain the
nature of Spanish popular art, or *costumbrismo*:

> It would be difficult for the person who
> catches these poetical emanations on the
> wing, as a boy catches butterflies, to
> explain to whoever might want to analyze
> them, why the nightingales and linnets
> lamented the death of the Redeemer; why
> the swallow pulled out the thorns from his
> crown; why the rosemary is looked on with
> a certain veneration, in the belief that the
> Virgin dried the diapers of the Child Jesus
> on a bush of that plant; why, or rather,
> how it is known that the elder tree is a
> sign of ill omen ever since Judas hung
> himself on one of them; why nothing bad
> ever happens in a house if incense from
> the rosemary is burned in it on Christmas

night; why all the instruments on the Passion can be seen in the flower given that name. And, in truth, there are no answers for such questions. The people neither have answers nor seek them, they have gathered those things like the vague sound of a distant music, without inquiring into their origin or analyzing their authenticity. The *sages* and *positivists* will honor with a smile of disdainful compassion the person who writes these lines. But for us it is enough to hope to find some sympathy in the heart of a mother, or beneath the humble roof of him who knows little and feels much, or in the mystical retreat of a cloister, when we say that for our part we believe there have always been and there are today mysterious revelations for pious and ascetic souls. The world will call these revelations the delirium of overexcited imaginations, whereas the people of obedient and fervent faith will look upon them as special favors of God. Henri Blaze has said: "How many ideas tradition puts in the air in the form of a germ and the poet gives them life with his breath!" It seems to us that this very same thought applies to these things; it obliges no one to believe but also authorizes no one to condemn. A mysterious origin put the germ of them in the air, and believing and pious hearts give them life. No matter how much the apostles of rationalism prune the tree of faith, if the tree has its roots in good ground, that is, in a sound and fervent heart, it will eternally throw out vigorous and flowering branches that reach to heaven.

These thoughts of Fernán Caballero permeate the *Recreational Readings*. Coloma professes to be speaking for the people, specifically, the Andalusian people. There are poetical emanations in the air, like unfertilized germs, and the poet or storyteller breathes into them, giving them life. This picture resembles the doctrines of the Generation of 1898, Unamuno's intrahistory, for example, or Baroja's little things, Valle-Inclán's pantheistic gnosis, or Azorín's quotidian cock crowing, hammer sound on anvil, and locomotive glowing in the night—except for one thing: Luis Coloma's Spanish people (*pueblo*) are traditionalists. They believe in "God, King, and Country" and the "altar and the throne," so that the popular emanations will primarily contain the seeds of religion: a swallow easing the pain of the Crown of Thorns by removing one of them, nightingales and linnets lamenting the death of the divine redeemer, the rosemary as a drying place for the Infant Savior's garments. For Luis Coloma, like the boy Manuel in *The Seagull*, there is no event for which he does not have "a story, joke or witty anecdote" of a religious nature, "whether they are to the point or not." Perhaps the observations of the narrators in Coloma's stories relate to his theological point, but they frequently seem impertinent through overstatement, as in *Half John and John and a Half*, where the author himself enters at the end to explain why two Spanish smugglers return a shipment of gold chalices and ciboria, stolen by the French, to the Church. In a well-told story, the act of restitution alone will show the common man's deep devotion, and the narrative will require no final expository essay telling how all Spaniards, even smugglers and ne'er do wells, revere the Christian religion.

Sages and *positivists* will question the "poetical emanations" in the air and also the "vague sound of a distant music," because these emanations and sound do not belong to the world of phenomena. The Catholic traditionalist, Fernán Caballero, will assent to them, and so will the heterodox Valle-Inclán, although he will give them a different reading. For both Fernán and Valle, there is a world beyond phenomena.[6]
    14. For Valle-Inclán, the second satan is P. Luis Coloma, S.J. (1851-1914), and yet here again one finds a paradoxical similarity.
    Chapter 28 of Coloma's novel *Boy* takes place in the midst of the Carlist civil war, where Boy is shot by the militia (*migueletes*). The page describing his interment is so unusual as to require commentary here. The *migueletes*, believing Boy to be a foreign citizen, are frightened and hastily bury him:

        Soon the hole was dug, wide and fairly
        deep, and first taking the watch and

money from the cadaver, they threw it into the pit . . . But it turned out that the grave was too short, and the feet of the dead man, which were well tied together now, stuck out over the end by about two hand lengths. The young miguelete wanted to lengthen the grave, but the old man violently opposed this with a devilish look, and he struck three or four blows with the edge of his pick on the dead man's legs; the bones crunched horribly on being splintered, and now that they were flexible like a sheet of paper, he folded the legs upward, and as quickly as he could began to throw earth in the grave until it was filled.

The young miguelete, as yellow as wax, turned his face away, horrified.

The *migueletes* leave, but one other person witnessed the burial, the Basque woman Juana-Mari, who was hidden behind a door: "She stuck her head out, trembling, livid with horror, her eyes still dilated by fright . . ."

It is curious that this terrible scene resembles the creations of Spain's great modern satirist, Ramón del Valle-Inclán (1866-1936). No one could be further removed from Valle than the devout Paco Burunda or his author Luis Coloma, S.J. Valle's *Sonatas* make a mockery of traditional values, and his aesthetic primer, *The Marvelous Lamp*, carries a subtitle, *Spiritual Exercises*, that is a patent spoofing of St. Ignatius Loyola's famous work of the same title. Valle's exercises proclaim an aesthetic gnosis based on a mixture of ancient pantheistic and Gnostic, particularly Manichaean, elements. In one part of *The Marvelous Lamp* he declares that gnostics like himself take delight in creating the grotesque, which accounts for the weird, uncanny scenes in his literature. Valle has been accused of a lack of seriousness, an inaccurate charge because his outlandish scenes and jokes are never merely that; sometimes they satirize, sometimes they provide an unforgettable experience of an era or event, for example, the Carlist War, and at all times they offer an artistic delight, which Valle would claim to be a gnostic pleasure.

What, on the other hand, will account for the grotesque interment of Boy? It certainly does not consciously come from anything as heterodox as *The Marvelous Lamp* or its anti-Jesuitic, anti-Catholic author Valle-Inclán. Valle would have likened Coloma to the hypocritical clergy of the *Sonatas*, with their "ojos entornados" (half-closed eyes), and Coloma would certainly have grouped Valle with Renan, Frazer, "revolutionary traitors," and even worse, with demonic forces, given the sacrilegious scenes of Valle's works. The answer then must lie somewhere beyond the conscious, and there we may find two reasons.

Coloma (1851-1916) and Valle-Inclán (1866-1936) were contemporaries, and they must have had similar experiences. Valle-Inclán's *The Marvelous Lamp* shows a formal Manichaean disdain of matter: the senses are evil and not to be trusted, and time, "the sterile Satan" as he calls it, is also evil. Valle does not like or place confidence in the world about him and seeks something outside it, the world of mystery, which can be captured somehow by the artist: "Listen to the music of my words, not to their meaning." Coloma, who believed in the Incarnation of Christ, could never disdain matter with the same intensity as Valle-Inclán, and he certainly could not call it inherently evil; nevertheless, there is in all his literature a certain antinomy between matter and spirit that has a nonorthodox savor. His otherworldliness seems excessive. Thus, both Coloma the Jesuit and Valle the anti-Jesuit may have had a common experience and sympathy; witnessing the last three decades of the nineteenth century, the Generation of Materialism as one historian has called it, they may both have reacted by creating grotesque scenes in their literature. In Coloma's case, this might mean that the *migueletes* could mutilate the body of Boy because his shriven soul had already ascended to heaven.

The second similarity between Coloma and Valle-Inclán can be seen in the former's active contradiction of his own verbal profession. He professed to be a missionary-novelist whose pulpit (*cátedra*) was the novel, and, to be sure, he seems to play that role throughout his *Recreational Readings*, some passages of *Bagatelles*, and a few parts of *Boy*. But, as we have seen, he is sometimes carried away by his satirical muse and talent for storytelling: the novelist acquires the upper hand. He is good at aesthetic deformation and enjoys doing it, so he creates his Villamelones, Frasquitos, Diogenes, and the final scene of *Boy*. He may not subscribe to the aesthetic gnosis of Valle-Inclán with its anti-Christian musical score, but he does experience a peculiar delight, a *gnosis* of sorts, in creating his marionettes and belittling them, and thus he resembles Valle. His antimaterialism and the pleasure he takes in narration make him a cousin, albeit distant, of the goat-bearded, one-armed, turban-hatted sage of Galicia. The similarities I have suggested stop short at the threshold of prose style. Coloma condemns materialism harshly, in its own terms, *sans façon*, whereas Valle creates a superior music. Hence he calls his works *Sonatas*.

15. Two last remarks: (1) Fernán Caballero published *La gaviota* in 1849. More than a half century before Valle-Inclán, she looked beyond the phenomenal world to the noumenal, just as he was to do. The trouble with her, from a gnostic's point of view, was her orthodoxy. Her noumenal world was Catholic.

(2) Perhaps we can borrow a metaphor from one of the parables. The New Testament speaks of the field where cockle and tares have been sown with the wheat, and where they will be allowed to grow together until after the harvest. Given Valle's vision, we might change the parable at this point: The cockle and wheat will be bound into separate bundles, the phenomenal cockle for esperpentic burning, and the wheat for sonatic illumination, celestial poetic penetration. This will result in the pneumatic satisfaction of the *hermano peregrino*. Valle would draw a gnostic eye and write *Laus Deo*.

16. Let us turn now to Canto III, where the following works are considered:
    (1) *Visión estelar de un momento de guerra*
    (2) *Sonata de primavera*
    (3) The trilogy of the *Guerra carlista*
    (4) *Tirano Banderas*

48

CANTO III

Stellar Vision

1. If the code is universal, it should obtain everywhere. So let us take any work of Valle, *La media noche, Visión estelar de un momento de guerra*, number 20 on Valle's list, just before the deformation of *Divinas palabras*. *La media noche* is Valle's historiography, so in Canto III I shall observe this order: historiography, *esperpento (Tirano Banderas)*, sonata (*Primavera*). Valle's historiography is stellar vision; his *esperpento* a concave-convex look at historical events, a mirror vision: and his sonata a vision of a different order, stellar and beyond, a vision predicated on sounds, music. Glossolalia. Impressionism. Synesthetic intuition. The code.

Thus we have: stellar vision   (historiography)
                      mirror vision   (*esperpento*)
                      gnosis   (sonata)

2. The word *stellar* suggests extreme distance and light, darkness and brilliance, an obscure midnight with one bright ray shining through. This is the way to capture the quintessence of war: Focus on the blackness and penetrate the veil with a beam, to bring forth one moment's quintessential truth, one instant's truth; for once possessed of the truth you know the war. You are in it. You have a stellar vision.

3. A war correspondent, a phenomenalist, sends back statistics—numbers of troops, location, arms, munitions, maps, advances of so many yards, names, diagnosis, prognosis—in a word, he sends back a huge garbanzo bean. But a stellar poet sends back . . . a first chapter of just fifteen lines: the moon travels through skies of clear stars, blue skies, nebulous skies; the trenches smell of death like hyena cages; the Frenchman, offspring of the Latin she-wolf, and the barbarous German, bastard by all tradition, are again at war; hundreds of thousands of combatants but only the stars can see them all at once; and, ever present, the lightning flashes of powder and thunder of cannon rolling across the heaven. Only the stars pierce the veil.

The stars do not seek images made by the jail of clay (the body, the senses), no, they pierce the veil of phenomena and abstract, distill, producing a fine liqueur. But this liqueur is spirit, so the object of art is spirit. The object of aesthetic historiography is spirit.

One example is worth a thousand words, so here are Valle's first fifteen lines (*La Media Noche*, Capitulo I):

> Son las doce de la noche. La luna navega por
> cielos de claras estrellas, por cielos azules, por
> cielos nebulosos. Desde los bosques montaneros de

49

la región alsaciana, hasta la costa brava del mar
norteño, se acechan dos ejércitos agazapados en los
fosos de su atrincheramiento, donde hiede a
muerto como en la jaula de las hienas. El francés,
hijo de la loba latina, y el bárbaro germano,
espurio de toda tradición, están otra vez en guerra.
Doscientas leguas alcanza la línea de sus defensas
desde los cantiles del mar hasta los montes que
dominan la verde plana del Rhin. Son cientos de
miles, y solamente los ojos de las estrellas pueden
verlos combatir al mismo tiempo, en los dos cabos
de esta línea tan larga, a toda hora llena del
relampagueo de la pólvora y con el trueno del
cañón rodante por su cielo.

It is twelve at night. The moon sails through skies
of bright stars, across blue skies, across nebulous
skies. From the highland forests of the Alsatian
home to the craggy coast of the northern sea, two
armies lie in wait crouched in the moats of their
trenches, where it smells of death like a hyenas'
cage. The Frenchman, offspring of the Latin she-
wolf, and the barbarous German, bastard by all
tradition, are once again at war. The line of
defense reaches two hundred leagues from the
cliffs at sea to the hills overseeing the verdure of
the Rhine. They are hundreds of thousands, and
only the eyes of the stars can see them struggle all
at once, at both ends of this stretched out line, at
every moment filled with lightning flashes of
powder bursts and thunder of cannon rolling
across the sky. (End of Chapter I).

4. Each chapter is a spark, a thaumaturgic vision of reality,
not visible reality but something beyond, namely, the ultimate
form of war. And to capture this form, nay, this Form, the
stellar correspondent may send back medieval alexandrines: "los
ratones corren vivaces por los taludes" ("the rats do run
vivacious down the slopes"); "las ratas aguaneras por el fondo
cenagoso" ("the aguaniferous rats along the mudhole
depths")—Chapter II. This is not Europe at war specifically in
1914, 1789, 1618, or any other year, but a moment of War Itself:
The distillation of history, not the phenomenon, not its mere
fermentation, but the distillation.
5. *Ráfagas* are somehow perceived and heard and felt.
Ráfaga (gust), with *crepúsculo*, is the favorite word of the poet,
for they both help pierce the veil. "Ráfagas de viento traen frías
pestilencias de carroña"—"Gusts of Wind come bearing frigid

putrefying plagues" (Ch. II); "Se oye el cañón, cuándo lento, cuándo en vivo fuego de ráfagas"—"The cannonade is heard, now slow now in lively gusty fire." (Ch. III). You cannot literally see a gust, gusts are impalpable, they are air, wind, approaching the pneuma; but you can experience their effect, perceive it so to speak, the thundering of mighty artillery and stink of fetid flesh. But not the gusts themselves, which hail from a metaphysical world.

In his book on *Santa Teresa de Avila* (1923), Gaston Etchegoyen speaks of the *terminologie traditionelle* of the mystics, which includes *air, fire,* and *water,* the least material of all elements (the most spiritual so to speak). A *ráfaga* is air. When reading Valle-Inclán, one should always keep in mind a mystical or quasi-mystical attempt.

6. Since *ráfagas* are vague, imprecise, distant, uncanny, now here and now gone, seen but not seen, they resemble *crepúsculos.* They belong to the same order. And linguistically they are *esdrújulos,* not *llanos,* not Spanish precisely, but *esdrújulos.* Valle's antepenults don't belong to the phenomenal language of the Spanish nation because they are metaphysically inspired. They do, however, belong to a stellar vision of war, or for that matter, to any stellar vision.

Many other *esdrújulos* are also trans-phenomenal, suggesting the existence of another, higher world; for example:

... destacábase en la penumbra inmóvil
... cerca del amanecer, cuando la luna ya muy pálida
... y sus ojos inmóviles, abiertos sobre el infinito
... entre mirtos inmóviles

These examples are taken at random from *Primavera,* where their number is legion. Pallid hands and pallid fingers (*manos pálidas* and *dedos pálidos*) and fluttering hands and fingers, which belong to women, also make trans-phenomenal suggestions. They engage in a manual choreography leading to the penumbral horizon and beyond.

7. Consider these vision-of-war chapters! Exactly forty of them in fifty-odd short pages, many of them just a paragraph! What a way to report a war, nay, to reveal a war! Stars are not like mortal men. They do not have to gather, cull, reason, edit, publish. They twinkle, cast a ray on the morass, and there, there it is, a moment of war, an instant of war captured forever:

Este soplo de inspiración muestra la eternidad del momento y desvela el enigma de las vidas.

51

This breath of inspiration shows the eternity of the moment and reveals the enigma of lives.

Stars capture the essence; no, that's not quite right, it's not the essence, nor even the quintessence, but something beyond. Stars capture a moment of eternity. The thing-in-itself! That's the code, that's where the code leads, Das Ding-an-sich! Noumena.

> 8. Del fondo de las trincheras surgen cohetes de luces rojas, verdes y blancas, que se abren en los aires de la noche oscura, esclareciendo brevemente aquel vasto campo de batallas. (Capítulo II)

> From the trenches' depth, red, green, white light rockets surge, bursting open in the air flow of the dark night, briefly clarifying that vast battlefield.

The world we live in is a dark battle field where the stellar poet sends forth a rocket, or flare, or *sonata*, or *clave lírica* briefly clarifying all. Briefly, for one eternal moment, the brother pilgrim can glimpse "un feliz desleimiento en el seno de todas las cosas." (*Lámpara*, 73), "a felicitous clearing up in the bosom of all things." Except for the eternal moment, made possible by stellar vision, the form of things is always uncertain; in the eternal moment, the form or bosom of all things is, so to speak, thinned, cleared up (*desleimiento*), made perceptible.[1]

Eternity lies outside of Time, which is sterile; sterile certainly when it comes to interpreting the Universe. Thus in an idealist instant, an aesthetic, timeless instant, the poet can capture the eternal forms of Plato, or the mystical communion of the Christians, or the Alma Mundo of Valle, in modern parlance, the noumena. Stellar vision will lead to the noumena.

9. Pilots in their planes throwing explosives are:

> . . . locos del *vértigo* del aire, como los *héroes* de la tragedia antigua del *vértigo erótico* (emphasis mine)

They are *esdrújulo* pilots (*vértigo, héroes, erótico*), and something about them attracts the stellar vision. *Vértigo erótico*: In the phenomenal world sex appears so awkward, so bestial even, but beyond it lies Eros itself . . . or Himself.

The orthodox always speaks of God the Father, but can a masculine creation account for Nature, *la gran fiera fecundada*, ardent woman? Could a man or man principle alone create the *Tierra Caliente*, the Niña Chole, ardent woman? In her shewings, which are mystical, Julian of Norwich speaks of the motherhood of God, and even the hypocritical Christians have a Mother of God, a God Mother, which Unamuno called the Fourth Person of the Blessed Quaternity. Female and male; female—the basis of existence. And the Gnostics of yore, ancient, millenary, timeless, aesthetic, metaphysical, fascinating spirits, who deplored the senses, the jail of clay and phenomena, had the Alien God, the Pleroma, Sophia, Ialdabaoth and his horrible creation, but notice, Sophia stands at the center. Were it not for her and her mischievous son, Ialdabaoth the Demiurge (who is the hypocritical God of the Christians), creation would never have taken place and the Light would be the Light, without a shell of darkness. Were it not for her there would be no midnight, no war, no phenomena, no piercing the veil, no abracadabra, just Light, the light light, just Poetry. Creation is Sophia's labor, *she* made it necessary, so it always has its *vértigo erótico*. You can see it there in the eternal moment, beyond the barrier of images, beyond the barrier of phenomena!

10. Valle's war vision is but a tiny step removed from the *Sonatas*. It is as close to history as the magic, thaumaturgic historian cares to go. Given a few more evocative roses:

> . . . los cohetes abren sus rosas (Capítulo III, IV, V),

and given some pale hands dancing, some more *trémulos* and *estremecimientos*:

> . . . un estremecimiento la recorre (la línea de ataque) . . . (Capítulo XXX)

and given another *revoloteo*:

> . . . Revoletean los pájaros, y en lo alto de las columnas, sobre los capiteles mutilados pían las nidadas.[2]

> . . . Las hojas de los árboles caen revoloteando, y por el tejado de una casa terrena brotan penachos de llamas.[2]

and given a few more evocative musical bars, and it would be a full-fledged *sonata*. We might call it the *Sonata de media noche*. Listen to this sonatic line:

> (The pilots) . . . vestidos de pieles, con grandes gafas redondas, y redondos cascos de cuero, tienen una forma embrionaria y una evocación oscura de monstrous científicos. (Capítulo IV)

(The pilots) dressed in skins, with great round goggles, and rounded helmets of leather, have an embryonic form and a dim evocation of scientific monsters.

Embryonic form: Perhaps this is the larva of the *krausistas*. We seek an eternal unity beyond the multiplicity, an eternal harmony beyond the cacophony, beauty beyond esperpentic phenomena, and we find them through musical evocation. It behooves us here to speak of the three potencies of the soul: the intellect, the will and memory (spiritual memory as distinguished from mere animal memory).[3] The Dominicans assigned first place to the intellect, which throws light on the other potencies, without which they cannot operate. The Franciscans placed a premium on the will, the source of love, which moves the stars. But Gnostic poets, easterners at heart, resort to the karma memory for stellar visions and evocations. Millenary cathedrals, centenary cypresses, ballads of yore, ancient myths and legends, distant voices, the gift of tongues, heartfelt reincarnation, embryonic forms, *all the ineffable*—to these the gnostic poet must turn, and when he does so turn, leathered pilots become chimerical monsters[4] (in a sense, he does not turn to them but is acted upon by them).

Just as the Christians could see Christ in Saint Francis Assisi, who evoked His Person, so the stellar poet can see Things-in-themselves behind ever-recurring phenomena, nay, they are evoked for him in his ancient memory. War and esperpentic pilots (scientific monsters) are weather vanes, pointing the way: and once given this proper direction, the brother pilgrim can arrive at Edenic Beauty and Love (through the sonata and musical miracle). An aesthetic gnostic is the converse of a Christian: For the latter, love will move you to memory, whereas for the former, memory will move you to love. Raymond Lull, *el loco, el fatuo por amor*, was furious because people didn't remember his Beloved, and they didn't remember Him because they didn't love. The new Raymond, Valle, Ramón *el loco el fatuo por belleza*, is furious because people don't love Beauty, and they don't love it because they don't remember. Lull wanted others to love his Beloved, Valle wants others to remember his. Aesthetic gnosis and karma memory constitute the epistemology of stellar poets.

11. I chose *La media noche, visión estelar de un momento de guerra* at random, merely because I read it *long ago* and liked it. But I also liked the Carlist books and Iberian ring and Santos Banderas and *Primavera* and *Otoño*, which are unforgettable. Perhaps I chose it because it was short, a good brief appetizer as it were, to excite the palate before I came in with the best wine.

But that's not so, Valle's works are like the *Psalms*; you can read them all, or only one, or in and out of order, it makes no difference.

> Upon my back the plowers plowed
> Long have they made their furrows.

This Psalm is a bible in itself; with proper meditation it will lead you to the truth of Mount Sinai. You see, according to Valle, if you rub the marvelous lamp all his works will lead the pilgrim home. Sonatic music and esperpentic penumbra are everywhere.

12. Saving some of my thoughts for Valle's other works, I shall sum up *La media noche*. But 'summing up' is unfair to a thaumaturgic artist creating the musical miracle for the light light beyond phenomena. Strictly speaking, you can sum up garbanzo beans, but you can't sum up stellar vision, there is only one. Unity. You don't sum up unity, and this will account for the abracadabra.

13. Historically, *Media noche* provides the reader with a few significant details: A machine gun cuts down a fir tree; a dog delivers a communiqué: two scouts hit an electrified wire and become *peleles*, two stuffed figures, mere objects, their helmets flashing flame and their cartridges exploding in their belts; a town burns, a baby dies, again the soldiers are like *peleles*; the batteries open fire, she-cats giving birth to dead litters; bloated bodies float in the water; the soldiers put sails on the bloated bodies, which navigate out to sea; two pregnant girls in a cart; a dead horse in a pool of sticky blood; Indian troops in turbans; a headless cadaver; an old doctor in a field hospital commenting on the enemy; a convoy of wounded soldiers. . . . all these and several more:

> Es una sucesión de imágenes desoladas que no se interrumpe desde la costa norteña a los montes de Alsacia. (Capítulo XL).

> It is an uninterrupted sequence of desolate images from the northern coast to the hills of Alsace-Lorraine.

> Es la religión de la guerra, y como las almas tienen hermandad sus palabras son breves . . . cobran aquella expresión radiante que las santas apariciones ponían en el rostro de los místicos. (Capítulo XXII)

> It is the religion of war, and since souls are related like brothers their words are brief . . .

they take on that radiant expression which holy apparitions used to put in the countenance of mystics.

This is not the total profile of war but only forty or so significant details, forty bagatelles as it were in an impressionist painting. Valle does not give the entire realistic profile of the war but only enough vague details (spots, stains, patches) to make the profile loom in the reader's eye. In this respect, *Media noche* resembles those short impressionistic chapters of Azorín's *Don Juan*; indeed, in one chapter Valle writes an Azorinian word, *mancha*[5]:

> . . . al borde de la carretera, aparece confusamente una gran *mancha* (emphasis mine) de ganado que acampa en el fondo de las praderas. (Capítulo XV)

> . . . near the edge of the highway, in the background of the fields, appears indistinctly a large blur of cattle.

The literary painter does not draw lines giving the height, width and length of objects, he simply brushes a series of spots that become the objects in the reader's eye: Visual impressionism, to which Valle will add musical impressionism.

Media noche speaks of the radiant expression on the countenance of mystics before holy apparitions. The reader should always heed a reference such as this, for according to Valle his aesthetic gnosis is similar to the gnosis of an orthodox mystic; it is not the same of course but it is similar.

In *Media noche* the reader encounters esperpentic irony:

> El Teniente Breal los anima con una gran voz:—¡Viva la Francia! ¡Arriba los muertos! (Capítulo VII)

> Lieutenant Breal cheers them with a loud voice: "Long live France! Long live the dead!"

> —¡El dolor de la guerra estremece y conforta el alma de Francia! (Capítulo IX)

> "The sorrow of war thrills and comforts the soul of France!"

Exclamations are an invariable source of irony in don Ramón María del Valle-Inclán. A French martinet, a rigid clown, a puppet, a *fantoche* shouts: Long live the dead! ¡Abracadabra pata de cabra!

Several passages of this prose poem on quintessential war evoke the sonatas. Things and events are always nebulous, the predilect word being *bruma* (*fog, mist*):

> ... el vaho de la bruma (Capítulo XVIII)
>
> ... the vapor of the mist

And events seem to begin in the dark of night and end in the twilight of dawn:

> ... alborean los gallos (Capítulo III)
> ... ya cantó dos veces el gallo (Capítulo X)

with flashes of rockets and bombs in between, briefly illuminating the sky. The poet's stellar light penetrates the veil. And certain *estribillos* (refrains) evoke the litanies of María del Rosario in *Primavera*:

> ¡Se me abre el cuerpo de dolor! ... ¡Ay Virgen
> Santa! ... ¡se me rompe el cuerpo de dolor!
> (Capítulos XV, XVI).

Finally, events are sonatically indistinct, always taking place in the distance or on the horizon (*a lo lejos*). I shall further discuss these ideas when I come to the *Sonata de Primavera*.

14. Stellar vision of a moment of war. The quintessence of war. The ancients were mistaken when they spoke of four elements, earth, air, fire and water. There is a fifth element, namely, stardust. Stardust, the poet's historiography.

15. Lest the reader has not experienced a stellar vision, I shall copy here unforgettable Chapter XII:

> La marinería se arremanga y entra chapoteando por el agua llena de fosforencias. A lo largo de la playa flotan más de cien cadáveres alemanes inflados y tumefactos. Uno hay que no tiene cabeza; otros descubren en el vientre y en las piernas lacras amoratadas, casi negras. Comienza la faena de ponerles velachos con las pértigas y lienzos de las tiendas. Valiéndose de los bicheros, les hacen brechas en la carne hidrópica, y clavan los astiles donde van las lonas. Luego, supersticiosos y diestros, los empujan hasta encontrar calado. Sesgan la vela buscando que la llene el viento, y, al tobillo o al cuello, les

57

amarran las escotas. Los muertos se alejan de la
playa como una escuadrilla de faluchos. Se les ve
alinearse bajo la luna, y partir hacia el horizonte
marino empujados por la fresca brisa que sopla del
tercer cuadrante. Pasa un aliento de alegría sobre
aquellas almas infantiles y crédulas. Un grumete,
con la gorra en la mano, y las luces de las estrellas
en los ojos fervorosos, clama en su vieja lengua
céltica:
—¡Madre del Señor! ¡Ya no tengo miedo a los
muertos!

The seamen roll up their cuffs and enter,
splashing through the water filled with
phosphoresences. Along the beach are floating
more than a hundred German cadavers, bloated
and protuberant. One of them has no head; others
reveal in their belly and legs dark purple marks,
almost black. The task begins of putting topsails
on them, with the poles and canvas from the tents.
Availing themselves of boathooks, they open up
holes in the swelling flesh and hammer down the
shafts where the sail cloth will go. Then,
supersticiously and dexterously, they push them to
where they'll find their depth. They turn the sails,
hoping the wind will fill them, and on their ankle
or their neck they fashion the sheet. The dead go
off from the beach like a squadron of lateen-
rigged ships; they are seen in formation under the
moon and setting off for the sea's horizon
impelled by the fresh breeze blowing from the
third quadrant. A spirit of joy passes over those
child-like credulous souls. A cabin boy, cap in
hand and the rays of the stars on his fervid eyes,
cries out in his old Celtic tongue:
—Mother of God! I no longer have fear of the
dead!

Quintessential war: Salamis, Carthage, Navas de Tolosa,
Lepanto, Thirty Years, Marengo, Austerlitz, Antietam,
Chichamauga, Passchendaele, Marne: Here is earth, air, fire,
water and stardust. Some would say that quintessence is
surrealistic, but surrealism belongs to the code, which exceeds
garbanzatic realism, the doctrine of the hylic, Auguste Comte. A
better word than *essential* or *quintessential* or *surrealistic* is
noumenal. The code is aiming at the Thing-in-itself, at the world
of things-in-themselves.

CANTO IV

The Shadows in Plato's Cave, or, Comte Revisited

1. Santos Banderas. Let us hold up the mirror to reality, alleged reality, the shadows in Plato's grave. What do we see? Not very much though we think we do. 2. Men sit in a dungeon where it is midnight. There are shadows on the wall, shapes of friars, money lenders, caciques, caudillos, ambassadors, generals, obese queens, doctors, lawyers, notaries, scribes, princesses, constables, plaintiffs, shopkeepers, hypocrites, grotesque shapes all. These are shadows on the wall. 3. Chickpea boys, the *garbancistas*, look at the wall and say, this is our essence, this is what we are, Santiago, Pelayo, Cid, San Fernando, Isabel, lanzas de Breda and the Cross, this is what we are. *Casticismo. Garbancismo.* This is what we are.
4. There was a young *garbancista*
who used to say *casticista*
but put to the wall
he had a great fall
and now shouts *realista*.
5. Marcel Bataillon translated *En torno al casticismo* as *L'essence d'Espagne. Casticismo* means essence, systematic essence. Unamuno may have had the right idea, getting away from ancient essence, but he got caught up in his own quiddities, in his SYLLOGISM:

> Major premise: All Nature is in a state of intrinsic contradiction.
> Minor premise: Man is part of Nature.
> Conclusion: Ergo, Man is in a state of intrinsic contradiction.

Abel Sánchez, San Manuel Bueno, Alejandro Gómez, Dr. Montarco, Tía Tula, Augusto Pérez, all of them are third premise conclusion shadows, created by a great ergotist, the greatest no doubt, but an ergo man nevertheless. There is no *intrahistoria*, as Unamuno would have it, *intrahistoria* is merely a word play for shadows within shadows; there is the wave and the ocean, to be sure, but Unamuno's deep ocean is just shadow waves put together; it is but an illusion of eternity. See not *intrahistoria* but *metahistoria*, if you must use such a ghastly unmusical word; *metahistoria* is the stellar light outside the cave. The truth is *outside* what we see, *beyond* it, not within it. See not phenomena but . . . noumena. That is the code.

Unamuno's shadow figures are just a bunch of vapid Aunt Gerties.

In this section I have tried to interpret what might be Valle's

reaction to Unamuno's ontology. I don't entirely agree with this reaction, so I shall return to it in a concluding chapter on Unamuno, Azorín, Baroja and others.
6. The Gnostics had the right idea. Damn St. Irenaeus and all those who suppressed these *cathari*:

El espíritu de los gnósticos descubre una emoción estética en el absurdo de las formas, en la creación de monstruos, en el acabamiento de la vida . . . La belleza está en el acto creador. (*Lámpara*, pp. 70-71)

The spirit of the gnostics reveals an aesthetic emotion in the absurdity of forms, in the creation of monsters, in the termination of life. Beauty lies in the creative act.

This statement accounts for the extreme formalism of Pedro Salinas, and for musical creations with sacrilegious themes. The sacrilege is without meaning, only poetic creation counts:

. . . aniquilando el significado ideológico de las palabras (*Lámpara*, 29)

. . . annihilating the ideological meaning of words.

This is the glossolalia, the musical miracle, the abracadabra.
7. Although the Alien God, Pure Light, exists outside the cave and will have nothing to do with it, His Existence is such that His stellar illumination can be seen by rubbing the magic lamp, by listening to its visual music. Synesthesia. Sound-light.
8. The poet alone can pierce the veil, reaching beyond the shadows, beyond grotesque phenomena. The libertine reader, or listener, a free spirit pilgrim, can journey with him by absorption in his musical miracle. The poet is a Master, the pilgrim a brother journeyman, and together they travel beyond the cave. To the noumenal light. To the light light.
The dancer too is a poet:

El baile es la más alta expresión estética, porque es la única que transporta a los ojos los números y las cesuras musicales. (*Lámpara*, p. 54)

Dance is the highest aesthetic expression, because it alone will bring to the eyes musical numbers and caesurae.

Visual music and dance. Sound, light, touch. Synesthesia.
Dance, the highest aesthetic expression, includes sexual
union, which is the most sublime dance of all. This will account
for the *logos espermático* of the *Lámpara*:

La primera rosa estetica florece del concepto
teológico del Logos Espermático. (*Lámpara*, p.
144)

The first aesthetic rose flowers from the
theological concept of the *Logos Espermático*.

Elsewhere Valle mentions *la lujuria de las formas (Lámpara*, p.
55-56)
Perhaps the best example of dance, the sexual union, art and
the gnosis comes from another modernist (read *gnostic*), Joan
Maragall:

DE LA DANZA (*Elogios*, pp. 120-124)
Parece que el primer impulso de expansión
artística del hombre debió ser la danza; que en su
primera percepción de la belleza del mundo (de
Dios revelándose en la forma de las cosas), sintió
el hombre agitarse dentro de sí todo el misterio de
la vida . . .

It would seem that man's first impulse toward
artistic expansion must have been the dance; that
in his first perception of beauty in the world (of
God revealing himself in the form of things), man
felt stirring within himself all the mystery of
life . . .

Beauty, then, according to Maragall, is God revealing himself in
the form of things, and on first perceiving this, man began to
dance:

Por esto es, pues, que en la mujer danzando
hallamos el mayor deleite artístico, porque ella nos
representa entonces el compendio de la creación:
nos representa el esfuerzo creador con su ritmo,
nos da la forma reveladora del supremo grado
espiritual . . .

That is why then in woman's dancing we find the
greatest artistic delight, because she then
represents for us the compendium of all creation,
she represents the creative force with its rhythm,

61

she gives us the revealing form of the supreme
spiritual order . . .

If beauty is God's revealing himself in the form of things, he
does this above all in the form of woman, especially in a woman
dancing.

> Y asimismo, paralelamente, en la danza
> encontramos el principio y el fin de todas las
> artes: desde la danza caótica de las olas en el mar
> y de toda multitud confusa y primitiva, hasta
> aquélla absolutamente individualizada y más pura
> que podemos imaginar, y que sentimos latir ya en
> el fondo de nuestros amores, de una Unica
> atrayendo a un Unico a confundirse con ella para
> siempre en amor en la suprema cima de la Belleza
> inmortal.

> And likewise, in a similar way, in the dance we
> find the beginning and ending of all the arts: from
> the chaotic dance waves in the sea and of that
> multitude of things that are hazy and primitive, to
> that most absolutely individualized dance, and
> most pure that we can imagine, and which we
> find beating in the depth of our love, of One
> Woman Alone attracting One Man Alone who will
> unite with her forever in love, in the supreme
> height of immortal Beauty.

Beauty: God's revealing himself above all in the rhythmic
embrace of a man and woman, at the feast of Hymen.
I believe that Valle's *Lámpara* will suffer Maragall's
interpretation. Sexual rhythm is part of the code, the Logos
Espermático. Every time the reader encounters *esdrújulos*
—ráfagas, párpados, crepúsculos, sacrílego, atusándome,
destacábase (en la penumbra inmóvil), pálida, quimérica, &c.—he
should consider them dancing words that are part of the code,
pointing to beauty in the form of things. And when he detects
any rhythmic movement in imagery and language, he should
consider that a dance also:

> Los mirlos cantaban en las ramas, y sus cantos se
> respondían encadenándose en un ritmo remoto
> como las olas del mar. Las cinco hermanas habían
> vuelto a sentarse: Tejían sus ramos en silencio, y
> entre la púrpura de las rosas revoloteaban como
> albas palomas sus manos, y los rayos del sol que
> pasaban a través del follaje, temblaban en ellas

como místicos haces encendidos. (*Primavera*, p. 22)

> The blackbirds were singing in the branches, and
> their songs were returned, weaving themselves into
> a remote rhythm like the waves of the sea. The
> five sisters had seated themselves once again: They
> were weaving their rose branches in silence, and
> amongst the purple of the flowers their hands
> were fluttering like white doves, and the rays of
> the sun coming through the foliage trembled over
> them like mystical flaming sheaves.

Whenever the reader, or listener, sees a garden where pale
fingers or hands or eyelids are fluttering[1], he should contemplate
them as he would a dance, a woman's dance, revealing the divine
form behind the appearance of things (phenomena), revealing
Beauty. Frequently the dance will be followed by *inmovilidad* or
lo inmóvil: One has arrived at the eternal moment, at the
quietude of the noumenon.

Fountains dance also, voluptuously, as in a feminine form:

> En el jardín las fuentes repetían el comentario
> voluptuoso que parecen hacer a todo pensamiento
> de amor, sus voces eternas y juveniles. (*Primavera*,
> p. 22)

> In the garden the fountains kept repeating the
> voluptuous commentary they seem to make on
> every thought of love, their voices eternal and
> young.

Everything is capable of the dance, in more or less degree, the
blackbirds' songs creating a remote rhythm like the waves of the
sea; the babble of the fountains . . . hands weaving flowers . . .
everything.

In the *Sonata de estío* all Nature becomes a *gran fiera
fecundada*, an unbridled *logos espermático*, which accounts for
the Niña Chole. I myself find a discordant note in *Estío*. I believe
that Valle's aesthetic gnosis is far more antinomian than
Maragall's. Were I to accept the gnosis, I should prefer a gentler
attitude.

Don Ramón María del Valle-Inclán and Joan Maragall.
Modernists. Aesthetic gnostics.

9. Plotinus, they say, hated the Gnostics, but even so a sort
of neo-Platonic gnosticism is the answer to so-called Realism;
Realism, which is about as real as a worm-eaten garbanzo bean.
All shadows are worm-eaten garbanzos. It is time now to prove
this dictum, or sort of prove it: *Esprit de géométrie, esprit de*

finesse. Since we have been finessing all along, it is time for esperpentic geometry, which unlike Euclidean geometry should reveal an aesthetic emotion.

10. There is in all of Valle-Inclán a kind of aesthetic anagnorisis, a going home to familiar sights, a *deja vu*, a recognition of the self and others, which he called karma memory. Santos Banderas is a Latin American caudillo, he is Rosas in Argentina, Estrada Cabrera in Ecuador, Batista in Cuba, Trujillo in Santo Domingo, but he is more than that, he is Tammany Hall's Tweed, Boss Crump, the don Primitivo of Pardo Bazán, the destroyers of Villaamil, and even some of the ecclesiastical politicians of Anthony Trollope. He is hypocritical, ubiquitous, universal. Through him we recognize someone we did not know before, our neighbors and ourselves. Anagnorisis. Recognition. Valle's is an art of recognition.

11. Santos Banderas is the one furthest removed from the light at the mouth of the cave, and the one closest to the wall. Shadow of shadows. Do you remember when you were six years old and went to the movies and ran to sit in the very first row where the figures on the screen were so big you couldn't really make them out, you could a little but not really? The hylic reader of Valle is like that and probably won't finish the book. The hylic reader won't understand. But most of us are hylics.

If you want to understand, to pierce the veil between the two worlds (the phenomenal and the noumenal), sit in the back row and watch. And listen. Forget the ideological significance of words, which is literal. Let the critics do that, the professors, they're all Aristarchs anyway, proud, inflated puppets, "con la botarga inflada." Just listen. See what I mean. Valle is an impressionist, and impressionist works should be viewed from afar, from the back row not the first row (*a lo lejos*). The critics, the professors, they're all in the first row. Damned hylics.

12. The hylic reader may finish some pages but not the book. Should he become psychic, he will experience the anagnorisis, recognition of self, be aesthetically moved by the *¡Chac! ¡Chac!* of Santos Banderas, and turn to the sonatas, where he may also experience the musical miracle, to pierce the veil. That is, he will turn around, away from the wall, and face the mouth of the cave.

13. The opposition between the Generation of 1898 and Modernism has been overstated. *Generation* has become a platitude. It is all Modernism, a systematic upturning or around-turning of values. Don't face the Church-and-State values on the wall of the cave, the shadow men, Padre Claret and Cánovas del Castillo. Do an about-face and see the mouth of the cave, the light and *Más Allá*, Humanity as it might be. Listen! See!—The stellar vision and sound. ¡Abracadabra! The Ideal.

Idealism, which a dictionary defines as:

(1) A theory that ultimate reality lies in a realm transcending phenomena
(2) A theory that the essential nature of reality lies in consciousness or reason
(3) Literary or artistic theory or practise that affirms the preeminent value of imagination as compared with *faithful copying of nature* (emphasis mine)—compare REALISM

Let us apply these three definitions to the works of Valle-Inclán:

(1) We must transcend phenomena. Pierce the veil between the two worlds. Arrive at noumena. The student of Valle should first study Immanuel Kant.
(2) Valle's system, his *eternal moment*, is subjective. The world about us depends for its existence on our consciousness of it.
(3) Idealists, gnostics, poets use their imagination (they are impressionists) whereas realists, *garbanceros*, take snapshots (snapshots: faithful copying of nature).

Valle's is an idealist, subjective, impressionist literature.

14. Aristotle speaks of *mythos* and *dianoia*, plot and theme, what happens in the story and what's it all about; and to these he added diction, spectacle, setting and characterization.[2] Were I writing a conventional critique of Valle-Inclán, I would follow Aristotle's method and write a monograph, for in spite of modern literary theory, I believe that Aristotle is still the greatest of critics. But mixing geometry and finesse and Valle's own *Lámpara*, I have chosen a somewhat different course. Valle himself would have us ignore the plot, which I construe to be "the ideological meaning of words:

Hagamos de toda nuestra vida a modo de una estrofa; donde el ritmo interior despierta las sensaciones indefinibles aniquilando el significado ideológico de las palabras. (*Lámpara*, p. 29)

Let us make our entire life a kind of strophe; where the interior rhythm awakens indefinable sensations annihilating the ideological meaning of words.

I would remind the reader that the Greek strophe is both a choral ode and a dance, music and the dance (Valle: "Dance is

65

the highest aesthetic expression . . .")

Substitute the phrase *nuestra novela* for *nuestra vida*, and we annihilate the ideological significance of words, that is to say, we annihilate the plot.[3]

15. *Tirano Banderas* is simply the story of a dictator's fall, and of the hypocrites around him: I have just paid tribute to Aristotle's opinion, I have just described the plot, which he says is the soul of a story. It seems to me that no matter how one tries (how Valle tries, and Unamuno too) one cannot avoid discursive reasoning and the *syllogism*, not the syllogism explicitly stated but syllogistic thought, by which one implicitly creates a chain of premises and proceeds from one to the other. It is not in the nature of things for men to argue otherwise, and here of course I differ from Valle.

Let me put it this way: I shall simply try to write about matter and form in such a way that I will leave a convincing impression on the reader. Matter is what Valle calls "ideological meaning" and form is the mode of presentation, e.g., *crepúsculos; ráfagas; lejanía; a lo lejos: forma incierta de las cosas*; the dance; vague, ineffable, mysterious words.

16. One might call Pascal and Valle essayists, in a way. Pascal employs *géométrie* and *finesse* in an attempt to convey his thought; Valle employs impressionism, which he calls the musical miracle. And so I too shall try to be an essayist. I shall unite matter and form, geometry and finesse, *esperpento* and sonata. I shall attempt to leave a convincing impression. Impressionism.

Thus we have:
Pascal	science	finesse
Valle	*esperpento*	music and dance
the critic	matter	form

17. The *esperpento*, grotesque geometry, but geometry nonetheless. A measure of the earth. A measure of the shadows in the cave. A measure of phenomena. The measure causes delight, although the phenomena themselves do not cause delight:

El espíritu de los gnósticos descubre una emoción estética en el absurdo de las formas, en la creación de monstruous . . . (*Lámpara*, p. 71)

The spirit of the gnostics reveals an aesthetic emotion in the absurdity of forms, in the creation of monsters . . .

Para los gnósticos la belleza de las imágenes no está en ellas, sino en el acto creador . . .

For the gnostics the beauty of images is not in them themselves, but in the creative act . . .

Las imágenes are phenomenal. The *acto creador*, which is the artistic measure, approaches the noumenal. Noumenal perception can take delight in the absurdity of forms.
18. The sonata: Musical finesse. An intuition of things-in-themselves. The sonata is an impression of noumena, although the statement seems contradictory. This leads to the *balbuceo* of the artist and the mystic.
19. The code. Numbers 17 and 18 belong to the code. I have contravened Lope de Vega's advice and revealed the denouement. I hope the reader will not desert me, for there are two or three acts to come.
20. There was an old man named Kant
    who used to love to rant;
    while playing phenomenal
    and playing the noumenal
    he produced Spain's hierophant.

Antiphon: ¡Abracadabra! ¡Pata de cabra!
           ¡Chac! ¡Chac!
           ¡Fue Satanás! Fue Satanás!
Don Ramón María del Valle-Inclán: The chief priest of the Eleunisian mysteries.
21. *Tirano Banderas*: Let us hold up the concave-convex mirror to reality or to what passes for reality, to the phenomenal shadows in Plato's cave. Let us experience an aesthetic emotion before the absurdity of forms by witnessing the creation of monsters. Let us delight in the termination of life. Let us witness Valle's *esperpento*. ¡Chac! ¡Chac!
22. *Tirano Banderas*, the esperpentic history of Latin American dictators, has a Pythagorean, cabalistic structure of seven parts, divided into three, three, three, seven, and three, three, three books respectively, and these are again divided into Roman numeral sub-parts varying from three lines to several pages. Let us start with Roman numeral I of the Prologue:

> Filomeno Cuevas, criollo ranchero, había dispuesto para aquella noche armas a sus peonadas con los fusiles ocultos en un manigual, y las glebas de indios, en difusas líneas, avanzaban por los esteros de Ticomaipu. Luna clara, nocturnos horizontes profundos de susurros y ecos.

> Filomeno Cuevas, creole rancher, had provided for that night arms for all his laborers, with rifles hidden in a thicket field, and the glebes of Indians, in extended lines, were advancing through the swamplands of Ticomaipu. A clear moon, deep pitch dark somber horizons filled with whispers

and echoes.

The language is pithy. If there are *criollos* then there must be *peninsulares*, gachupines, Europeans who will be the object of the hidden rifles. The *criollo* is arming his *peonadas*, gangs of laborers, with rifles, so he must be a very powerful and wealthy man. He must have hundreds of workers under him—one does not start an uprising with a score of men—and he must have a single, powerful unusual enemy, for ordinary men of his high estate resist revolutions, they do not start them. Who can this enemy be? The class structure, moreover, is much more rigid than first meets the eye, for there are not only *peonadas* but glebes of Indians, glebes, *siervos de la gleba*, "slaves bound to an estate who are not released from it when there is a change of owner." This definition comes from the Royal Academy dictionary of the narrator. Thus we have Indians, hundreds of them, perhaps thousands, *peonadas* by the score and hundreds, *mestizos* probably, and the *criollo* who, like Simón Bolivar before him, is probably, white:[4] in section II of the *Prólogo* we learn that "Atilio Palmieri, primo de la niña ranchera," is *rubio*.

The enemy, then, must be *peninsular*, a white European (we learn later that Santos Banderas himself is not European, but the diplomatic community supporting him are; this community is the ultimate enemy).

Since so many Indians and laborers cannot live on a few acres of land, the *criollo* must be a *latifundista* with enormous holdings, several thousand acres or perhaps even an entire province. Hereditary land: This division goes back to colonial times or at least to 1810-1825; nevertheless, even the conservatives are rebelling. These lands, moreover, belong to a hot climate, the *tierra caliente* of the title (*Tirano Banderas, novela de Tierra Caliente*), because *manigual*, where the rifles are hidden, is a Cuban word; *manigua*: "terreno de la isla de Cuba cubierta de malezas," according to the narrator's Royal Academy dictionary. This tells us something about the glebes of Indians. The *criollo* has armed his laborers with rifles hidden in thickets, but the Indians simply advance in broken lines through the tideland swamps of Ticomaipu. Surely the Indians are not going unarmed, and if they don't have rifles they must have . . . machetes. This is going to be a horrible uprising, swamps, water, thickets, rifles and machetes to behead a man.

Upon reflection, one remembers that Indians don't abound in Cuba but on the mainland, in Mexico and Guatemala. Thus this country of Santos Banderas and the revolution are fictitious; they are composite rather than particular; they are not Cuban or Mexican or Guatemalan or Peruvian etc., but all of them put together. This is not Filomeno Cuevas, *a* criollo, but *the* criollo, the quintessential criollo, and his armed men are not *mestizos* or *indios* but the quintessential mestizo and Indian.

The last line of Roman numeral I in the prologue strikes a different note, or I should say, a different rhythm:

> Luna clara, nocturnos horizontes profundos de susurros y ecos.

Although the horizons are pitch dark, distant, vague and somber, above them shines the rays of the moon (stellar vision), and whispers echo a strange music, namely, the sonata. No matter how grotesque the phenomena may appear (the mummy Santos Banderas, the effeminate *carcamal* Benicarlés, the miser Quintín Pereda), no matter how absurd the forms, the music is there behind them.

On reading the opening lines of *Tirano*, I was reminded of Sean O'Faolain's argument concerning the short story, which must exercise an economy of language and cling to the original subject like a sonnet; it must not state an argument but only suggest. Valle-Inclan's *esperpento* resembles that. *Tirano Banderas* reads like a series of short stories and sonnets, woven together. You can take any one of the Roman numeral divisions—there are more than seven score of them—and read it by itself and you have a completion, a work of art, a short story or sonnet. They can be read alone or as part of the whole. They are monads.[5]

23. The tyrant Santos Banderas is an aggregate of all Latin American dictators; in his mask, his *persona*, he is the caudillo incarnate, and his country Santa Fe de Tierra Firme is all of Latin American. The monetary units of the novel are *bolivianos, soles, pesos, bolívares*, currencies from Bolivia, Peru, Mexico, Argentina and Venezuela, and even the eighteenth century *tlaco* is mentioned. Furthermore, hosts of words appear, two or three per page, from all the former colonies: *macanear, coca, chinita, chicote, mucama, quitrí, catinga, mecate, cholo, no me vea chuela, mambí, tilingo, mero mero, mocho, vos no vendés* (el voseo), *atorrante, congal, guagua, auras, zopilotes, ñanduti, ñata, morocha, chancho, cocal*, to name a few; indeed, all future editions of *Tirano Banderas* should contain a glossary, with listings nation by nation. As the full title suggests, this is a novel about *tierra caliente*, and there are vague references to its location:

> "frente al mar ecuatorial" (p. 197)
> "frente al vasto mar ecuatorial" (p. 143)
> "el indio de estas Repúblicas del Mar Pacífico" (p. 47)

The novel has a certain Mexican-Cuban bias (as a young man Valle lived in Mexico for a year), so Banderas's country is rather like the Caribbean coast transported to Ecuador with some La

69

Plata and Andean elements added.

24. I once saw a staging of Goldoni's *The Liar* in which the actors dressed before the performance on the stage, in full view of the audience, putting on plastic frames to make themselves look fat, oversized shoes for clumsiness, and extravagant makeup to complete the ridiculous appearance. Here was the *commedia dell' arte* apprising you of its nature even before you saw it: an awkward, bumbling, ridiculous, funny show. Valle's art is like that. In *Tirano Banderas*, where Valle is the doyen of puppeteers, the Maese Pedro, the Master, he also apprises you of the puppet strings without destroying the illusion: It is all right to reveal the strings as long as you don't display the hand of the puppeteer. The tyrant is a *momia* (this is said a score of times) with a skin of *pergamino*; he has a *verde máscara india*, and when he sits framed by a window, he is a *garabato de lechuza*, a cramped calligrapher's grotesque scrawl. The *honrados gachupines* and el Coronelito Domiciano have *botargas* (clown suits) that inflate with pride and deflate before adversity; these *botargas* seem to be identified with their bellies, *búdicos vientres*. On the Night of All Saints the whole atmosphere of Santa Fe is a "guiñol de mitote y puñales." ¡Chac! ¡Chac!, as the dictator chews his coca cud.

The reader constantly encounters literary strings, as in a puppet show:

"no dejar títere sano"
"la cera de las manos"

these puppets have the rigidity of wood, the brilliance and unctuousness of wax.

"Bailarín de alambre"
"empaque farsero"
"muñeco automático"

in a few words: The characters are automatic, waxen, farcical, unctuous dancing puppet dolls stretched on a wire. But the reader does not see or sense the puppeteer, because even though the irony and satire are not lost on him, the adversaries of the tyrant mummy are not melodramatic, polarized good guys. They are frequently *fantoches* themselves, whose patriotic speeches sound like operatic arias. They may not inflate their clown suit and bellies like the honorable *gachupines*, but their most patriotic speeches are arias (see pp. 53, 122, 145, 150, 153). These operatic patriots later appear in the theosophical *calabozo* #3, one of Banderas's dungeons.[6]

25. They are phenomenal puppets, awkward and grotesque, because "the spirit of the gnostics discovers an aesthetic emotion

70

in the absurdity of forms, in the creation of monsters . . ."[7]
26. *Tirano Banderas*, like the sonatas, has a peculiar, remote, penumbral quality. Of Santos Banderas, the narrator writes:

> Desde la remota ventana, agaritado en una inmovilidad de corneja sagrada, está mirando las escuadras de indios, soturnos en la cruel indiferencia del dolor y de la muerte. (p. 20)

> From the remote window, boxed like a sentry with the motionlessness of a sacred owl, he is watching the squads of Indians, gloomy before the cruel indifference of sorrow and death.

> Tirano Banderas, en la remota ventana, era siempre el garabato de un lechuzo.[8]

> Tirano Banderas, in the distant window, was always scrawled there like a screech owl.

> Tirano Banderas, agaritado en la ventana, inmóvil y distante, acrecentaba su prestigio de pájaro sagrado. (p. 29)

> Tirano Banderas, boxed like a sentry in the window, motionless and distant, augmented his reputation as a sacred bird.

As we have seen, the horizon, which is remote, in the distance, lies at the threshold of things-in-themselves. It is near the last barrier. A completely phenomenal Banderas is a mummy chewing coca, a *¡Chac! ¡Chac!*, but on the horizon, remotely, we can immobilize him and glimpse his essence (era siempre garabato de un lechuzo): Eternal graffiti on the phenomenal wall. Dictators are an owlish scrawl; they are essentially remote, indistinct twilight birds of prey. At the horizon one can see the absurdity of forms.
   Another example: The Spanish Minister, the effeminate, hypocritical Barón de Benicarlés:

> . . . limitaba el azul horizonte de los ojos huevones, entornando los párpados.

> . . . narrowed the blue horizon of those bulging egg eyes[9], half closing his eyelids. (p. 180)

In *Primavera* "los ojos entornados" is a formulaic verse meaning "hypocritical clergy", just as "el de la barba bellida"

71

means the Cid in epic poetry. In *Tirano Banderas* all the
hypocrites have *párpados* or *ojos entornados*: this is perhaps the
only way you can say *good* or *bad* in an esperpento without
destroying the genre, because *all* phenomena look ridiculous.
How can the puppeteer directly call a revolutionary clown
singing his aria *good*, even though he is good. What he can do,
however, is not have him half-close his eyelids. He can indicate
the clown is good through omission. (Here is a sign: *El buen
fantoche no entorna los ojos ni los párpados*.)
   27. As we have seen in *Primavera*, the penumbral is remote
and the remote penumbral. Both are thresholds. Just before the
attack on Santos Banderas:

> El enemigo en difusas líneas, por los caminos
> crepusculares, descubría un buen orden militar. (p.
> 217)

> The enemy, with extended lines, displayed good
> military discipline down the crepuscular roads.

You can attack the owl only at twilight.
   Modernist prose is crepuscular, and remote. It is at once
sonatic and esperpentic:

> Un vaho pesado calor y catinga anunciaba la
> proximidad de la manigua y el crepúsculo
> enciende con las estrellas los ojos de los jaguares.
> (p. 36)

Read the Academy speeches of the nineteenth century, for
example, Ventura de la Vega's. They were not written the way
Valle writes. Then read Menéndez Pelayo, Ricardo León, Galdós,
Alarcón, Valera, Pereda, Pardo Bazán. Nobody writes prose like
Valle: hexasyllabic verses at times, alexandrines, Americanisms,
internal rhyme, stars and twilights illuminating jaguars' eyes.
This is a stellar vision of the sounds, smells and fecund heat of
nature. Remote. Crepuscular. Uncanny. On the verge of the
noumenal world, beyond the uncertain form of things.
   28. *Tirano Banderas* may throw light on the modernist slogan
azul (blue). Of Banderas's fort, the narrator writes:

> El tumbo del mar batía la muralla, y el oboe de
> las olas cantaba el triunfo de la muerte. Los
> pájaros negros hacían círculos en el remoto azul, y
> sobre el losado del patio se pintaba la sombra
> fugitiva del aleteo. (p. 147)

The tumbling of the sea was beating the wall, and

the oboe of the waves was singing the triumph of death. Black birds were flying circles in the distant blue, and over the courtyard's flagged tiles was painted the fluttering of their passing wings.

The *azul* is the natural color of the horizon. It is the state, the place, the vision, the intuition, the poetry, the remote threshold where the phenomenal ends and poets start to pierce the veil between the two worlds, where the events of the phenomenal world become aesthetic, the land of Novalis's blue flower. Banderas has executed so many victims that the sharks no longer seek them, and even the buzzards are reaching satisfaction; this is a horrible thought, but given the horizon vision in the distant blue and the musical miracle of poetry, the tumbling waves and circles and shades and fluttering wings become a dance:

> El baile es la más alta expresión estética . . .
> (*Lámpara* p. 54)

Even in death there is aesthetic joy! Perhaps we can coin a phrase in Spanish: "La danza macabre no lo es!" Death has lost its sting.

29. One sentence of *Tirano Banderas* evokes *Primavera* and the mystical verse of San Juan de la Cruz:

> Los bailes, las músicas, las cuerdas de farolillos, tenían una exasperacion absurda, un enrabiamiento de quimera alucinante. (pp. 132-133)

> The dances, the music, the little lamps strung out on cords, all had an absurd exasperation, all had a hallucinating, chimerical violent wrath.

Quimera will evoke *Primavera*'s "un no sé qué quimérica y confusa desventura," which in turn evokes San Juan's "un no sé qué que quedan balbuciendo." The mystical stammer. Aesthetic deformation in Valle never wanders far from the music of the sonatas nor from his alleged mysticism.

30. *Claves Líricas*: In *Tirano Banderas* Valle frequently leaves hints that are lyrical keys to his thought, or definitions of his art (to the extent that definition is possible.) He does this in all his works, so much so that one is tempted to consider the two books, *La lámpara maravillosa* and *Claves líricas* a compilation of these thoughts and definitions. I shall write several of these hints here and call them, prosaically, topic sentences:

> (a) El aguardiente y el facón del indio[10], la baraja y el baile lleno de *lujurias*, encadenaba una

sucesión de *imágenes violentas* y tumultuosas. Sentíase la oscura y desolada palpitación de la *vida* sobre una fosa abierta. Santa Fe, con una *furia trágica y devoradora* del tiempo, escapaba del terrorífico *sopor cotidiano*, con el grito de sus ferias, tumultuoso como un grito bélico. En la lumbrada del ocaso, sobre la loma de granados y palmas, encendía los azulejos de sus redondas cúpolas coloniales San Martín de los Mostenses. (p. 35, emphasis mine).

The brandy and the Indians' knife, the quarrels and the lustful dances, formed a chain of violent and tumultuous images. There could be felt the dark and desolate palpitation of life over an open grave. Santa Fe, with a tragic fury devouring time, was escaping from the terrifying stupor of daily life, through the outcry of its festivities, which was turbulent like a warlike cry. In the bonfire of the setting sun, on top of the hill of pomegranate and palm trees, San Martín de los Mostenses was igniting the glazed tiles of its rounded colonial cupolas.

Within the economy of Valle's gnosis, this passage accounts for the *esperpento*. It is sunset, the artist's hour, the witching hour, when one can descry what one would otherwise not see, when one can see beyond the immediate images of things to their ultimate meaning. This eve of the Feast of All Saints in Santa Fe, amidst the festivities, there are lusts, knives, whiskey, violent turbulent images, quotidian boredom, warlike shouting; but midst this phenomenal pandemonium, remotely, on a hill of swaying tropical trees, one picks out the cupolas of a millenary monastery. Beauty. A glimpse of eternity. The eternal moment. Blazing cupolas against the twilight.

An Aside: If we set aside Valle's aesthetic vision for a minute, the paragraph may have great philosophical value. The violence (knives, lusts, furies, cries, tumults, wars) of left wing and right wing movements unquestionably holds allure for soporific man. All those banners, speeches, words, slogans, drums, rhythms, arms, music (all that unity, five million people saluting their priest with one accord) give life a meaning:

> . . . sentíase la oscura y desolada palpitación de la vida sobre la fosa abierta.

This is an obscure beat before the edge of the grave but a beat nevertheless. A rhythm. Life.

(b) Vistosa ondulación de niñas mulatas, con la vieja de rebocillo al flanco.[11] Formas, sombras, luces se multiplicaban trenzándose, promoviendo la caliginosa y aluciante vibración oriental que resumen el opio y la marihuana. (p. 51)

The colorful undulation of mulata girls, with the old woman in a shawl on the flank. Forms, shades, lights were multiplying, braiding themselves, provoking the sultry and hallucinating oriental vibration which opium and marijuana induce.

The dazzling, hallucinating power of art, which has the strength of an opiate. It is not precisely the same, because anyone can light a clay pipe, but only the poet can light the Pipa de Kif and only the brother pilgrim, the psychic, can smoke it. Understand it. Amidst the shouts and forms of phenomenal reality, amidst alternating lights and shadows—IN A PENUMBRA—one can descry, adumbrate, intuit, hear the eternal undulation and vibration. Another glimpse of beauty, BEAUTY, which is there, there, there, behind what meets the eye. The thing-in-itself.

(c) An Aside: I have a theory concerning art and philosophy. The Greeks had a trinity of the Good, the True and the Beautiful. As I view history and literature, I find that great figures tend to latch on to one division of the trinity, perhaps at the expense of the others.

Let us take the Good. Bartolomé de las Casas was so interested in the good, in the welfare of his Indians, social justice for them, that he seems to have stretched the truth to effect legislation on their behalf; indeed, in his *Brevísima relación de la destrucción de las Indias* he has been accused of lying: Don Ramón Menéndez Pidal has leveled such a charge. I find that many reformers resemble Las Casas in our universities today, where they are so interested in social engineering, as they call it, that they ride rough shod over the truth and the Humanities.

Was Las Casas interested in Beauty? I don't know. His histories are imperishable, but I wonder if that was of great moment to him. Perhaps he was like St. Bernard of Clairvaux, the Doctor of Love, who they say spent his life in the Romanesque convent of Cluny but couldn't describe the refectory. Apparently he never saw the refectory, for he had a different vision. In any case, Erwin Panofsky deeply resented Bernard's failure to appreciate architectural beauty.[12]

Let us now take the emphasis on the truth. Here I should nominate René Descartes, who wanted his ideas to be absolutely clear and distinct. He had to have the truth, which could come

75

only from God. Yet Cartesianism has been accused of placing art in a strait jacket; literary art cannot suffer rules so rigid and unforgiving as his. The abuse of the three unities in the drama has been attributed to René Descartes. If this charge is certain, then we have a case of the true at the expense of the beautiful.[13] And finally let us take the Beautiful of the Greek trinity. Here I would nominate the humble Nicaraguan, Rubén Darío, and the haughty Galician, Don Ramón del Valle-Inclán, both of whom might be called gluttons of beauty. For Rubén a ruby is a diamond crimsoned with the blood of elves; for don Ramón, glazed eyeballs toasted in a chimney can be a source of beauty. I will not say that these two were untruthful or un-good, but I will say they found everything, perhaps truth and goodness too, in Beauty.

Was there any genius who incorporated all three, the good, the true and the beautiful? Pascal perhaps, scientist, artist and God-seeker (although he was rather harsh on the theater). San Juan de la Cruz?—poet, saint, a tiny man of boundless courage. I myself favor Raymond Lull for the honor, *Raimundo el loco el fatuo por amor*[14], author of that most beautiful *Libro del Amigo y del Amado*, and father of the Catalan language. To unite all three one would have to be crazy in the sense that Raymond was crazy.

Be that as it may, I shall only accuse Valle of being an aesthetic glutton: the Beautiful always. Whether in undulating sonatas or grotesque forms, his one concern was the Beautiful. Where? There, behind the veil. Beyond phenomena, beyond the uncertain form of things.

(d) Another Aside: Valle is a unitarian, not a trinitarian. The *Alma Mundo* is one.

> (e) . . . y todos se advertían presos en la acción de una guiñolada dramática . . . *Tirano Banderas*, p. 57)

> . . . and they all came to realize they were prisoners in a great dramatic *guiñolada* (puppet theater) . . .

Guiñol comes from the French *guignol* and literally means puppet theater; it was also the Gran Guignol[15], theater of the weird, outlandish, bizarre, uncouth, eerie, uncanny, grotesque, of *contes cruelles*, like the sultan who demanded a hundred pounds of human eyeballs.

The *esperpentos* of Valle-Inclán belong to the *gran guignol* and then some. I recall Benavente's prologue to *Los Intereses Creados*, where Crispín says he will follow the ancient *commedia dell' arte* with its rigid buffoons, Harlequin, Pantaloon,

Colombine and others:

> He aquí el tinglado de la antigua farsa . . . Es una farsa *guiñolesca*, de asunto disparatado, sin realidad alguna. Pronto veréis cómo cuanto en ella sucede no pudo suceder nunca, que sus personajes no son ni semejan hombres y mujeres, sino muñecos o fantoches de cartón y trapo, con groseros hilos, visibles a poca luz y al más corto de vista. Son las mismas grotescas máscaras de aquella comedia de Arte italiano, no tan regocijadas como solían, porque *han meditado mucho* en tanto tiempo. (Emphasis mine).

> Here is the stage of the ancient farce . . . It is a *guignolesque* farce, with a ridiculous argument, without any reality whatsoever. You will soon see how what happens in it could never happen, that its characters don't resemble men and women but puppets and dolls of cardboard and rags, with thick strings visible even where it's dark, visible also to near-sighted people. They are the same grotesque masks of that Italian *commedia dell' arte* of yore, not as joyful as they were wont to be because *they have meditated a lot* during the course of so many years.

Crispín is saying that *Los Intereses Creados* is *commedia dell' arte* but not pure *commedia dell' arte*; it is comedy directed by thought. The author's theme is love.

I should say that Valle's dramatic *guiñolada* is not merely *guignol*. I cannot say that Santos Banderas, he of the green saliva and ¡Chac! ¡Chac! has been changed by meditation, although he is an exceptionally intelligent man, perhaps the most intelligent in modern literature. Nor has Nacho Veguillas meditated, he who honks like a frog (¡Cua! ¡Cua!), no, the puppets have not meditated a great deal. Their cardboard-and-rags nature certainly shows through, as do the thick visible strings guiding them. The puppeteer, on the other hand, has certainly meditated: *Ha meditado mucho. Tirano Banderas* is a devastating satire of a political order; and within the novel, amidst all the wordiness, posing and ironical exclamations of both liberals and reactionaries[16], one comes upon succinct statements of political reality. Although the Europeans know that Banderas's system is unjust, they also realize it suits their economic aspirations. The revolutionaries understand that also, but nevertheless their "arias" do not reveal a superior rhetoric. The bombast of both groups is not without precedent in Latin American history. Thus we have a true historical picture.

Tirano Banderas is a most unusual reading experience. With all the *¡Cua! ¡Cua! ¡Chac! ¡Chac!* and *guignol*, one still comes forth with a profound appreciation of history. Quintessential history.

3. I have reserved three topic sentences, as I call them, for special mention:

> Los gendarmes comenzaban a repartir sablazos. Cachizas de faroles, gritos, manos en alto, caras ensangrentadas. Convulsiones de luces apagándose. Rotura de la pista en ángulos. Visión cubista del Circo Harris. (*Tirano*, p. 56)

> The police began striking out with their swords. Timbers and lanterns, shouts, hands on high, bloodied faces. A fit of lights going out. Cracks on the road surface in angles. A cubist vision of Circo Harris.

(In the Harris Stadium the journalists betray their profession, and Licenciado Larranaga delivers his speech, his *aria*, on the rights of the Indians and the sordid European civilization.)

> Sentíanse alejados en una orilla remota, y la luz triangulada del calabozo realzaba en un módulo moderno y cubista la actitud macilenta de las figuras. (*Tirano*, p. 162)

> They felt far removed on a distant shore, and the triangulated light of the jail emphasized in a modern and cubist module the emaciated posture of the figures.

(In jail the prisoners play cards and talk of their bleak future, especially Nacho Veguillas, who croaks like a frog, *¡Cua! ¡Cua!* They are all perfectly equal. They are all going to die.)

> En aquella sima, números de una gramática rota y llena de ángulos, volvían a inscribir los poliedros del pensamiento, volvían las cláusulas acrobáticas encadenadas por ocultos nexos. (*Tirano*, p. 184)

> In that abyss, numbers of a broken grammar filled with angles came to inscribe again the polyhedrons of thought; acrobatic clauses returned joined by hidden links.

78

(This passage refers to the thoughts of the homosexual Minister of Spain, the diplomatic old wreck (*carcamal*), who is about to be blackmailed.) The words *poliedros, triangulaba, ángulos y roturas gramaticales*, appear in adjoining paragraphs; and throughout the book appear the words *inmóvil, inmovilizado, inmovilizarse*, and also the word *geometría* (pp. 162, 186): "una geometría oblicua y disparatada." We are clearly here in a visual world, an abrupt, sharply defined world of angles, breaks, triangles, modules, numbers, polyhedrons, chains and nexuses. These units of measurement not only apply to the *fantoches* of this farce, and to their actions also, and to other bodies, but even to the language, thoughts and words of puppets like Benicarlés, the Minister of Spain. The contour of everything, even of thoughts and spirit, is reduced to a rectilinear, triangular or polyhedral scheme. Everything is crystallized, geometrically dehumanized. And, like crystals, everything will never change. Niño Santos Banderas will always be an owlish scrawl framed like a sentry in the embrasure of an old monastery. One may see in the scrawl, wax, sheepskin and skull, the latter colored coca green, but there are no identifying features, no nose, eyes, ears, throat, mouth. Nacho Veguillas will always be a *¡Cua! ¡Cua!*, a rectilinear triangular frog in a dungeon. Banderas and Nachito are two of the principal figures in this *guiñolada dramática*, and all we have is a scrawl and a triangle[17]. The coronelito Domiciano, hero of the whore house, has a *vientre búdico*, but picture this Buddha with a rectilinear belly, possibly triangular, and you have him in his inflexibility, his immobility. The thoughts of the decrepit Minister Benicarlés lack a curving contour: "Que me destinen al Centro de Africa. Donde no haya Colonia Española . . . ¡Vaya, Don Celes! ¡Grotesco personaje! . . . ¡Qué idea la de Castelar! . . . Estuvo poco humano. Casi me pesa. Una broma pasada . . ." Broken thought. Broken syntax. Lumped together. Piled up. Staccato. Rectilinear montage.

It is curious what reflections on literary art will do to you. As I think of Valle's music and geometry, his sonatic undulations and esperpentic cubes and triangles, I think of some diagrams I have seen in elementary Spanish textbooks, to explain the imperfect and preterite tenses:

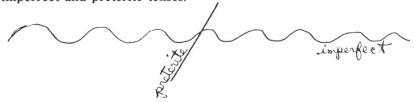

The imperfect tense undulates in the background while the preterite appears in the foreground as an abrupt straight mark, a slash mark across the curves of the imperfect:

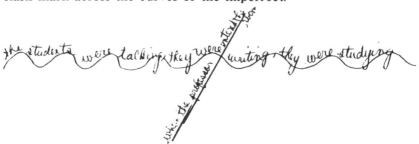

Valle's sonata is the undulating line, the imperfect so to speak, the distant and vague, that bends its way up and down and forward and back, a musical wave rolling towards the horizon, beyond which lies the promised land. Although it is vague out there, indistinct and remote, IMPERFECT in the sense of delineation, the direction is the true one. Meanwhile, in the foreground, we have an abrupt straight line, hash marks, slash marks, triangles and cubes, phenomenal polyhedrons, an emotional delight for the gnostic *who is aware of the undulation beyond*; but they are nonetheless grotesque, awkward, stupid, torpid, the coca spittle and frog grunts of reality, ¡Chac! ¡Chac! ¡Cua! ¡Cua! And if one doesn't know about the undulation, if one is hylic, an Emilio Castelar, a hypocritical *casticista*, a positivist rug-seller vending chickpeas, then one is, to say the least, gravely deprived, and to say it gnostically, one is damned. The prisoner of sterile satan, Time.

32. I have said that Valle is an impressionist, and here he himself speaks of cubism. Which is it to be? Why not both? Perhaps cubism is a form of impressionism. To reach the horizon and beyond, one must listen to the music of the poet. This spiritual journey will require lyrical keys, and finally, a musical miracle, something like a leap of faith to the reality beyond, the *Más Allá*. Close your eyes and listen!

But as you travel on your journey you will, if you open your eyes, see strange shapes and forms, shadows, images in time, humans bound in the jail of clay. Sonatic music will not avail here, for the sonatic is eschatological, *ultimate*, salvational, whereas the phenomena you see are temporal and *proximate*; but if you train your cubist eye on the phenomena you will discover an aesthetic emotion. There is Banderas, no, not the bloody dictator of history, but the owlish scrawl, framed for eternity in the embrasure of a monastery, a product of artful creation, which will evoke thoughts of beauty, which will awaken your memory to the eternal beauty, out there, Beyond. Phenomenal men are ridiculous and grotesque, but esperpentic man, arrested in a pirouette, a *dance*, or in an immobility, will point to the horizon, where the music will take command and convey you.

Just as gargoyles point to the cathedral's truth, which is Christ's Mystical Body, the Communion of Saints, so the *esperpentos* point to the sonatas and the noumenal world beyond: Proximately, *esperpento*; ultimately, sonata. The *esperpento* is the mole on the beautiful lady's face, luring the viewer to her countenance. I am mixing theology and metaphors about loveliness, but when you attempt to explain these truths you cannot help but stammer:

un no sé qué que quedan balbuciendo.

You can't avoid the *balbuceo*, which doesn't diminish my truth but enhances it.
33. Were this really my truth, it would be easily described. But I do not describe, and I cannot define. Attempting an exegesis of Valle, I stammer.
34. Read the newspapers' review of a recent musical concert. It will read something like this:

Mozart made magical
Nobody who believes in the magic of Mozart could have doubted the sorcery in store Monday night when Claudio Abbado passed his wand over the Chicago Symphony Orchestra.

For this Mozart night, Abbado, recently named as principal guest conductor effective in 1982, formed a charmed circle with violinist Salvatore Accardo, principal french horn player Dale Clevenger and an orchestra reduced to chamber proportions.

Accardo, an Italian virtuoso lately catapulted into the American limelight, applied his imposing art to a gently affectionate and deliciously droll interpretation of Violin Concerto No. 4 in D.

Between violinist and conductor existed a bond of understatement, and in that soft light Mozart's music shone. Against Abbado's smoothly spun backdrop. Accardo delivered a vividly personal reading of a work that begs, if quietly, for just such intimacy.

Yet the violinist also had his moments of flashing brilliance, notably in a sharply etched first-movement cadenza and a witty finale marked by stunning passages in double-stops.

With the same happy rapport, Abbado and Clevenger made a stylish joy of Horn Concerto No. 3 in E-flat.

In its first-chair occupant, the Chicago

Symphony boasts a horn player probably unsurpassed in the world. Few players could have matched Clevenger's pianissimo trills and daredevil octaves or the streaming silvery line with which he caressed the slow movement's nocturne-like romance.

Framing these concertos, Abbado began and ended his program with symphonies—a vivacious account of the brief though brightly colored Symphony No. 32 in G and a scintillating romp through the "Haffner" (No. 35 in D).

To the brilliantly scored "Haffner" Abbado brought the best qualities of his musicianship. He sorted out voices with absolute clarity, struck fetching contrasts within the minuet and whipped up a blistering finale of irrepressible rhythmic force.

And in all this, the Chicago Symphony illuninated Mozart's music with breathtaking detail, to say nothing of infectious spirit and, no matter how fast Abbado pushed, disarming precision. Conjury it was; collective prestidigitation.

It was a sad moment indeed when the witching hour passed.

Notice the abundant metaphors: magic, sorcery, wand, charmed, gently affectionate, deliciously droll, bond, understatement, soft light, shone, flashing, brilliance, etched, stunning, happy rapport, stylish joy, daredevil, streaming silvery line, caressed, vivacious, brightly colored, scintillating romp, brilliantly sorted out, sorted out voices, clarity, fetching contrasts, whipped, blistering force, illuminated, infectious, conjury, prestidigitation, sad, witching hour.

The critic has pulled out all the stops, with metaphors from magic, human affection, comedy, light, graphics, acrobatics, chromatics, love, élan vital, frolics, art, coercion, disease, melancholy, and back to magic. Not one of these metaphors is based on sound (although music is sound), but on light, physical movement and human emotions. Perhaps two words have something to do with sound, *voices* and *trills*, although the former's being sorted out evokes literature as much as musical sound, and *trills* is a flat statement indeed compared to the sorcery of witching hours. The critic obviously is stammering, as all musical critics do when they attempt to describe their experience: *Balbuceo*.

I am not suggesting that music is the same as mysticism but only that it is similar. It certainly cannot be defined, or even

82

described well, for when critics employ metaphors they usually resort to something resembling air, fire and water, the *terminologie traditionelle* of the mystics.[18]

I believe, however, that don Ramón María del Valle-Inclán y Montenegro would disagree with my judgment. He is surely suggesting, nay, he is declaring, that the musical miracle is mysticism. He is saying that through music the artist can in an eternal moment transcend phenomena and arrive at ultimate reality, which he calls the *Alma Mundo*. Thus we may call his system, and his code, LYRICAL IDEALISM. This philosophy is extremely subjective, being based on one's awareness, one's consciousness.

Stated in humble terms: There is sonatic music, a little cubism, and a gnosis to show you the horizon and what lies beyond.

35. An afterthought: The remarks concerning cubism and polyhedrons in *Tirano Banderas* brought to mind Picasso's *Demoiselles d'Avignon* (1907), with the designs on one side of the picture and the three recognizable figures on the other. Perhaps *Tirano Banderas* is like that; on the one side, the owlish scrawl and triangulated lights of the Circo Harris, and on the other, some recognizable figures, especially Zacarías el Cruzado, his wife, and Quintín Pereda, the miserly *honrado gachupín* whom Zacarías executes by dragging him with his horse.[19]

Les Demoiselles d'Avignon. Pablo Picasso. Paris (June-July 1907). Oil on canvas, 8' x 7'8". The Museum of Modern Art, New York. Acquired through the Lillie P. Bliss Bequest.

CANTO V

The <u>Sonata de Primavera</u>: Deciphering Valle-Inclán

1. In the *Sonata de Primavera*, the epitaph opposite the first page reads:

NOTA
Estas páginas son un fragmento de las "Memorias Amables," que ya muy viejo empezó a escribir en la emigración el Marqués de Bradomín. Un Don Juan admirable. ¡El más admirable tal vez! Era feo, católico y sentimental.

NOTE
These pages are a fragment of the "Affable Memoirs" that the Marquis de Bradomin, already quite old, began to write during his emigration. An admirable Don Juan. Perhaps the most admirable! He was ugly, Catholic and sentimental.

This epitaph resembles the subtitle to *La lámpara maravillosa, Ejercicios Espirituales*, and is to be taken as a joke. Bradomín is neither ugly nor Catholic nor sentimental, and the grouping of *católico* with *feo* and *sentimental*, likening them, is clearly a devaluation. Here is one evidence of Henri Bergson's *raideur mécanique*, mechanical rigidity. If your aim is laughter, juxtapose the spiritual and the corporal, the Bergsonian example being a funeral oration in which the homilist says: "The deceased was a good man and fat."; Valle's example being: "He was Catholic and ugly." *Sentimental* is a bonus word[1], because higher religions are supposed to be cerebral, with the sentiments held in good order. You would never call Calderón *sentimental*. "Bradomín is Catholic and sentimental" means Catholic and not too cerebral. The so-called "Affable Memoirs," moreover, are not affable, that is, they are not friendly, courteous and kind, but quite the opposite.

On another plane, Bradomín is obviously not ugly, Catholic or sentimental. He is extremely attractive to women, he mocks every part of the Creed and he cynically destroys women, tweaking his moustache as he does so.

Exclamation marks in Valle-Inclán are frequently ironical. The phrase "The most admirable perhaps!" means he is most certainly, and not perhaps, the least admirable. One can speak with certitude about Valle's literature, Valle, the most resolute of Spanish authors. His jokes are deadly serious.

2. In spite of his amorous flippancy Bradomín is not really a

Don Juan. The Don Juan of Tirso de Molina is a theological figure committing various sins: lust, murder, prevarication, contumely and presumption, the sin against the theological virtue of Hope—"¡Qué largo me lo fiais!" Presumption is his specific sin. Don Juan goes to hell believing in divine justice, which is why he asks the stone statue for time to repent. He has been presumptuous.[2]

Bradomín believes in nothing of the sort. From the orthodox viewpoint, the specific sin of this attractive, anti-Catholic ruthless figure is contumely, an insolence aimed at devaluing traditional beliefs. Bradomín is a *títere desvalorizador*. This is why the sonatas have scandalized so many people. This question of scandal is real. I once knew an instructor who used the sonatas (especially the Niña Chole-Statue of the Christ Child episode) to tease his American, mostly Protestant, students. The young boys were truly offended by the embellishment of such an episode. Such cheapness of course is never in season, but I am not interested in cheapness, I am interested in ruthless devaluation.

3. Given the doctrine of the *Lámpara*, the orthodox point of view is despicable. A hierophant has discovered a marvelous new (and yet very ancient) doctrine and art, a hypnotic *Pipa de Kif* that he proposes to use for aesthetic magnetism. But ancient rubbish surrounds him, ancient *casticismo* and platitudes hem him in. He must clear the way by creating a dehumanized puppet, Bradomín.

4. René Descartes also aspired to clear the way. He disdained the evidence of the senses; he wanted clear and distinct ideas, a brand new epistemology, the *cogito ergo sum* and ontological proof of the existence of God. The Scholastics before him, who had argued that all knowledge begins with the senses, had created a deceptive city, and so he likened himself to the architect of a new city. Such an architect must first tear the old city down before he can build, although he will set up a temporary builder's shack while doing the demolition. This shack is the laws of his Church and King, because he is reverent and loyal. He may have ended up scandalizing the *casticistas*, his Jesuit professors, but that was hardly his intention. He first brought his new doctrine to them, he drew his new plans with reverence.

5. Valle wanted to create a new city, but he is irreverent and disloyal to ancient essences. There is no temporary builder's shack, no apartment for replanning and reconsideration. The ancient city must go at once, on the instant, as if mowed down by a scythe. Valle's soft, gentle sonata, that mellifluous language, those delicate nights in the garden, on the one hand, and the devastating scythe on the other, are paradoxical, and their apparent self-contradiction, their incongruity, has caused grave misunderstanding. The scythe is a bulldozer, leveling the ground, preparing the foundation, whereas the sonata is the new edifice,

which should reach the stars. Stellar sound and stellar vision.

6. The orthodox will be scandalized by the sonatas whereas the heterodox will bind them in leather, like breviaries, prayer books and missals. Since there is no room for skepticism here, the Montaignes of this world can decide nothing. There is no backshop of the mind, no alternative; you have to choose.[3] Even so, even though you are orthodox, to understand the sonatas you must look at them internally, as if you were a disciple of the hierophant, the priest of the Eleunisian mysteries, Don Ramón del Valle-Inclán y Montenegro. But what are those mysteries?

7. I am unable to agree with Pedro Salinas's formalism, which skirts the issue:

> El que crea como yo que la literatura, en su altísimo punto, es un procedimiento de objetivar, con ánimo de salvación perdurable, las experiencias humanas mediante un uso especial, o sea un arte, del lenguaje, de las palabras, verá la supremacía de una obra no derivada capitalmente del asunto o tema dado por la experiencia y sí del acierto de la operación subjetivante o poetizadora, fuente de la hermosura.[4]

No, as far as Valle-Inclán is concerned, Salinas is mistaken. You must make the wager on the *asunto* or *tema*. You must make the choice. To separate the matter from the form, as Salinas does, is to kill the sonata. Aristotle was right, you cannot separate matter from form.

Valle-Inclán, the central figure of modern Spanish literature, was not naive. He knew what he was doing. To the critics one can only say: Please don't make him a *¡Chac! ¡Chac!*, a *¡Cua! ¡Cua!* author, an *esperpento*. Don't separate matter from form.

8. In 1962 a British Hispanist said to me: "Valle has created a ruthless synthesis." Ruthless, not sentimental, ruthless. Bradomín is ruthless.

9. What is the plot of *Primavera*? It is the era of Pope Kings, before Italy's unification in 1870 and two score years after the death of Casanova, Marqués de Seingalt (1725-1798). Into this ancient atmosphere, on a mission from Rome, comes the young Marqués de Bradomín, who tweaks his moustache when people suffer or die. Employing a diabolical pose, he destroys a saintly girl and her family. He leaves, professing to be covered with sadness. A joke.

10. The plot is as simple as that and were the sonata no more than that we would have the work of a fool delighting in the attention of other fools. But the literal plot is only proximate. The sequence of events is really an ingenious scythe, a large finely honed blade lopping off ancient doctrines, such as the

cardinal and theological virtues, the beliefs of the Church, and the tenets of a decrepit retrograde society. The real target of course is not the virtues in themselves but a priest-ridden reactionary society hypocritically professing them. We must tear down the old city before we can build the new one.

11. So much for the plot, which is the scythe. Bradomín may say he is a "carlista por estética," but only for aesthetic reasons, the truth is his narrator despises Carlism. He hates everything it stands for, except the literary myth, of which fanciful dreams are woven. We have something like this in the United States of America, in the northern regions. The Blue and the Gray! Billy Yank and Johnnie Reb! Even in the north the gray is the sentimental favorite, the land of better fighters, better generals (Lee, Jackson, Stuart), courage, loyalty, better dreams (¿Soy suriano por estética?), but nobody really wants the South to have won. That would mean a journey back to the oxcart. More gray souvenirs are sold than blue, but remember, they are only toys.

12. In the U.S.A. people like the rebel flag, but they don't like rebellion. Valle likes royal ritual but he doesn't like royalism. A vision, yes: "¡Carlos VII, Duque de Madrid!," but not Carlism itself.

Valle detests all privilege not based on art. Money, aristocracy, ecclesiastical privilege—he despises them all. But he adores the creators of *romances*:

> No sé lo que tienen, madre,
> las flores del camposanto,
> mas cuando las mueve el aire
> parece que están llorando.

> I don't know what it is, mother,
> the flowers by her side,
> but when the night air moves
> it's just like they would cry. (Anonymous)[5]

13. So much for the plot, which has razed old streets and houses. Now let us get to the sonata. What's it all about? The *dianoia*.

14. Five sentences of *La lámpara maravillosa* will tell us what is going on in the *Sonata de Primavera*. Again I, in my prosaic way, shall call these *topic sentences*. But you are too logical, you say, too cold and calculating; Valle despised topic sentences. That may be, but if I were to act any other way I would simply write another *sonata*. That's all Gómez de la Serna and those other blabbers ever did, attempt to write another sonata, proving they were able writers, though never so able as the prodigious ropewalker from Galicia. *Les funambules*. So why should I turn funambulist and add to the confusion? Besides, I

could never write a sonata, I don't have the talent. I see things as they are, not as I would have them be, and I see them so because I haven't been smoking the *Pipa de Kif*. If you deny me this academic freedom, then no literary criticism is possible, only an endless chain of would-be sonatas. And in lesser hands, sonatas become cacophonous.

15. Very well, I select five topic sentences:

(1) Hagamos de toda nuestra vida a modo de una estrofa, donde el ritmo interior *despierta* las sensaciones indefinibles aniquilando el significado ideológico de las cosas. (*Lámpara*, p. 29; emphasis mine)

Let us conduct our entire life as if it were a strophe where the interior rhythm *awakens* ineffable sensations, annihilating the ideological meaning of things.

(2) Toda la vida pasada era como el verso *lejano* que revive su *evocación* musical al encontrar otro verso que le guarda consonancia, y sin perder el primer significado, entra a completar un significado *más profundo*. (*Lámpara*, 29; emphasis mine)

All of past life was like the *distant* verse that revives its musical *evocation* when it meets another verse with which it holds a consonance, and without losing its first meaning it starts to complete a *more profound* meaning.

(3) En todas las cosas duerme un poder de evocaciones eróticas . . . El conocimiento de un grano de trigo, con todas sus evocaciones, nos dará el conocimiento pleno del Universo . . . En este mundo de evocaciones sólo penetran los poetas, porque para sus ojos todas las cosas tienen una significación religiosa, más próxima a la significación única. (*Lámpara*, p. 26)

In all these things there slumbers a power of erotic evocations . . . The knowledge of a grain of wheat, with all its evocations, would give us the complete knowledge of the Universe . . . Only the poets penetrate this world of evocations, because for their eyes all things have a religious meaning, closer to the one and only meaning.

88

(4) El espíritu de los gnósticos descubre una emoción estética en el absurdo de las formas, en la creación de monstruos, en al acabamiento de la vida. (*Lámpara*, p. 70)

The spirit of the gnostics reveals an aesthetic emotion in the absurdity of forms, in the creation of monsters, in the termination of life.

(5) El baile es la más alta expresión estética porque es la única que transporta a los ojos los números y las cesuras musicales. (*Lámpara*, p. 54)

The dance is the highest aesthetic expression, because it is the only one that brings to the eyes musical numbers and caesurae.

Now I hope to take these five topic sentences and examine the first third of the *Sonata de Primavera* with them, up to the scene where Bradomín recites the *¡Os adoro!* litany to María del Rosario. Just what is the meaning of this introductory dance? What is it supposed to awaken in us? What is it supposed to evoke? What deeper meaning does it contain? And why do absurd forms appear in the dance, or perhaps I ought to say, before it? Why does Valle see himself as the Great Choreographer? (I should remind the reader of Joan Maragall's identification of the dance with supreme sexual union: *ut supra*, Canto I, #9, and End Note 3.).

16. I am tempted to write a score of topic sentences and examine all the sonatas in their light. Take this sentence for example:

Sólo buscando la suprema inmovilidad de las cosas puede leerse en ellas el enigma bello de su eternidad. (*Lámpara*, p. 97)

Only by seeking the supreme immobility of things can one read in them the beautiful enigma of their eternity.

For deciphering the choreography in Valle-Inclán no word is more important than *inmovilidad (inmóvil, inmovilizarse)*. Nevertheless, I shall add no more topic sentences from the *Lámpara*, for were I to do so I would compile an interminable list with hundreds and hundreds of references to Valle's twenty-odd sonatas. The repetition might be overwhelming, but then, I have always found Valle to be an unusually repetitious author, his opera being a sort of vast anadiplosis. Indeed, codes by nature are repetitious. Picture him as a celestial musicologist assuming the appearance of a plain organ grinder with a simian on his shoulder performing absurd actions: he grinds and grinds and grinds until your eyes turn from the simian to the music to a miraculous heavenly ballet in which everything takes its place. Its proper place. *Inmovilización*. Quietude. (These last two are code words). Picture that and you have an idea of what is going on in Valle.

Since I want to draw attention to the ballet rather than the grinding, I shall content myself with a few sententious sayings and one sonata, *Primavera*. And don't let your eyes deceive you. Phenomenally this goat-bearded spalpeen will appear as a mere organ-grinder, but he is really much more than that. He is the clown *que no lo es*. He is the apparently awkward, but central figure of modern Spanish letters.

17. Wave your wand! The sonata is about to begin:

Anochecía cuando la silla de posta traspuso la Puerta Salaria y comenzamos a cruzar la *campiña llena de misterio y rumores lejanos*. (emphasis mine)

Night was falling when the post chaise went through the Salarian Gate and we began to cross the *countryside filled with mystery and distant indistinct sounds*.

Anochecer and similar words (*amanecer, misa de alba, penumbra, media luz, caída de la tarde*: all of them taken from the opening page of *Primavera*) are part of the lexicon of Valle-Inclán; let us reduce them all to the word *twilight* in English, or *crepúsculo-penumbra* in Spanish. In the sonatic ambience actions take place and objects are seen in a diffused light, when things are dim, uncertain, vague, indistinct. People, for example, travel in a penumbra, and it is no accident that Bradomín is journeying to the ancient ecclesiastical city of Ligura as night is falling. He is traveling, as all of us in life travel, to the unknown, the uncanny, the different, and it is fitting that he do so at twilight. In broad day everything is clearly seen, in deep night nothing is seen unless there be a moon, but then the moon's rays compose a twilight rather than dark night. There is something out there, we are not quite sure, but we sense it is there, we know it is there, and so we find ourselves in twilight. Not full assent, not negation, but a kind of uncertain certitude, a penumbral epistemology. Bradomín arrives at Ligura just before dawn, when the moon, already pale, is disappearing.

The youthful Bradomín passes through a countryside filled with mystery and distant indistinct noises. Remember your days as a young man or woman in May, the month of flowers, aromatically stirring flowers, the flower of youth, and in the crepuscular darkness of a moonlit night you can't really see but you can sense and you can hear, and you can sense mystery, something secret, something evocative but obscure and hard to understand, but you know or think you know it's there, and then you hear strange distant noises (imperceptible erotic stirrings perhaps) suggesting the existence of an unseen, unknown presence. You have so to speak a visual hearing or an audible sight (synesthesia) throwing dim light, throwing rumors on the landscape, and there is a moon of sorts and now it wanes just as life wanes and then it is dawn and the end of the night. You can't *prove* anything but you just *know* something was there, you'll assent to that, as we all did when we were on a balmy country road in the stirring month of May. We all have such a memory, and the city is no good for evoking memories because in the city there are garish lights and noises and traffic and buildings and . . . hubbub, but not in the country where the sounds (the rumors—low indistinct murmurs) are distant (*lejanos*). That is the key word, *distant sound*, which is a synesthetic synonym for *crepuscular*. Just as twilight objects are indistinct and vague so distant sounds are indistinct and vague. Here lie truths vaguely known, faintly and remotely apprehended, but they are truths nonetheless and far more substantial than the quotidian phenomena of midday, when you and I hustle in the marketplace, and policemen, merchants, generals, queens, clergymen and other hypocrites go through their awkward daily motions. In the distance lies the horizon where the two worlds meet, the phenomenal and the noumenal, and it calls to mind the saying from Celtic mythology, said of Halloween:

This is the night when the veil between the two
worlds thins . . .

Twilight and remote distance are the setting of a strange knowledge, a sonatic epistemology. The realization of this valleinclanesque truth comes from the first sentence of the *Sonata de Primavera*:

Anochecía cuando la silla de posta traspuso la
Puerto Salaria y comenzamos a cruzar la campiña
llena de misterio y de rumores lejanos.

These are just twenty-three select words. Imagine reading all the sonatas like this—and imagine writing them!—but that is what

you must do, Brother Pilgrim, if you really want to know. If you desire the gnosis.
    18. The fifth line of *Primavera* reads:

> Antiguos sepulcros orillaban el camino y mustios cipreses dejaban caer sobre ellos su sombra venerable.

> Ancient sepulchres were bordering the road and faded cypress trees were casting on them their venerable gloom.

The graves are ancient, and the shadows of the cypresses venerable, commanding respect because of their great age. In another sonata, *Flor de santidad*, admiration is expressed, nay, whispered, for centenary cypresses and millenary trees; and in still another sonata, the *Lámpara* itself, for thousand year old cathedrals. Again we have indistinctness: a crepuscular light, distant sounds and old graves, and faded, gloomy trees, in a word, antiquity; because the further back you go the vaguer things[6] become, and if you retreat far enough, only some sort of a memory, call it a karma memory, can evoke them, a karma memory stimulated by music. Let the rigid Scholastics and John Locke argue that all knowledge begins with the senses, the infallible senses according to them, and let that Frenchman Descartes have his clear and distinct ideas issuing from his infallible God, they are all of them wrong, hylics and fools. We know from experience this is a brutal, disordered world filled with phenomenal puppets, hypocrites, *fantoches*, so if you want the truth, which brings unity and beauty, you must descry it in a twilight zone, a whispering, murmuring zone, long ago and far away, on the horizon, where phenomena fade away, before the advent of time. And how do you descry it? Through the evocations of memory, aided by musical mnemonics, as in a sonata or dance.
    Western philosophy emphasizes the intellect or the will, which romantics called the heart, but the Galician hierophant emphasizes memory. His thought has an eastern divergence, as he indicates in his *Lámpara*:

> El idioma de un pueblo es la lámpara de su karma.
> Toda palabra encierra un oculto poder cabalístico:
> Es grimorio y pentáculo.

> The language of a nation is the lamp of its karma.
> Every word conceals a hidden cabalistic power: It is a five-pointed star and book of magic spells.
> (*Lámpara*, p. 41)

92

Karma: in Hinduism, one of the means of reaching Brahma. Brahma is the ultimate ground of all being. The evocations of karma memory educed in penumbral music, with its numbers and caesurae, will bring us to an ultimate ground, which Valle calls the Alma Mundo. Reading the sonatas, we are meant to enter the world of soteriology *sans* Jesus Christ, although one can always use his name in the spirit of Docetism. The sonatas are the agent effecting salvation. Perhaps that is why they are bound like prayerbooks by many disciples of the turbaned sage from Galicia.

Mustios cipreses: These cypresses, perpetual symbols of death[7], are faded, indistinct and ancient, like the graves they border, or dance over in the breeze. One might call Valle's sonatas an art of synonyms: twilight, remoteness, age, graves, death, trees, gardens, countryside, act of fading, shade, act of withering, horizon—although they all seem to differ semantically, in the sonata they mean the same thing, indistinctness, that which is not clearly recognizable or understandable. They are synonyms; let us call them musical variations of the same theme. And added to this indistinctness of images are all those verbs in the imperfect tense, hovering in the background, undulating, whispering, murmuring, softly, vaguely, while Bradomín arrives at Ligura.

There is of course another kind of undulation:

. . . y sus colinas, que tienen la graciosa ondulación de los senos femeninos.

. . . and their hills, which have the gracious undulation of female bosoms.

Whenever sex appears in the sonatas a peculiar vagueness always attends it: tears clouding the eyes, a languid light, a fainting, hands fluttering, a penumbra, a mysterious garden, a sigh, a "mundo de recuerdos lejanos," an evocation, tears slowly, dolorously sliding down the cheek, a stammer, a tremor, a trembling, a gust, a dream, a nostalgia, a lap filled with roses, eyes open to the infinite—none of them defined and all of them strangely moving. Sex is crepuscular, distant, ancient, undulating, imperfect in time, sonatic, and more than that a choreography (pálidas manos—an esdrújulo—and fluttering fingers are a dance.) The Catalan poet Joan Maragall likens the supreme union of a man and woman to a dance:

Y asimismo, paralelamente, en la danza encontramos el principio y el fin de todas las artes: desde la danza caótica de las olas en el mar

93

y de toda multitud confusa y primitiva, hasta
aquella absolutamente individualizada y más pura
que podemos imaginar, y que sentimos latir ya en
el fondo de nuestros amores, de una Unica
atrayendo a un Unico a confundirse en ella para
siempre en amor en la suprema cima de la Belleza
inmortal. (*Elogios*, p. 124)

And likewise, in a parallel manner, we find in the
dance the beginning and end of all the arts: from
the chaotic dance of waves on the sea and of
every obscure and primitive multitude, to that one
dance that is the most pure and absolutely
individualized we can imagine, and that we
already feel pulsing in the depth of our love, of a
Woman, one alone, attracting a Man, one alone, to
unite himself with her forever in love in the
supreme height of immortal Beauty.

An uncanny erotic rhythm, a *logos espermático*, undulates behind
the veil of this world, which the lyrical poet must pierce for us
to arrive at gnosis. Sex, the mysterious life force.

19. One other phrase in the first paragraph of *Primavera*
commands our attention:

. . . y el golpe alegre y desigual de los cascabeles
despertaba un eco en los floridos olivares . . .

. . . and the happy and uneven clang of the jingle
bells was awakening an echo in the flowering
olive groves . . .

The "ideological significance" of the sentence is relatively
unimportant; as the post chaise was traveling along, the merry
uneven beat of the jingle bells was arousing, was recalling an
echo in the olive groves. The bells were echoing, but in these
Memoirs of Spring, Bradomín says *despertaba*; they were
awakening, arousing, recalling an echo that was already there. In
a sense, then, it wasn't an echo as we know it, but something
that was already there. This language comes from the Magic
Lamp, where, as we have seen:

Hagamos de toda nuestra vida a modo de una
estrofa, donde el ritmo interior *despierta* las
sensaciones indefinibles aniquilando el significado
ideológico de las cosas.

Let us make of our lives a sort of strophe[8], where

94

the interior rhythm awakens those ineffable sensations that annihilate the ideological meaning of things.

Ineffable, indefinable, that is to say, indistinct sensations. If we live well, our lives will be a poem, the music of a dance, an interior rhythm through which we'll arrive at certain ineffable sensations, intuitions, that will erase the ideological meaning of things; not the meaning of words alone, but of things. We'll arrive at a higher, non-phenomenal meaning. Listen to the echoes aroused by all the *despertabas* and evocations you encounter in the sonata, and you will intuit a higher meaning. We know the means, the road if you will, which is music, dance, intuition. But where will the road lead the brother pilgrim? What lies at the road's end?

20. Valle reminds me of St. Augustine, in reverse. St. Augustine admired Plato, through Plotinus, because of his sense of finality, his knowledge of final matters (final things); one might say his instinct for heaven and the Form of Goodness. The Platonists could see the top of the mountain they were journeying to, but being pagans they didn't know how to get there:

> By reading these books of the Platonists I had been prompted to look for truth as something incorporeal, and I *caught sight of your invisible nature, as it is known through your creatures* (the emphasis is in St. Augustine). But how could I expect that the Platonist books would ever teach me charity? I believe that it was by your will that I came across these books before I studied the Scriptures, because you wished me always to remember the impression that they had made on me, so that later on, when I had been chastened by your Holy Writ and my wounds had been touched by your healing hand, I should be able to see and understand the difference between presumption and confession, between those who see the goal that they must reach, but cannot see the road by which they are to reach it, and those who see the road to that blessed country which is meant to be no mere vision but our home. (St. Augustine, *Confessions*, Hammondsworth: Penguin Books, 1975, p. 154—Book VII, Section 20).

In contrast to the Platonists, according to St. Augustine, the most humble Christian peasant, illiterate, quite ordinary, knows the road. St. Augustine, you might say, Platonized the Christian religion but always gave precedence to supernatural charity. The heterodox Valle seems to have a converse problem. He professes to know the road to a blessed land, the road being poetry, but his disciples still can't see the mountain top; indeed, they still don't know where the mountain is, where they are going. Valle himself professes to have that knowledge, which refers to the *Alma Mundo*. It is hidden in the *Lámpara*.

> 21. A lo lejos, almenados muros se destacaban, negros y sombríos, sobre celajes de frío azul. Era la vieja, la noble, la piadosa ciudad de Ligura.

> Afar, merloned walls loomed forth, black and gloomy, from clouds of cold blue. It was the old, the noble, the pious city of Ligura.

We have been told that the highway (*calzada*) was old (everything in the background worth mentioning is old, faded, indistinct), and now, afar, walls with battlements, millenary medieval walls, ancient walls *se destacaban*—they were standing out, they were looming, they were coming into view, indistinctly and enlarged against cold blue clouds, that is, flat, dull clouds. Bradomín does not use words like *estaban, se encontraban, había*, but the word *se destacaban*.[9] On the distant horizon, afar, *a lo lejos*, things were not there in the sense of *estar*, they were looming up, rising up, coming forth, vaguely, for that's the way things are, or were, or were being evoked, when you arrive at the wall edging phenomena. Things that have a modest metaphysical movement, they slowly come to meet you, vaguely however, because they are not seen with the eyes or heard with the ears but are evocations of memory; or they are immobile. The walls are dark and dismal, but in the penumbra against the one cold blue, the colorless blue so to speak, you can just pick them out, you can descry them. *Blue, azul* from the land of poetry, near the phenomenal wall. What lies beyond? Things-in-themselves. Noumena. The *Alma Mundo*.

Ligura, ancient, noble and pious. Historically (according to the tone of Bradomín's *Memoirs*), nobility and piety are the alleged virtues of fanatical princesses and hypocritical clergy, but even so, aesthetically they can be the objects of art. We have spoken of Platonic Forms and noumena, and now we find ourselves with an ancient fortress looming up before us, but, . . . but, there is a hint of what is to come:

> La silla de posta caminaba lentamente, y el cascabeleo de las mulas hallaba un eco burlón, casi sacrílego, en las calles desiertas, donde crecía la yerba.

The poet chaise was traveling slowly, and the bell
jingling of the mules was finding a scornful echo,
an almost sacrilegious one, in the deserted streets
where weeds were growing. (I deliberately
translate *hallaba* as *was finding*.)

In this land, a never-never land, an edge-of-the-horizon-land
known only to vatic bards who pierce the veil, grass grows in
deserted streets at dawn, and sounds are found evoked,
summoned forth as echoes, but these echoes have a mocking
almost sacrilegious overtone. Unfortunately, within this
mysterious scene repugnant phenomena will appear, not the thing-
in-itself (things-in-themselves) but the Princess Gaetanis,
Polonios, beadles and clergy of this world, fanatics, hypocrites,
with their fleshy pale hands and half-closed eyes. And
Bradomín's *Memoirs* will scorn them, flog them, quarter them,
even by sacrilege. They are phenomenal fools and hypocrites,
grotesque puppets who destroy this potential Garden of Eden.

There is of course a certain irony here. The gnostic can
always draw a distinctive esperpentic delight in the creation of
grotesque figures. Polonio is cousin german to Nacho Veguillas
and his *¡Cua! ¡Cua!*. Sonata and esperpento are never entirely
separate.

22. Tres viejas, que parecían tres sombras,
esperaban acurrucadas a la puerta de una iglesia
todavía cerrada, pero otras campanas distantes ya
tocaban a misa.

Three old women, who looked like three shades,
were waiting curled up at the door of a church,
still closed, but other distant bells were already
sounding for Mass.

Three: a Pythagorean number, cabalistic, abracadabristic, is the
predilect cipher of the sonatas; three old women, three shades,
three doors, three knocks on the door, *tres veces*, adjectives in
groups of three[10], and *se santiguó tres veces*. For the brother
pilgrims, however, who are somewhat advanced now,
aprovechados rather than *principiantes*, it is no longer necessary
to dwell on cabalistic threes, which may only distract them in
their meditation.
    Within orthodoxy, Santa Teresa de Avila spoke of four states
of prayer, likening them to irrigation: the bucket, the *noria*, the
rains and finally the floods. When the ardent soul is inundated
with infused knowledge, prayerbooks, rosaries and sacred images
(which are ordinarily desirable) might only distract the soul from

97

union with the Beloved. Similarly, within valleinclanesque heterodoxy, it would be unwise for the pilgrims approaching sonatic wisdom to dwell on literal numbers, three and five.[11] The numbers might distract them. Strict numerology is all right for neophyte psychics, but *hermanos peregrinos* nearing the wall containing phenomena, with noumena just beyond, are almost pneumatics; indeed, some of them have already received the poet's word (*Verbo*), the eucharistic grace of art.

Aprovechados! Advanced ones! Forget threes and fives, triangles and pentacles, rings of Giges, Molinos and three aesthetic roses, souls in jail and aesthetic circles; forget the abracadabra and spiritual exercises, that is all behind you now. You have become part of the trans-phenomenal miracle, the musical miracle, the Dance! The true Self! Beauty! Lyrical transcendentalism.

23. I haven't read the sonatas in twenty years, and I must say reading them again is like going home. And that's what they are meant to be, going home. The definition of a sonata, if there is one, is "going home." Not the home on 123 Elm Street, where trees are short or tall or stripped for winter, but *home*, the true home, where *tree* looms, the Form *Tree*, where you see it-in-itself, you, not the you of this jail of clay, the persona, the mask, the phenomenal you, deformed, distorted, an owlish scrawl like Banderas, but *you*, the real *you*, and where everything is-as-it-is, where the Universe, devoid of multiplicity, becomes One:

> El conocimiento de un grano de trigo, con todas sus evocaciones, nos daría el conocimiento pleno del Universo. (*Lámpara*, p. 26)

> The knowledge of one grain of wheat, with all its evocations, would give us the absolute knowledge of the Universe.

The aesthetic gnosis (*conocimiento*) of Ramón del Valle-Inclán requires an extraordinary act of faith.[12]

> 24. Bajo los aleros sombríos revoloteaban los gorriones, y en el fondo de la calle el farol de una hornacina agonizaba.[13]

> Beneath the gloomy eaves were fluttering sparrows, and in the further depth of the road, the lamp of a niche was on the verge of dying.

Again, the light is indistinct, uncertain. The eaves are penumbral, lit only by a dying, waning lamp recessed in a niche back at the end of a street. In this vague light sparrows are fluttering, they are only wings really, you can barely make them out; you descry a waning, flickering lamp and flying fluttering whirling spinning—*dancing*—shades; you can't see the profile of things, realistic, lined, detailed profiles, instead you sense a kind of presence, a spirit so to speak in the penumbra, fluttering beings; and remember, the lamp is in the distant background, ill-defined, not in the foreground where you might see its lines, and the lamp is dying, so we are left with a vague impression, twilight, shades, fluttering, flickering, off in the distance. This is the place where the two worlds meet, the phenomenal and the noumenal, and

> This is the night when the veil between the two
> worlds thins . . . (Celtic mythology)

a sort of Halloween.

As you pass from the phenomenal world, things (dare I call them things?) are like that. They aren't there in the sense of *estar*. They loom, they flicker, they flutter, they rise up briefly, for otherwise the eye could not contain them. Philosophers have said that although light is the proper object of the eye, the eye cannot look at the Sun without being blinded, it cannot take in All Light at once; it will see nothing. Similarly, the soul cannot see God, its proper object, its end (what a horrible, philosophical, unpoetic word, *object*, better to say BEAUTY) without being blinded. It too will perceive nothing. Bradomín is saying in effect that the soul can't see things-in-themselves, it can only divine. Penumbral, adumbrative knowledge.

St. Paul said it for the orthodox: We now see only darkly, but we shall see then face to face. Bradomín says it for the heterodox: you will see only darkly, but if you persevere you will catch it in the eternal moment. The eternal moment of the lamp. Light. Not twilight. Light. Gnosis. The orthodox vision is personal, whereas the heterodox vision seems pantheistic (*Alma Mundo*).

25. In the previous passage, the reader (or listener!) is drawn to the sound and evocations of *agonizaba*. *Agonizaba*: it is a slow, prolonged word, a *lentamente* word, drawn out, and we remember that the spirit of the gnostics discovers an aesthetic emotion in "el acabamiento de la vida," the termination of life. In the *Sonata de primavera*, the lamp *agonizaba*, and the bishop *agonizaba* (this is repeated several times). Death looms there in the distance at the thither side of the phenomenal wall, and Death is indistinct, the same as age, twilight, gloom, melancholy (the women of *Primavera* are sad figures[14]), and flutterings. Death is indistinct. It is a vague, mysterious presence.

26. Perhaps we can call Valle's method a new *conceptismo*.

Statements have several layers of meaning, the least apparent being the final one, the *terminus ad quem*. We needn't pay attention to hylics, they're not worth it, and as for *garbanceros*, we can take them at face value. But poets well that's different, we take them for their background value.[15] Poets like Valle destroy doctrines they consider false, then they place a doctrine (poets are the legislators of the world), and then, in the case of Valle, a background doctrine, and this is the one the reader must look for, or listen to. Read Valle in this order:

Sacrilege   (destroys old doctrines)
Story
Background.

Look for the background.

27. We have come through two paragraphs, and we have the whole sonata. Two paragraphs, like two sonnets. Cling to the original idea. Everything will be repetition now. Anadiplosis. Variations on the theme.

Just two short paragraphs. Great prophets are like that. Christ said: "The sabbath was made for man, man was not made for the sabbath;" thirteen brief words, only one of them duosyllabic in English, and today they call it Existentialism. Ponderous Germans and Frenchmen write thousands of ponderous tomes on being and essence and beingforitselfness, and all the Prophet did was say thirteen words. Perhaps He couldn't even read and write, He just said them. Christ also said: "Render to Caesar the things that are Caesar's and to God the things that are God's," sixteen words this time, a slightly longer sonnet, and today they call it Separation of State and Church, and American professorial and Supreme Court *carcamales* write tomes and tomes on it, just like El Tostado. That's what they are, Tostados. Two aphorisms will do, two sonnets.

And that other prophet, Valle the hierophant, puts it all there for us in two paragraphs (two short sonnets), but we are so hylic, so jailed in clay he has to repeat it and repeat it and repeat it until the Grand Sonata overwhelms us with its musical miracle. His was a lonely aesthetic existence meant only for sufferers. Poets. Funambulators who have to funambulate the funambules. They even have to pretend they are fakers. Caftans. Turbans. Rings. *Ceceo. Manquedad poética.* Prestidigitation.

28. We have just examined the first two paragraphs of *Primavera*. Let us select a few words and phrases from the following paragraphs, up to the *¡Os adoro!* litany recited by Bradomín to María Rosario. Some phrases will be discussed, others only listed in an effort to show Valle's repetition. These repeated utterances are not unlike a prayer wheel that a Buddhist or a Raymond Lull might have devised to aid you in your journey; you might say that the sonatas are lyrical keys and prayer wheels. Perhaps that is why Bradomín disciples religiously

bind his *Memoirs* to look like mantras or prayer wheels.

(a) . . . Las Memorias del Caballero de Seingalt
(Casanova)

. . . the Memoirs of the Knight of Seingalt
(Casanova)

Bradomín's sonatas are called *Memoirs* on the title page. Any
reference to or suggestion of memory is important in the sonatas,
whose very theme is memory, not the historical memory of
Gabriel Araceli in Galdós's *National Episodes* (Galdós is a
garbancero), but an ancient, ineffable, ancestral, crepuscular
karma memory that will take us beyond the phenomenal wall. In
this sense the sonatas, as lyrical keys, may be called a virtuoso
performance in musical mnemonics. By synesthesia this is called
Pipa de Kif, but it is really musical mnemonics.

(b) ¡Acatemos la voluntad de Dios!

Let us revere the will of God!

Bradomín says this to two beadles, while talking about the dying
bishop. This exclamation, like most exclamations in Bradomín, is
ironical. Bradomín's words are rigid, farcical, esperpentic, set
against the suave, undulating sonata of the background, rather
like a drum clap against soft music. Or, you are listening to
Mozart—the door bell clangs—back to Mozart.

(c) . . . y el argentino son de la campanilla
revoloteaba glorioso sobre las voces apagadas y
contritas.

. . . and the silver sound of the bell fluttered
(was fluttering, imperfect tense) over the voices,
contrite and subdued.

Synesthesia: a fluttering silver sound. *Voces apagadas* are barely
discernible. Indistinctness. Death is on the horizon, the
phenomenal horizon.

(d) La cámara donde agonizaba . . .

The room where he lay dying . . .

Agonizaba has been discussed above.

(e) . . . y su corvo perfil de patricio romano

101

destacábase en la penumbral inmóvil, blanco,
sepulcral, como el perfil de las estatuas yacentes.

. . . and his arched profile of a Roman patrician
stood out in the motionless penumbra, white,
funereal, like the profile of statues at rest.

The bishop is in his ancient bed (*lecho antiguo*), dying
(*agonizaba*). The scene is penumbral and the profile vague,
patrician and statuesque, massive perhaps, graceful and beautiful.
That is all. There are no details. The vague profile rises up
before you. The word *inmóvil* is frequently repeated in Valle-
Inclán. In the quotidian world, which is phenomenal, the puppets
and shadowy beings are constantly in motion, Chac-chacing, Cua-
cuaing and talking hypocritically, but there, on the horizon,
where the veil between the two worlds thins, things tend towards
immobility. And on the other side of the horizon, in the *Más
Allá*, Plato's Forms and Kant's noumena are surely immobile. As
we shall all be one day.

(f) La voz de la Princesa Gaetani *despertaba* en mi
alma un *mundo* de *recuerdos lejanos*, que tenían
esa *vaguedad risueña* y *feliz* de los *recuerdos
infantiles*. (Emphasis mine).

The voice of Princess Gaetani *was awakening* in
my *soul* a *world* of *distant memories*, which had
that *happy* and *cheerful vagueness* of *childlike
memories*.

This sentence, which contains perhaps all the archetypes of the
Lámpara, may be construed thus: "Once upon a time there was a
happy, carefree world where everyone was childlike and
innocent, but that is all vague now, distant, dim in memory, long
ago, and the only way it can be evoked now, awakened, is for
the soul to experience something special[16], like the sound of a
woman's voice, yes, music and sex are evocations. Oh to be in
that world again!" This is the true myth of the Golden Age, the
time of faery and poesie, and since it is there everyone must
share it. Sex here is not like it is today, in the *congala*[17] of
Tirano Banderas or amongst the conniving men and women of
our quotidian world; it is more a music, a *voz*, a poetry, a dance,
yes, it is a grand celestial ballet, mystical and mysterious, and
through it we can be happy again. By inference, we can think of
all those gargoyles in *El ruedo ibérico*, all those maimed ones,
and realize that they, and by they I mean we too, do not share
the golden age myth. We do not even know of its existence. We
go about our daily routine, digging ourselves deeper into the

mud, and think we are virtuous. But there is an exit if we will only try: Phantasize, dream, transcend, listen to the music and remember. I recall reading Denis de Rougemont's book on love in the west, where he spoke of Tristan and Isolde as a Manichaean myth. A myth is spellbinding, uncanny, for it holds some truth so profound and awesome it cannot be told directly, it must be told as a simple story that all will delight in. Valle-Inclán is like that. He the mythmaker stands on Parnassus in the presence of ancient bards who set it all down: Creation, Garden of Eden, Deluge, a baby cast on the waters, the dying God, a new season, resurrection. The sonatas are pagan myths of cosmogony, fall, Manichaean redemption and the final things (*postrimerías*). Archetypical, they contain the original pattern. That is why in their decadence they appeal to so many readers, who understand their letter but not their meaning, similar to the way some Christians understand *Genesis*. Theologians call this a religious mystery; in the case of Valle it is a pagan religious mystery.

(g) Y callé evocando el pasado . . .

And I remained silent, evoking the past . . .

This phrase requires no explanation.

(h) María del Rosario era pálida, con los ojos negros, llenos de luz ardiente y lánguida.

María del Rosario was pale, with black eyes, eyes filled with ardent and languid light.

Pálida, lánguida: these *esdrújulos* are choreographic words, especially in Spanish, which ordinarily stresses the penult. Whenever you meet an *esdrújulo* in Valle, look for a lyrical key, which you have here of course in erotic intimation and the sensual vagueness of *lánguida*, the languor of a faint, feeble passive woman (sexual longing always has a peculiar vagueness to it, a sort of mystical *no sé qué*).

Valle-Inclán, like Unamuno, does not describe the woman's profile. Black eyes and a feeble penumbral light, that is all. Sonatas necessarily belong to impressionist art.

(i) Don Antonino juntó las manos con falsa beatitud, y entornó los ojos.

Don Antonino joined his hands in false beatitude, and half-closed his eyes.

103

Con falsa beatitud is pleonastic, because, like the bards of yore, Valle employs certain formulaic verses, the most common being *entornando los ojos*. Just as we say of the Cid, *el que en buen ora nació*, or, *el de la barba bellida*, so in Valle *entornando los ojos* means that a certain man, usually a clergyman, is a hypocrite, a Tartuffe, a *fantoche*, a clown caught in a rigid attitude. Perhaps in the passage just cited Valle is only establishing his formula, because in the future the beadles and theologians will say something insincerely, their eyes half-closed, and the "con falsa beatitud" phrase will not appear.

I thought of the Cid and also of the *Romancero*. Having likened Valle's paragraphs to sonnets, I want now to liken them to the ballads, which cover . . . everything. Hegel once said that the *romances* (Spanish ballads) are the Iliad and the Odyssey of Spain; similarly, the paragraphs of the sonatas are the Iliad and the Odyssey of . . . Spanish literary modernism, of the *azul*, the modern myth, of the systematic attempt to pierce the veil concealing things-as-they-are-in-themselves.

I believe that Valle also looked upon the sonatas as *exempla*, exemplary novels, novelistic manifestations of the truths he professed to establish in the *Lámpara*.[18]

> (j) ". . . que una lágrima le resbalaba lenta y angustiosa por la mejilla."

> ". . . a tear slowly and dolorously slipped down his cheek."

the bishop is dying and a tear slides down his cheek. This motion of the tear is a dance pointing to death, "el acabamiento de la vida;" a new and different *danse macabre*, a source of gnostic emotion. It also points to the most important single word in the sonata, for after the phrase about the sliding tear, we read:

> Al cabo de un momento pudo decir con afanoso *balbuceo* (emphasis mine) . . .

> After a moment he managed to say with a laborious *stammer* . . .

The *balbuceo*, or stammer, also appears in the dark night of the garden, when Bradomín likens himself to St. John of the Cross. Since this garden scene takes place after the *¡Os adoro! ¡Os adoro!* litany, I shall discuss it and the *balbuceo* in its place.

The sonatas are *balbuceos*, stammerings. Valle's entire work is a *balbuceo*. The *Lámpara* tells us that; after all, music is transrational.

(k) *Temblor, estremecer, trémulo, temblar* (here is a list of these formulaic, choreographic words. The emphases are mine. And notice the *esdrújulo, trémulo místico):*

Sus labios . . . parecían agitados por el temblor de un rezo.

Her lips seemed to be stirred by the *tremor* of a prayer.

Yo apenas pude oprimir un estremecimiento.

I could scarcely keep back a *shudder.*

Y los rayos del sol que pasaban a través del follaje temblaban en ellas como místicos haces encendidos.

And the rays of the sun which came through the foliage *trembled* above the girls like flaming mystical sheaves.

Temblaba en las agujas el hilo de oro.

The golden thread *trembled* on the needle. (A reference to knitting. Notice that the words I translate as *trembled* are in Spanish in the imperfect tense.)

Ella nos miraba con los labios trémulos . . .

She was looking at us with tremulous lips . . .

En su mejilla temblaba la sombra de las pestañas . . .

On her cheek the shadow of her eyelashes was *trembling . . .*

. . . y yo comprendía con un estremecimiento . . .

. . . and I understood with a shudder . . .

De pronto me estremecí . . . (a rather rare preterite tense in such a key word.)

Suddenly I shuddered . . .

Y sin volver la cabeza, azorada, trémula, huía por

el corredor.

And without turning her head, bewildered,
tremulous, she ran (was running) through the hall.

... el amor, ardiente y *trémulo*, como una llama
mística ...

... love, ardent and tremulous, like a mystical
flame ...

All these examples come from the first third of *Primavera* (only
twenty-odd pages), and of all the formulaic phrases they occur
most frequently. Lips, bodies, fingers, rays of light, lamps,
eyelids, hands, landscapes, air—something is always trembling,
flickering, stirring, shaking, waving, quaking, quivering,
shuddering[19] in the sonatas; something is always moving, if ever
so slightly, to suggest an added presence, a Mover behind or
beyond what is being moved, an invisible presence greater than
what meets the eye. In the first place, these formulaic verses[20]
are a tremolo ("the rapid fluttering reiteration of a tone or chord
without apparent breaks"), part of a sonata composed to induce
the musical miracle, the intuition of a greater impalpable reality;
in this sense, let us call them CHORDS.

Secondly, and perhaps on a higher plane, these words are
dance words, a patterned succession of movements ("el baile es la
más alta expresión estética."). Whenever you see a series of words
in the sonatas suggesting a measured motion, or an abrupt change
of motion, or a complete cessation of motion (*rígido,
inmovilizado*) you are in the *presence* of a ballet; I was going to
change this phrase to "You are witnessing a ballet," but on
reflection *presence* is the apt word here. The sonatas are always
suggesting, indicating, awakening, raising, evoking hidden
presence. In addition to the formulaic verses already mentioned, I
would say that the following words are choreographic: *esdrújulos*,
especially when accompanying female anatomy, e.g., *pálidas
manos*; imperfect tenses, especially in onomatopoeic words like
murmuraba and *susurraba*; fountains *borboteando*; adverbial
esdrújulos such as "desmayaba *lánguidamente*" and *sus labios se
movían débilmente*;" the act of fainting; air in motion of any
kind, such as *ráfagas, hálito*; the word *revolotear*; sighing;
polysyllabic words, *insensiblemente, misterioso*; a breeze in a
garden—I am beginning to repeat myself, but then, repetition of
words and movements is the very nature of the sonatas, so you
might say I am adding an example to my precept.

Music and dance have rhythm, which, sensed over and over
again, evoke a higher rhythm. And a Rhythm Maker.

One definition of *estremecer* is "to astound," a word calling to mind the Baroque amazement of Cervantes. Do you remember in the *Exemplary Novels*, all those *embelesados, atónitos, suspensos, pasmados, admirados*, and *maravillados*; some one was always amazing someone or being amazed: Preciosa with her beauty, ballads and dance; a licenciado telling a story about talking dogs; English Spanish girls; sages who thought they were made of glass; deceitful marriages. The sonatas with their strange plots and movements are rather like that. Their words are one thing but their music evokes another, professing to bring to mind an interior illumination, as by a magic lamp. They are exemplary. Yes, that's it, the sonatas are exemplary novels, spiritual exercises with Baroque *admiratio*.[21]

> (l) El prelado hizo un gesto doloroso.

> The prelate made a painful grimace.

A painful grimace or gesture is a movement in a dance; a dying, agonizing, tremulous man is moving in a dance; not the *danse macabre* of yore, although it could be that esperpentically, but a dance moving slowly now, midst whispers and murmurs towards the horizon, and finally, beyond phenomena. Beyond the shadows on the wall of the cave. To the Forms. The Noumena. *Alma Mundo.*

> (m) Allá abajo *exhalaba*, su *perpetuo sollozo* la *fuente* que había en medio de la plaza. Y se oían voces de unas *niñas* que jugaban a la rueda. (Emphasis mine).

> There below, the fountain in the middle of the plaza was exhaling its perpetual sobbing. And the voices of girls were heard, who were playing in a circle.

Here we have the imperfect tense, an exhaling, a sobbing, a fountain bubbling, vague musical voices, the feminine sex dancing in a circle, a gnostic circle. They all have perpetuity. Our quotidian life is not perpetual, but this scene is; it is the eternal moment.

> (n) Yo, pecador de mí, empezaba a dormirme . . .

> I, sinner that I am, began to doze . . .

A man is dying in a sad, mysterious, quivering scene, so Bradomín snoozes. Here is a Byronic ending with an *eco burlón* and *sacrílego*, soon to be echoed and re-echoed throughout the sonata.

(o) En aquel instante, no sé decir qué vago aroma
primaveral traía a mi alma el recuerdo de las cinco
hijas de la Princesa.

At that moment, I don't know how to say it, what
vague aroma brought (was bringing) to my soul
the memory of the five daughters of the
Princesses.

Vague light, vague sound and now vague aromas to evoke a
memory in the soul. *Synesthesia*: the evocations of all the senses
blended harmoniously are part of the *balbuceo* (stammer).
Visually things[22] are penumbral, and audibly, distant and
quivering. The olfactory sensations are also vague as we approach
a higher reality. Cabalistic catechumens will want to investigate
the pentacular reference of *five* daughters, but we *aprovechados*
(advanced ones) have passed beyond that stage. The abracadabra
will only distract us now.

    Hijas, feminine. Eros. The *logos espermático* of a masculine
Bradomín.

(p) . . . el hálito de la Primavera me subía al
rostro.

. . . the breath of Spring rose to my face (was
rising to my countenance)

A breath, a breath of air, a breeze of Spring was rising to my
countenance. One doesn't smell the aromas of Spring, they dance
to the countenance, aloft, in the imperfect tense, before an
ancient evocative garden.

(q) Sobre la playa de dorada arena morían mansas
las olas, y el son de los caracoles con que
anunciaban los pescadores su arribada a la playa, y
el ronco canto del mar, parecían acordarse con la
fragancia de aquel jardín antiguo donde las cinco
hermanas se contaban sus sueños juveniles, a la
sombra de los rosáceos laureles.

The waves were dying gently on the golden sand
of the beach, and the sound of the horns from the
fishermen arriving at the beach, and the hoarse
chant of the sea, seemed to harmonize with the
fragrance of that ancient garden where the five
sisters were telling each other about their youthful

dreams, in the shade of rose-colored laurels.
The waves dance and agonize in keeping with the aroma of the ancient garden, and five sisters dream in the shade of rosaceous laurels. Waning water, ballet, death, music, aroma, antiquity, the garden, Eros, nebulous dreams, penumbra, roses—they are the road to the truth of unseen presence, to Reality. We find ourselves in the garden of the soul. In the words of the *Lámpara*:

Cuando yo era mozo, la gloria literaria y la gloria aventurera me tentaron por igual. Fue un momento lleno de voces oscuras, de un vasto rumor ardiente y místico, para el cual se hacía sonoro todo mi ser como un caracol de los mares. De aquella gran voz atávica y desconocida sentí el aliento como un vaho de horno, y el son como un murmullo de marea que me llenó de inquietud y de perplejidad. Pero los sueños de aventura, esmaltados con los colores del blasón, huyeron como los pájaros del nido. Sólo alguna vez, por el influjo de la Noche, por el influjo de la Primavera, por el influjo de la Luna, volvían a posarse y a cantar en los jardines del alma, sobre un ramaje de lambrequines . . .

When I was a lad literary glory and the glory of adventure tempted me the same. It was a time filled with obscure voices, with a vast ardent and mystical sound, for which my entire being became sonorous, like a snail shell from the depths of the sea. I felt the breath of that great unknown atavistic voice like the vapor from an oven, and the sound like the murmur of a tide filling me with puzzling discomposure. But the dreams of adventure, adorned with the colors of heraldry, fled like birds from a nest. Only once in a while, through the emanation of Night, through the emanation of Spring, through the emanation of the Moon, the dreams came to nest again and to sing in the gardens of my soul, over the twining branches of my coat of arms . . .

Just like Valle after his youth, we are adults now, caught up in phenomena and the web of time, and we don't remember; but a scene such as this in an ancient garden, may stir the soul. Memory. Gnosis.

(r) Las cinco hermanas se arrodillaron sobre la

yerba, y juntaron las manos llenas de rosas.
Los mirlos cantaban en las ramas, y sus cantos
se respondían encadenándose en un ritmo remoto
como las olas del mar. Tejían sus ramos en
silencio, y entre la púrpura de las rosas
revoloteaban como albas palomas sus manos, y los
rayos del sol que pasaban a través del follaje,
temblaban en ellas como místicos haces
encendidos. Los tritones y las sirenas de las
fuentes borboteaban su risa quimérica, y las aguas
de plata corrían con juvenil murmullo por las
barbas limosas de los viejos monstruos marinos
que se inclinaban para besar a las sirenas, presas
en sus brazos. Las cinco hermanas se levantaron
para volver al Palacio. Caminaban lentamente por
los senderos del laberinto, como princesas
encantadas que acarician un mismo ensueño.
Cuando hablaban, el rumor de sus voces se perdía
en los rumores de la tarde, y sólo la onda
primaveral de sus risas se levantaba armónica bajo
la sombra de los clásicos laureles. (*Lámpara*, p. 23)

The five sisters kneeled down on the grass, and
they joined their hands, filled with roses.
The blackbirds were singing in the branches,
and all their songs were answered, joining
together in a distant rhythm resembling the waves
of the sea. The five sisters had seated themselves
again: They were weaving their boughs in silence,
and their hands fluttered like white doves in
amongst the purple of the roses, and the rays of
the sun coming through the foliage trembled
above them, like flaming mystical sheaves. The
tritons and sirens of the fountains were bubbling
with chimerical laughter, and the silvery waters
ran with a youthful murmur down the slimy
beards of the old marine monsters, who were
bending down to kiss the sirens they held captive
in their arms. The five sisters arose to return to
the Palace. They strolled slowly along the
labyrinthine paths, like enchanted princesses who
cherish the one same dream. When they spoke, the
sound of their voices was lost in the evening
sounds, and only the Spring tide of their voices
rose up in harmony, beneath the shade of classical
laurels.

Very few verses are as sonatic as these. Five sisters kneel on the grass, their hands and laps filled with roses; the rose, the most erotic of all symbols, resembling erogenous zones of the body. In the words of Manuel Machado, speaking of a young girl in springtime:

Las rosas de su carne son la rosa.[23]

The roses of her flesh are the rose.

The blackbirds, which can imitate sounds, even the human voice, sing a song linking all Nature, the laughter of the girls and, one might infer, the undulating music of the waves of the sea. There is one remote rhythm. Unity. The girls' hands dance joyously weaving garlands of roses; the sun's rays and the fountains dance along. One discerns the unity of Nature, which evokes a mystical light, a mystical understanding.

The word *mystic* brings to mind a similar word, *misterio* (mystery), from the first line of *Primavera*: "campiña llena de misterio y de rumores lejanos." *Mystery* is a theological word meaning "an article of faith beyond human understanding," and the mystic is the one who, somehow, transcends ordinary human understanding, glimpsing religious mysteries.

Just think of this scene of girls and roses and song and dance and bubbling fountains and sounding sea, and meditate on its beauty, its unity, and you will perceive the light as if you had rubbed a magic lamp. You will sense an ancient harmony ("y sólo la onda primaveral de sus risas se levantaba armónica bajo la sombra de clásicos laureles"), a universal penumbral harmony. Oneness. The eternity of the moment.

In this scene there are tritons and sirens, monstrous men and insidious women, but they will not prevail, they cannot destroy the illusion, the remote rhythm and eternal harmony. They are grotesque figures, esperpentos, in the phenomenal foreground, whereas the harmony is ultimate and remote.

The *risa quimérica* of tritons and sirens also anticipates the dark night of the garden that is to come, with its *balbuceo* (stammer: "un no sé qué quimérica ilusión.")

(s) Una ráfaga paso por el salón y apagó algunas luces.

A gust passed through the room and extinguished some of the lights.

On reading this line we immediately know that the old holy bishop has died, and to be sure a few lines later we are told: "—¡Ya goza de Dios!" ("He is now with God!"). I find *ráfaga* to be one of the most stimulating words of the sonatas, because its

111

sound and meaning are one, and it suggests a teleology[24] behind it, a hidden presence, a hidden hand as it were causing a sudden movement of the air or flash of light. A group of people are sitting and talking and embroidering and worrying about the fate of a dying man, all this in the imperfect tense, in the background, and there is silence and vague trembling and embroidered roses and lilies born in the fluttering fingers of dancing hands, when, "Una ráfaga pasó por el salón." Something like that doesn't just happen, the gust is directed at the soft, undulating background. Where did it come from? Perhaps from the *Satanás* mentioned earlier in the sonata, whose presence will be evoked in the garden, and perhaps from a noumenal being called Death, but in any case that gust came from the land beyond, from beyond phenomena: A harbinger of ill fate, harbinger, one who has been sent ahead, a forerunner, from the other side of the horizon.

The sonatas, the dance and music, are forerunners of a higher reality.

(t) María del Rosario: "En su mejilla temblaba la sombra de las pestañas, y yo sentía que en el *fondo* de mi alma aquel rostro pálido temblaba, con el encanto misterioso y poético con que tiembla en el *fondo* de un lago el rostro de la luna." (Emphasis mine)

On her cheek the shadow of her eyelashes were trembling, and I felt that in the *depth* of my soul that pale countenance was trembling, with the same mysterious and poetical charm with which the moon's countenance trembles in the *depths* of a pool. (Emphasis mine)

Given the doctrine I have tried to develop, I find these verses to be most sonatic. Those two *fondos* reveal the sonatas as an art of depths and background, where real things happen. The background, apparently illusory and superficial, is real and deep, whereas the foreground and surface, apparently real and of great moment, are bagatelles. Depths and backgrounds pertain to the soul, the soul soul so to speak, just as Santa Teresa saw the light light. You can't express them directly, you must stammer when you try, and so you call them soul souls, or you write enigmatic, paradoxical sonatas. That is the only way you can express yourself, through a *balbuceo*. The sonata is a stammering, a *balbuceo*.

There is a mysterious and poetical *encanto* at work here; *encanto*-charm, fascination, delight, enchantment. If a mystery is beyond human understanding, then only the meta-human effort of poetry can pierce the veil and reach it, enchanting us, fascinating, delighting us. The sonata is an enchantment, an epistemological legerdemain, a *balbuceo*.

The moon brings to mind Federico García Lorca's *Luna* in *Bodas de sangre*, with a brilliant, cold, silvered chest wanting to warm itself with blood; the Moon, Gnostic symbol of Death. The moon appears, the bishop has died, the sonata must end in death. Like a Greek tragedy. Fate. Death.

When I beheld the countenance of the moon in the deep lake, the other lake, I also thought of *San Manuel Bueno* and Unamuno's *intrahistoria* (intrahistory), which, he tells us, transcends phenomena. History, according to Unamuno, is the waves on the surface of the sea (or lake), whereas intrahistory is the deep waters, the depths of the sea. Unamuno's *intrahistoria* also lies beyond the horizon of don Ramón María del Valle-Inclán. Both artists were seeking the noumena, the world of Things-in-themselves.

(u) Vino del mundo lejano, y pasó sobre mi alma como soplo de aire sobre un lago de misterio.

(The thought that María Rosario might be keeping vigil over the dead prelate) came from the distant world, and it passed over my soul like a breath of wind over a lake of mystery.

According to Gaston Etchegoyen, the mystics have a *terminologie traditionelle*, which consists largely of metaphors from air, fire and water. The terminology of the heterodox neo-mystic, Valle-Inclán, includes air words, water words and everything from the distant horizon that quivers and quavers.

Air, water, quivering, quavering: Sonata.

(v) Se hablaban en voz baja con tímida mesura, y en los momentos de silencio, oíase el péndulo de un reloj.

They were speaking to one another in a low voice and shyly, and during the moments of silence you could hear a clock's pendulum.

Max Picard once wrote a book on silence, in which he bestows on silence an ontological dignity. The world of Being is silent, the world of God is silent. All our human phenomenal activity is a sort of grand cacophony. Similarly, in Valle, in the interstices of esperpentos (of cubistic polyhedrons) there are moments of silence where you can break through the walls; and in the sonatas you must look for those silences too, caesurae, the interstices where you can barely detect the pendulum of a clock (time is all but subdued, the pendulum pointing to the silence); and you can seize the eternal instant, moment of Universal Rhythm. Ecstasy. The sonatic man is ecstatic. Rather like a heterodox beatific vision.

Perhaps that is why Valle's sonatas are bound by the heterodox as prayerbooks.

(w) We come to the end of the *Sonata de primavera's* prelude and encounter *¡Os adoro! ¡Os adoro!* eight times, Bradomín's sacrilegious litany (*eco burlón, casi sacrílego*) to the saintly, innocent and humble María del Rosario. He tweaks his moustache as he recites the words, and their meaning will not be lost on Spanish readers who remember the litanies they recited in school as children:

House of Gold	Pray for us
Star of the Sea	Pray for us
Tower of Ivory	Pray for Us
Ark of the Covenant	Pray for Us

These are a litany to the Blessed Virgin Mary, Mother of God, recited five times eight, or forty. The *¡Os adoro!* sequences, then, are no ordinary *estribillos* (refrains), but litanies, a series of invocations announcing that Bradomín's devaluation (*Umwertung aller Werte*) has begun. To build the new city, one must first tear down the old; to build sonatic doctrines with their heterodox gnosis, one must destroy the Catechism of Ripalda.

Right after the litany comes an outstanding *clave lírica*:

Su boca, pálida de ideales nostalgias, permanecía
anhelante, como si hablase con las almas invisibles,
y sus ojos inmóviles y abiertos sobre el infinito,
miraban sin ver.

Her mouth, pale with ideal nostalgia, remained
filled with longing, as if she were speaking with
invisible souls, and her eyes, immobile and open
to the infinite, looked without seeing.

Bradomín may jeer at ancient venerable doctrines and destroy María del Rosario, but he is no materialist. There are invisible realities, call them noumena, call them souls, and one can look out over the infinite. That is what the sonatas are all about, that is their *dianoia*: to apprehend the higher realities.

29. The second movement of the *Sonata de Primavera* begins at dawn:

Ya cerca del amanecer me retiré a la biblioteca.

Now near dawn I retired to the library.

And it ends after the second night in the garden, when Bradomín is wounded by Polonio. Within this movement Bradomín begins the destruction of María del Rosario. The sonata is still penumbral, midst two dark nights: "cerca del amanecer;" "Empezaba a decaer la tarde;" "En el salón medio apagado:" "Las luciérnagas brillaban;" "poco a poco mis ojos columbraron la forma incierta de las cosas;" "Las dormidas olas fosforecían;" "Al caer de la tarde;" "Desde el salón distinguíase el jardín, inmóvil bajo la luna, que envolvía en pálida claridad; . . ." "y la claridad de la luna penetró en la estancia;" "Un rayo de luna esclarecía el aposento." Two dark nights in the garden, framed in twilight, with faint rays of light even at the darkest hour. In this crepuscular scene, the form of things is uncertain, without profile. The forms are there all right, THEY ARE DEFINITELY THERE, but not being phenomena they are indistinct.[25]

There is more narrative now, so that time seems to pick up its pace, except for the atemporal states in the garden. The emaciated figure of Polonio moves in and out of the scenes, praising María del Rosario, building his Float of Christ's Falls, for the Holy Week parade, watching over María and finally stabbing Bradomín. We see the saintly girl giving alms to the poor, receiving her nun's gown and trying to avoid Bradomín, who resolutely seeks her destruction. We must remember that in the *Sonata de primavera* Bradomín is not a human being from a realist novel, a Villaamil, a Maximiliano, a Torquemada, but a figure, an attitude, a pose, a systematic devaluator setting the foreground for a sonata; his tears are not real tears, his sighs not real sighs, his remorse not remorse, but posed, ironic emotions bent on tearing down the old city. One of his psychological states holds true, however, the irrepressible sexual longing and nostalgia of a young man, so that he does have a shred of humanity. (On narrating his *Memoirs*, Bradomín must have sensed this.)

We see the burial of the bishop, which is an ancient ecclesiastical scene recalling the opening paragraph of the novel, the description of Ligura. And we see Bradomín enter the library and garden and salon and garden again, and finally his chambers, to be attended by his servant Musarelo. But the highlight of this part, and of all the sonatas, is that garden.

30. THE FIRST NIGHT OF THE GARDEN

The first Spring night in the garden is silent, fragrant, soft, penumbral, mysterious, quiet, serene, although Bradomín senses a long tremor:

Era una noche de Primavera, silenciosa y fragante.

115

El aire agitaba las ramas de los árboles con blando movimiento, y la luna iluminaba por un instante la sombra y el misterio de los follajes. Sentíase pasar por el jardín un largo estremicimiento y luego todo quedaba en esa amorosa paz de las *noches serenas*. En el azul profundo temblaban las estrellas, y la quietud del jardín parecía mayor que la quietud del cielo. A lo lejos, el mar misterioso y ondulante exhalaba la eterna queja. Las dormidas olas fosforecían al pasar tumbando los delfines, y una vela latina cruzaba el horizonte bajo la luna pálida. (Emphasis mine.)

It was a Spring night, silent and fragrant. The breeze was moving the branches of the trees with a soft movement, and the moon threw light for a moment on the shade and mystery of the leaves. One could feel a long tremor pass through the garden, and later everything remained in that amorous peace of the *noches serenas*. In the deep blue the stars were trembling, and the quietude of the garden seemed greater than the quietude of heaven. Afar, the mysterious undulating sea exhaled its eternal complaint. The somnolent waves were phosphorescent as the tumbling dolphins passed by, and a Latin sail crossed the horizon beneath the pallid moon.

This is the garden of a young man's soul:

Sólo alguna vez, por el influjo de la Noche, por el influjo de la Primavera, por el influjo de la Luna, volvían (the dreams of adventure) a posarse y a cantar en los jardines del alma, sobre un ramaje de lambrequines. (*Lámpara*, p. 11)

Only sometimes, through the emanation of the Night, through the emanation of Springtime, through the emanation of the Moon, the dreams of adventure returned to nest again and to sing in the gardens of my soul, on a bough of heraldry.

Bradomín goes out on a path bordered by flowering rose bushes, a crepuscular path lit by fireflies, and all the senses are pleased. This is not the path of the serene night (*noche serena*) of St. John of the Cross; for in spite of the amorous peace (*amorosa paz*), Bradomín experiences Wertherian extremes, let us call them "Wertherian polarity:"

116

Con extremos verterianos soñaba superar a todos
los amantes que en el mundo han sido. (*Primavera*,
p. 41)

With Wertherian extremes, I dreamed of surpassing
all the lovers who have ever been in this world.

The reader will recall Goethe's Werther (in *Las cuitas del joven
Werther*) and his extreme love for Lotte. Werther was either
absolutely accepted or absolutely rejected, in amorous heaven or
hell, there was no middle ground, and finally in his anguish he
committed suicide. Bradomín dreams of surpassing other lovers,
romantically, a la Werther, but this glory is denied him:

Desgraciadamente, quedéme sin superarlos, porque
tales romanticismos nunca fueron otra cosa que un
perfume derramado sobre todos mis amores de
juventud. ¡Locuras gentiles y fugaces que duraban
algunas horas, y que, sin duda por eso, me han
hecho suspirar y sonreír toda la vida! (*Primavera*,
pp. 41-42)

Unfortunately, I failed to surpass them, because
such romanticisms were never anything else than a
perfume poured over my youthful loves. Charming
and fleeting follies that lasted a few hours, and
which undoubtedly for that reason, have made me
smile and sigh all my life!

This scene, for all its beauty, is jocular, devaluing that other
noche serena of San Juan.
    In the garden, time is suspended, time, the sterile satan
forbidding us to see the true nature of things (the form of
things):

Dios es la eterna quietud, y la belleza eterna está
en Dios. Satán es el estéril que borra eternamente
sus huellas sobre el camino del Tiempo. (*Lámpara*,
p. 27)

God is eternal quietude, and eternal beauty is in
God. Satan is the sterile one who eternally erases
God's traces along the road of Time.

While experiencing the quietude of the garden, we should have
an insight into supreme beauty and Things-as-they-are-in-
themselves, that is, the form of things beyond Time. We should

also remember that the garden is a *jardín del alma* (garden of the soul) (*Lámpara*, p. 11); so perhaps we can define the garden as the place or state where the soul ventures forth to the noumenal world.

Orthodox mystics, however, speak of the *vicissitudo*, the mutability of the mystical state, and of *sequedades*, dry spells. Mystics do not enter a permanent state of rapture. Similarly, the heterodox Bradomín, does not enter a permanent state of ecstasy; his rapture, his poetic trance has come and gone:

> De pronto huyeron mis pensamientos. (*Lámpara*, p. 42)

> Suddenly my thoughts fled away.

Against (so to speak) the imperfect tense of ecstasy, that is to say, no tense or no time at all, the preterite tense of the outside world (*huyeron*) breaks Bradomín's spell and his thoughts escape him. The clock sounds twelve midnight, in this first night of the garden, and Bradomín returns to the drawing room where he has seen a woman seated on a sofa. It is María del Rosario, suffering in the darkness.

Returned to time, we next see the emaciated figure of Polonio, painter and sculptor, author of the *Float With Christ's Falls*. A marvel to behold! Another Leonardo da Vinci! And the Italian *beatas* are his Maecenas! Bradomín describes "el último perfil" of the Float, with its bloody, livid Christ, its four fierce-looking Jews, and a paper bearing Pilate's sentence, the latter being a sheet of music because the musical notes look like Semitic scrawl. And the figures are made of pasteboard! Edifying! This is the world of phenomena. Edifying!

Right after this scene of rigid puppetry, we return to the background of the garden. The sonatas are composed like that, background, foreground, background, imperfect, preterite, imperfect; melody, cacophony, melody; and the brother pilgrim (*hermano peregrino*) will be lured to the background, where beyond the phenomenal wall the aesthetic gnosis awaits him.

31. THE SECOND NIGHT OF THE GARDEN

This night the five daughters of Princess Gaetani are on the terrace, beneath the moon, like fairies in a story. They form a circle (there are always gnostic circles) around a young beautiful girl friend of theirs, who keeps looking at Bradomín (he is certainly not *ugly!*: not "católico, feo y sentimental"). The old women converse, and smile as they hear the "perfumed gusts" of young voices. The garden lies motionless beneath the moon, in penumbral light; the moon:

> . . . que envolvía en pálida claridad la cima

mustia de los cipreses . . .

. . . which enveloped in pale clarity the gloomy
tops of the cypress trees . . .

The background is a delight to the spirit, soft, gentle, attractive;
even the cypresses, harbingers of death, have a calm, ethereal
quality.[26] But now we come to the foreground, where Bradomín
the Devaluator tries to get near María del Rosario:

. . . sólo por turbarla . . .

. . . just to trouble her . . .

This phrase calls to mind Segismundo's throwing a man from a
balcony, in Calderón's *Life Is A Dream*:

. . . sólo por ver si puedo . . .

. . . just to see if I can . . .

Here is an evocation of arrogance, pride, haughtiness. Unless he
is stopped, Bradomín will destroy her.
He cannot find her:

Una nube de tristeza cubrió mi alma . . .

A cloud of sadness covered my soul . . .

Sadness, a true psychological state when a man longs to be with a
girl, but jocosely insincere from the pen of Bradomín. He
contemplates the garden. In the silence a nightingale sings in
harmony with the fountains. We are entering sonatic territory
now, and Bradomín sees a mystical path:

El reflejo de la luna iluminaba aquel sendero de
los rosales que yo había recorrido otra noche.

The reflection of the moon was illuminating that
path of rose bushes I had gone along another
evening.

The air is soft, breezes murmur, and in the distance, amongst the
myrtles, sacred to Venus, undulates the water of a pond:

Yo evocaba en la memoria el rostro de María
Rosario y no cesaba de pensar:
—¿Qué siente ella? . . . ¿Qué siente ella por mí?—

119

In my memory I evoked the countenance of María Rosario and I couldn't stop thinking:
—What does she feel? . . . What does she feel for me?

The erotic litany has begun, *¿Qué siente ella?*, recalling the *¡Os adoro!* of the first movement, and foretelling the stark, *¡Fue Satanás!* litany at the end, when María Rosario is insane. Perhaps we can call the first litany (*¡Os adoro!*) Marian, the second (*¿Qué siente ella?*) Venery, and the third (*¡Fue Satanás!*) Diabolical, flowers of evil. Thus the *Sonata de primavera* has three movements corresponding to the role of Bradomín: Ligura is Marian when he arrives, venereal while he is there, and diabolical on his departure, its inhabitants being conversant with evil. This is the work of a true Devaluator.

Bradomín enters the garden, the garden of the soul, and his first words are:

. . . mi corazón presentía no sé qué quimérica y confusa desventura . . .

. . . my heart had a premonition of an I don't know what chimerical and vague misfortune . . .

To understand the sonata and its stammering (*balbuceo*) one must consider this *no sé qué (qué-qui)*.

In order to have a definition, one must first have a genus and species; for example, "man is a rational animal." *Animal* is the genus and *rational* the adjective limiting it. One can define *man* but one cannot define this man, an individual, for example, *John Jones*. There is only one of him, he can only be described, not defined. Consequently, individual experiences can only be described, and the more subtle or dignified the experience, the harder it is to describe it. To illustrate my point, I shall now reproduce a review about music from the newspapers (I repeat the argument I gave under #34 of the Fourth Canto):

Mozart made magical
Nobody who believes in the music of Mozart could have doubted the sorcery in store Monday night when Claudio Abbado passed his wand over the Chicago Symphony Orchestra.

For this Mozart night, Abbado, recently named as principal guest conductor effective in 1982, formed a charmed circle with violinist Salvatore Accardo, principal french horn player Dale Clevenger and an orchestra reduced to chamber proportions.

Accardo, an Italian virtuoso lately catapulted into the American limelight, applied his imposing art to a gently affectionate and deliciously droll interpretation of Violin Concerto No. 4 in D. Between violinist and conductor existed a bond of understatement, and in that soft light Mozart's music shone. Against Abbado's smoothly spun backdrop. Accardo delivered a vividly personal reading of a work that begs, if quietly, for just such intimacy.

Yet the violinist also had his moments of flashing brilliance, notably in a sharply etched first-movement cadenza and a witty finale marked by stunning passages in double-stops.

With the same happy rapport, Abbado and Clevenger made a stylish joy of Horn Concerto No. 3 in E-flat.

In its first-chair occupant, the Chicago Symphony boasts a horn player probably unsurpassed in the world. Few players could have matched Clevenger's pianissimo trills and daredevil octaves or the streaming silvery line with which he caressed the slow movement's nocturne-like romance.

Framing these concertos. Abbado began and ended his program with symphonies—a vivacious account of the brief though brightly colored Symphony No. 32 in G and a scintillating romp through the "Haffner" (No. 35 in D).

To the brilliantly scored "Haffner" Abbado brought the best qualities of his musicianship. He sorted out voices with absolute clarity, struck fetching contrasts within the minuet and whipped up a blistering finale of irrepressible rhythmic force.

And in all this, the Chicago Symphony illuminated Mozart's music with breathtaking detail, to say nothing of infectious spirit and, no matter how fast Abbado pushed, disarming precision. Conjury it was; collective prestidigitation.

It was a sad moment indeed when the witching hour passed.

Notice the abundant metaphors: magic, sorcery, wind, charmed, gently affectionate, deliciously droll, bond, understatement, soft light, shone, flashing, brilliance, etched, stunning, happy rapport,

121

stylish joy, daredevil, streaming silvery line, caressed, vivacious, brightly colored, scintillating romp, brilliantly sorted out, sorted out voices, clarity, fetching contrasts, whipped, blistering force, illuminated, infectious, conjury, prestidigitation, sad, witching hour. The critic has pulled out all the stops, with metaphors from magic, human affection, comedy, light, graphics, acrobatics, chromatics, love, élan vital, frolics, art, coercion, disease, melancholy, and back to magic. Not one of these metaphors is based on sound (although music is sound), but on light, physical movement and human emotions. Perhaps two words have something to do with sound, *voices* and *trills*, although the former's being sorted out evokes literature as much as musical sound, and *trills* is a flat statement indeed compared to the sorcery of witching hours. The critic obviously is stammering, as all musical critics do when they attempt to describe their experience: *Balbuceo*.

I am not suggesting that music is the same as mysticism but only that it is similar. It certainly cannot be defined, or even described well, for when critics employ metaphors they usually resort to something resembling air, fire and water, the *terminologie traditionelle* of the mystics.

Very well, then, what is the meaning of this *no sé qué quimérica y confusa desventura?* What is it *trying* to say? (*trying*: a sonata is a musical essay). It is an obvious parody of the verses of San Juan de la Cruz, who is mentioned later in the same paragraph. San Juan writes:

... un no sé qué que quedan balbuciendo. ...

... an I don't know what what stays behind stammering ...

This is part of the mystical tradition and *terminologie traditionelle*. The soul, the Bride, has reached union with its heavenly Bridegroom, and San Juan writes to . . . to tell it to us . . . to describe it . . . to let us know what it is, to communicate his joy, . . . but he can't because his finite words are inadequate to the task; they are weak vessels, unable to contain infinite joy and being, and so he blurts out . . . *yo no sé, yo no sé decirlo*, I can't, nobody can, nobody knows how, it is a *no sé qué que quedan balbuciendo, que-que-que*, the mystical stammer. If a music critic can't say it properly for a concert but is reduced to a stammer, how can San Juan say it, even remotely, for the Loved One, Who is Infinite, or better said, Who Is?

And so the poet must use air, fire, water, any quasi-spiritual element he can find to . . . somehow . . . suggest his individual experience. Definition is out of the question.

Valle is obviously parodying San Juan. In this venereal garden of the young man's soul, Bradomín is confused, bewildered, beside himself, and he blurts out *no sé qué quimérica*. He can't define what he wants to say, nor can any man, although he has experienced it. But Bradomín's *no sé qué* goes far beyond erotic impulse. This is not only a Spring garden, it is a sonatic garden, and the sonata by its nature is a *balbuceo*, a literary, musical, choreographic stammer trying to convey to the reader the doctrine of *La lámpara maravillosa*. There is Beauty, Rhythm, Eternal Harmony, Forms, the forms-of-things, and they can be descried there, in the garden beyond the senses, in the distance, beyond the horizon, beyond the phenomenal wall, beyond the veil, in crepuscular light (which is not light as we know it), in celestial chords, in the dance, in Eros . . . The critic can say no more; listen to it, listen, you, the true you, not the phenomenal you, listen the true you, in consonance with the rhythm behind visible reality, the rhythm of the Universe. "Prove it, critic." *Yo no sé, no puedo.* But I can perhaps lead you to intuit it.

In San Juan's poetry, in his celebrated garden so to speak:

Aminadab no parecía.

Aminadab did not appear

Aminadab, spirit of discord. But here in Bradomín's Garden of Venus, frogs abound and "el canto de un sapo" ("the chant of a toad") distracts Bradomín from his quasi-mystical erotic reverie. This *sapo* suggests diabolical presence, adversarial presence opposing a young man's erotic desire, and it paves the way for Bradomín's later pretense of angelical, diabolical intuition, which so distorts María del Rosario that she finally becomes insane, repeating for all her days the last litany:

¡Fue Satanás! ¡Fue Satanás!

It was Satan! It was Satan!

We might also gather that within the economy of Valle's *opera*, phenomenal and temporal distractions are satanic, sterile, drawing us away from eternal beauty, eternal harmony, the eternal moment:

Satán es el estéril que borra eternamente sus huellas sobre el camino del Tiempo. (*Lámpara*, p. 27)

Satan is the sterile one who eternally erases God's

123

traces along the road of Time.

In the garden, the Devaluator intervenes:

> Yo, calumniado y mal comprendido, nunca fui
> otra cosa que un místico galante, como San Juan
> de la Cruz.

> I, calumniated and misunderstood, was never
> anything but a gallant mystic, like St. John of the
> Cross.

Bradomín the Contumelious is hardly a kindred spirit of San Juan de la Cruz. As for Valle himself, in spite of his many similarities to San Juan—his courage, his asceticism, his detachment, his devotion, his poetry, even his diminutive size—it is difficult to think of an author more different from the humble Juan de Yepes, who was only interested in Uncreated Being.

This passage now turns from background to foreground (from background music to foreground action), from a garden of love to a lustful Bradomín. That night the horned monarch "fired my blood, awakened my flesh;" a "violent gust raised the curtain;" his mortal eyes saw María del Rosario kneeling; he had an "ardent impulse;" "I looked around;" "I listened for a minute;" "I jumped inside," in front of her; "she gave a shout;" "she doubled over . . . fainted." And amidst all these violent actions, performed by Bradomín when the devil was "whipping my flesh with his black tail," he remembers one thing, María Rosario's hands:

> —¡Manos diáfanas como la hostia!—

> Diaphanous hands, like the host![27]

A sort of Black Mass, which of all the devaluations is the greatest. Sacrilege. Remember the "eco burlón, casi sacrílego" of the second paragraph: In the sonatas the reader (or listener) always remembers having seen something or heard something, somewhere before. The sonatas have a very vivid and phonetic structural unity.

Bradomín carries the unconscious girl to her room, but someone is following him. He leaves her, hears the toad again under the cypresses, is stabbed on the terrace and returns to his quarters, where his servant binds him. The second movement of the sonata ends with the second night in the garden.

The journey is a descent now, not from the mystical hill of Mount Carmel, but from the Venereal Garden of Youth, a perpetual state of the soul.

32. I have been reading the *Contes Cruelles* of Villiers de L'Isle Adam, which may throw some light, a crepuscular light, on the doctrine we have been developing. Although Villiers's stories are hardly as sonatic as Valle-Inclán's, they contain many of the same words, phrases and ideas. Here are some of those words (in Spanish translation): *evocaba, magnetismo, recuerdos, el cisne, última armonía, ideal, las vibraciones de las cosas eternas, nuestra melancolía, en este mundo todo es ilusión, el infinito que llevamos en el fondo del corazón, una especie de triste jardín, íntima armonía, inmóvil, esa música inefable, recuerdos de infancia,* and scores, nay hundreds, more. Two stories stand out in my mind, *El Deseo De Ser Un Hombre,* where a man seems to be looking for his real self and performs grotesque acts to find it:

> Pero el Dios que invocaba no le concedió este favor; y el viejo histrión expiró, siempre declamando en vano énfasis su gran deseo de ver espectros . . . *sin comprender que era él, él mismo, lo que buscaba.* (The emphasis is Villiers's.)

> But the God he was invoking didn't grant him his favor; and the old actor died, always exclaiming emphatically, and in vain, his great desire of seeing spirits . . . *without understanding that it was he, he himself, what he was looking for.*

The other story is *Vera,* where the autumnal Count d'Athal ("Fue un crepúsculo otoñal de París") refuses to accept his wife's death, acts as if she were still alive, doubts for a moment and then receives a magnetic (hypnotic) invitation from beyond the grave. These stories seem to have an ontological meaning, as if existence consisted of the imposition of the subject on the object, of the illusory world on so-called external reality, which may not even be there. Man is lost and in search of something, his own identity, in search of he-in-himself. He doesn't even know himself, that is, not the phenomenal self but the person behind it, beyond it; indeed, he knows this self least of all.

The theory that ultimate reality lies in a realm transcending phenomena, in a realm of things-in-themselves, where consciousness accounts for existence, is generally called idealism. And in the nineteenth century, idealism will lead us to the philosophy of Immanuel Kant. To understand Valle and Villiers de L'Isle Adam, one must turn to Kant.

The difference between Valle and Villiers is the music. Villiers (1838-1889), an able teller of tales, creates a mood luring the reader to read on until he is surprised by the strange turn at the end: *Admiratio.* Nowadays we have become accustomed to a vulgarized rendition of this sort of story by TV's twilight zone series; but Villiers rises above such entertainments with a consistent philosophy of mind over matter. And this Frenchman of a very sad life lived his own philosophy, creating legends and walking across the borders of illusion and reality. You might say Villiers never had a home. Valle, on the other hand, creates the mood of Villiers and much more. I have suggested that his paragraphs resemble sonnets, clinging to the original idea, and so they may be read in isolation or all together; whereas you can't read Villiers's paragraphs in isolation, they lack the charm. Valle is right: he does create a background music, call it an artistic miracle, that is worth attending. His Epistemology? Knowledge through music, aesthetic gnosis. His ontology? That depends on the reader's orthodoxy.

If you are orthodox, Valle is either making God's Creation depend on your consciousness of it, which is a hubristic, sterile, blasphemy; or he is arguing that a proud human being can redeem his existence by pulling on his own bootstraps, lifting his Pelagian self into Eternal Mystery.

If you are heterodox, a true *hermano peregrino*, then you will say yes, the Word of the artist is the Logos with its grace, beauty, truth and harmony, which will lead us to Eternal Beauty, Ideal Harmony, the Oneness of the Universe. And that way lies Pantheism:

> La Contemplación es así como una exégesis mística de todo conocimiento, y la suprema manera de llegar a la comunión con el Todo. (*Lámpara*, p. 7)

> Thus Contemplation is like a mystical exegesis of all knowledge, and the supreme way of arriving at communion with the All.

> Quietismo y panteísmo son las dos claves místicas, representadas en Bohas y Jakin. (*Lámpara*, p. 74) El quietismo es la comunión con el Paracleto. Y contrariamente, el éxtasis panida representa la suma en el arcano sideral y los desposorios con el Alma Creadora: Así, por modos diversos, quietismo y panteísmo rompen el Divino Ternario. (*Lámpara*, p. 75)[28]

> Quietism is communion with the Paraclete (the Holy Spirit). And on the other hand, pantheistic ecstasy represents the highest point in the astral arcanum and betrothal with the Creator Soul: Thus, in different ways, quietism and pantheism pierce the Divine Trinity.

As I see it, you cannot avoid in Valle-Inclán a sort of Pascalian wager: You are either orthodox or heterodox, you must wager. Valle himself would want it that way, for he was not a pompous ass, a mere turban-hatted clown on a tightrope, although he may have created that legend. That pose was simply his method. He was a great artist, I should say the greatest, the central figure of modern Spanish literature; and although proximately he seems not to call bread *bread* and wine *wine* (after all, his *ráfaga* is not merely a *ráfaga*), ultimately he does just that (call a spade a spade, as we say in English). In 1916, halfway through his career, he took the trouble to spell it all out, in the *Lámpara maravillosa*, which he placed as #1 of his collected works.

33. In the third movement of *Primavera*, the Devaluator takes over, preparing the way perhaps for the future seasonal sonatas, a San Juan Bautista *a lo infernal*, so to speak. All the Ligurans know who Bradomín is now, and what he is up to, but before he leaves he must first destroy María del Rosario.

34. An Aside: Unamuno once spoke of the Spanish Quaternity, that is to say, the Holy Trinity plus the Mother of God. Perhaps his witticism will throw some light on the present essay. If you are anxious to change the old *casticismo* (Spanish essence), the Quaternity must be the first to go, and with it all those debile men and foolish *beatas*, people bowing to superstitious tales.

It seems odd that when Henry Adams, the American from the "black Protestant" nation, made his *Wanderjahr* to Europe, he saw the Force of the Woman, Mary Mother of God, and was gladdened. He admired the force. Incalculable power.

But when you are a Devaluator, you don't see it that way; you see a nation bowed beneath the weight of centuries; you see a priest-ridden society. No, the Virgin must go.

As an explanation of Valle's meaning and form (*fondo y forma*), Pedro Salinas's extreme formalism is wanting; contrary to what he says, one must take the "ideological meaning" of the sonatas very seriously, giving it a primary position. Salinas was a fine poet and his critical work *Reality and the Poet* a masterpiece; but when it came to Valle his excessive formalism and admiration for the great artist blinded him. He couldn't see the woods for the trees. (I also recall what a British Hispanist said to me in 1962; he spoke of "the ruthless synthesis of Valle-Inclán.")

35. The third movement of *Primavera* might be labelled "Atusándome el mostacho," which is the formulaic verse of the second paragraph:

Con la sonrisa en los labios y atusándome el

mostacho entré en la biblioteca. (*Lámpara*, p. 55)

With a smile on my lips and tweaking my
moustache, I entered the library.

"Tweaking my moustache," or grooming it in a nonchalant way,
is the mark of the Devaluator, who scandalizes other persons and
then plays with his moustache as if scandal were a bagatelle.
Bradomín knows that the others hate him and fear him, but he
toys with them, speaking without emotion:

Me pareció oíros, y no quise pasar sin saludaros,
Princesa. (*Lámpara*, p. 55)

I thought I heard you, and I didn't want to go by
without greeting you, Princess.

Bradomín resolves to stay in Ligura, saying that pride has always
been his greatest virtue! Pride, of course, is the first of the seven
capital sins.

From here on the plot prevails, with intermittent satanic
background. The theme of this third movement is satanic.

A Capuchin priest comes to tell Bradomín that his life is in
danger, that an ancestral ring of his is missing, and that he must
recover it at all costs from an old woman "who lives in an
earthen house, with an ox skull on the roof." He must use money
and guile to get his ring back. Bradomín replies:

Sí, Reverendo Padre, seguiré la inspiración del
Angel que os trajo. (*Primavera*, p. 60)

Yes, Reverend Father, I shall follow the
inspiration of the Angel who brought you.

This *Angel* is an obvious reference to Lucifer, author of black
magic.

Bradomín goes to the garden, where he teases María Rosario
about her mystical reading. She prefers the *Mystic City* of Sor
María de Agreda, but he says he has the humble Caballero de
Casanova for a spiritual father. The ingenuous María fails to see
the joke, because she knows nothing of Casanova. Finally she
tells him to leave, right now, for his life is in danger. Bradomín
leaves her and as he does his *Memoirs* make another diabolical
allusion:

Empezaba a declinar la tarde, y . . . se arrullaban
dos palomas que huyeron al acercarme.

128

The afternoon began to wane, and . . . two doves
were cooing who fled on my approach.

Two doves, symbols of peace and concord, flee as Bradomín
approaches, he, an apostle of Discord. Henceforth Bradomín will
play a satanic role. He goes to the hut of the old witch, who, with the aid of his
ring and a crude figurine, has prepared a cursèd charm.
Everyone believes in the efficacy of her sortilege, everyone is
superstitious, the Capuchin, the Princesa Gaetani, Polonio the
steward and María del Rosario—everyone except Bradomín, who
amusedly puts on diabolical airs. Polonio even believes that
Bradomín has caused the downpour which has destroyed his
Float, softening his fierce-looking Jews, making them kneel and
look repentant. What a joke this is, especially when two old
women who have seen the repentant Semites exclaim:
"¡Edificante!"
Bradomín has been denounced to the Holy Office and must
depart. Just before he goes he again teases María del Rosario,
who believes he is a warlock, and when her baby sister falls from
a window killing herself, María goes insane. The Satanic Litany,
which will last three score years for the demented woman, has
begun:

> ¡Fue Satanás!   ¡Fue Satanás!
> ¡Fue Satanás!   ¡Fue Satanás!
> Me contaron que ahora, al cabo de tantos años, ya
> repite sin pasión, sin duelo, con la monotonía de
> una vieja que reza: ¡Fue Satanás! (End of the
> sonata.)

> It was Satan!   It was Satan!
> It was Satan!   It was Satan!
> They have told me that now, after so many years,
> she still repeats without passion, without sorrow,
> with the monotony of an old woman at prayer: It
> was Satan!

There is more to the plot than meets the eye. There is a
crescendo of violence; *crescendo*—one cannot avoid a musical
lexicon when discussing this work, which is designed to induce a
musical miracle. Bradomín's *Memoirs* mention "ráfagas de una
insensata violencia" (*Primavera*, p. 68), "gusts of a senseless
violence." This appearance of violence is accounted for in the
Lámpara, in a chapter on quietism:

> Entonces la ráfaga de violencias adquiere la
> significación de la quietud, porque un instante

basta a revelar el sentido inmutable de la órbita. (*Lámpara*, p. 99)

Then the gust of violence acquires the significance of quietude, because one instant is enough to reveal the immutable meaning of the field of action.[29]

Thus, even within Bradomín's destructive actions, which permeate *Primavera*, one can, in the eternal moment, arrest the form of things, perceiving immobility, immutability. Such a state leads to the apprehension of Beauty and quietude in union with the Alma Mundo.

A restatement here might be helpful. In spite of its mellifluous language, the *Sonata de primavera* gives expression to a peculiar, gusty violence. Events flow smoothly, then:

> Ráfagas de una insensata violencia agitaban mi alma . . .

> Gusts of a senseless violence were stirring my soul . . .

Events resume their flow, and then:

> Una ráfaga aborrascada pasó sobre me cabeza . . .

> A stormy gust passed over my head . . .

There is an ancient gentle city, Ligura, a quiet penumbral garden, calm peaceful meditation, and then, an abrupt action destroying the scene (the abruptness is stressed in the *esdrújulo*, *ráfaga*). This is particularly true of the story of María Rosario, with whom Bradomín goes to great lengths to create a gentle, loving, Christ-like figure, and although there is a devaluation here, I don't think it is merely that. It is never mere devaluation, because tearing down the old city is a prelude to building the new; it is a means to an end, not the end in itself. Perhaps the *Lámpara maravillosa* can help us here:

> Descubrir en el vértigo del movimiento la suprema aspiración a la quietud es el secreto de la estética. Amamos la vida porque sabemos que al final del camino está la muerte, y somos como las sombras de una tragedia que sólo alcanzan plenitud de belleza en aquel gesto que presagia su Destino. Entonces la ráfaga de violencias adquiere la significación de la quietud, porque un instante

basta a revelar el sentido inmutable de la órbita. Decía Leonardo que el movimiento sólo es bello cuando recuerda su origen y define su término, y lo comparaba con la línea de la vida en los horóscopos. El quietismo estético tiene esta fuerza alucinadora. Inicia una visión más sutil de las cosas, y al mismo tiempo nubla su conocimiento porque presiente en ellas el misterio. Es la revelación del sentido oculto que duerme en todo lo creado, y que al ser advertido nos llena de perplejidad. Cuando los ojos quieren mirar fuera de la caverna oscura, quedan ciegos de luz, divina Cáligo de cuantos alcanzan una comprensión del mundo más allá de la eñsenanza temporal y mortal de los sentidos. Como Ireneo Alejandrino, el iniciado no mira el vuelo de la flecha porque penetra en la conciencia del arquero. Sabedor de los destinos, es sabedor de los caminos, sin ser ellos desenvueltos. Y el camino de la flecha estuvo antes en el ojo y en la mente del arquero.

Para el ojo que se abre en el gnóstico triángulo, todas las flechas que dispara el sagitario están quietas. (Lámpara, p. 98-99)

The secret of aesthetics is to reveal the supreme aspiration to quietude, within the vertigo of movement. We love life because we know that at life's end is death, and we resemble the phantoms in a tragedy, who can only realize the fulness of beauty in the action presaging their Destiny. Then the gust of violent movements acquires the significance of quietude, because one instant is enough to reveal the immutable meaning of a sphere of action. Leonardo used to say that movement is beautiful only when it recalls its origin and defines its terminus, and he compared it to the line of life in horoscopes. Aesthetic quietism has this power of hallucination. It initiates a more subtle vision of things, and at the same time it clouds its knowledge, because it has a presentiment of mystery in them. It is the revelation of the hidden meaning that sleeps in all of creation, and which, when we notice it, fills us with perplexity. When the eyes try to look outside the dark cavern, they are blinded by the light, the divine Darkness of all those who reach an understanding of the world beyond the temporal and mortal experience of the senses. Like Ireneus

Alejandrinus, the gnostic initiate doesn't look at the flight of the arrow, because he penetrates the consciousness of the archer. Since he knows destinies he knows the roads to them, although these are not easy to ascertain. And the road of the arrow was first in the eye and mind of the archer.

To the eye that opens in the gnostic triangle, all arrows that the bowman lets fly are quiet (motionless, still, peaceful).[30]

Since the sonatas are Spiritual Exercises, we may say that the goal of man is tranquillity, repose, quietude, which he can reach through his response to beauty, and beauty is universal. Take the example of an archer who lets his arrow fly, perhaps at a stationery target, perhaps to mutilate a deer or human being. The phenomenal object is not important, whereas the origin of the flying arrow is. Proceed in the opposite direction; if you have the gnosis, you will go from arrow to bow to archer to the eye and mind of the archer, to the occult meaning in all creation, which is One. Similarly, if you are a literary archer, you can create a celestial music, a sonata, sending forth a movement that will accord with the Universal Rhythm, an ideal harmony; and from time to time you can if you will shoot an arrow, a ráfaga, a gust that will distract the reader only if he is a hylic phenomenally bound in the jail of clay, that is to say, the senses; but if he follows the arrow's proper course, from itself to bow to archer, he will appreciate the ideal harmony so much more. Violent arrows, gusts, cacophony, so to speak, are like the cosmetic mole on a beautiful woman's face—they enhance beauty; or perhaps they are like the Arcipreste's reasoning that in his Book of Good Love he will put both good love and foolish love, because without the latter you cannot really appreciate the former. Properly heard and seen (from arrow back to archer), violence, devaluation, destruction and even Satanism will lead to a more subtle vision of things and to quietude, that is, the certain form of things, the vision of things-in-themselves.[31]

For the hermano peregrino, the psychic, this aesthetic quietism has a dazzling, hallucinatory force, more properly called perhaps intuition. For the artist, the pneumatic, the one who creates the sonata with its rhythm allied to Eternal Rhythm, punctuated by calculated gusts of violence, this vision is more properly called infused knowledge.[32] The artist received this infusion from the Alma Mundo.

The Sonata de primavera has come to an end. One might move on and study the other sonatas for certain refinements, but not for a basic understanding of the sonatic idea. The background music is ever the same, necessarily, because it harmonizes with the Universal and Eternal Rhythm. Let us take an example from orthodoxy. The Sacrifice of the Mass is always the same, three hundred and sixty-five days a year, year in and year out. The gospel changes, the epistle changes, and a lesson here or there, and you might get a preacher schooled in homiletics to give you a fine sermon, but the Mass itself doesn't change, not one iota. It is simply the Last Supper. Similarly, you might prefer the *tierra caliente* of *Estío*, where sex is emphasized rather more, or the autumnal sadness of Concha in *Otoño*, or the civil war of *Invierno*, but these facets are like gospels, epistles, fine sermons, the sonata is still the same. And how could it be otherwise? The noumenal world doesn't change nor does the eternal rhythm found there, the oneness of the Universe. The violent gusts, promiscuous arrows, take on different external appearances (incest and nymphomania in *Estío*, unshriven adultery in *Otoño*) but that merely means the arrow is heavier or lighter, faster or slower, it doesn't mean you can't trace its proper direction, from arrow to bow to archer to Idea.

Consequently we shall not examine all the sonatas but establish another itinerary. Thus far we have considered:

I. Some proems and a series of *pensées* attempting to establish a principle of proof-intuition called "textual control of the imagination."

II. *La Media Noche. Visión estelar de un momento de guerra*, in which we tried to account for Valle's sidereal vision, his discernment of the quintessential.

III. *Tirano Banderas.* Aesthetic deformation.

IV. The *Sonata de primavera*, a musical *exemplum* composed to lead the brother pilgrim (*hermano peregrino*) to the outer wall of phenomena and beyond.

V. Now we shall study the trilogy called *La guerra carlista (The Carlist War): (1) Los cruzados de la causa (Crusaders For The Cause), (2) El resplandor de la hoguera (The Bonfire's Glare),* and *(3) Gerifaltes de antaño (Falcons Of Yesteryear).* I am very fond of these novels, owing to their historicity. Strangely, *Tirano Banderas*, with all its rigid puppets, also seems quite historical.

VI. The *esperpentos, Tirano Banderas,* and *Luces de Bohemia (Bohemian Lights).* Graphically, I picture the proems and cantos like this:

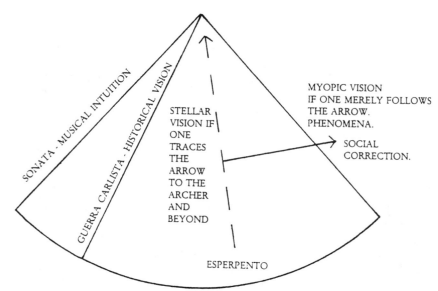

This graph is not rigid, since sonatas have esperpentic gusts (*ráfagas*), whereas *esperpentos* can have their sonatic moments. I believe that the graph allows for the ordering Valle gave to his books, with the *Lámpara* in first place, then the sonatas, the histories in the middle, and finally *El ruedo ibérico*.

> VII. An attempt to explain mysticism and the code of Valle-Inclán. (By Valle's standards, this explanation will be prosaic). The anthology of *Mysticism*, edited by F.W. Happold.
> VIII. A restatement of Plato's Allegory of the Cave.
> IX. Compline, with corollaries. Some remarks concerning Unamuno, Azorín and Pío Baroja.

CANTO VI

La Guerra Carlista

1. *Los cruzados de la causa*
When writing about works of art it is invidious to say that this work is better than that, or that work better than the other, which is like saying an oak is better than an elm or an elm better than a maple. They all have beauty; put it this way, the mighty oak, or the graceful elm, or the frondiferous maple happens to conform to the idea of beauty you have in your mind. Although Beauty is not within the eye of the beholder, preferences within Beauty are. Very well, then, of Valle's works I prefer *La guerra carlista* and *Tirano Banderas*. For me they are the best fruit of this poet's garden.

The Carlist trilogy provides us with a stellar vision of the humble and diminutive, and so we attain a profound understanding of that fratricidal war. The authors of 1898[1] had a special love for diminutiveness. Pío Baroja praised old accordeons and merry-go-rounds, a village Quixote, a glass of wine and fire on the hearth. Azorín gave a name to this humble sentiment—*¡Viva la bagatela!*—long live the sound of a hammer on anvil, of a cock crowing at dawn, and the red glow of a locomotive in the middle of the night. Small experiences hold the true meaning of life. A later author, Gregorio Marañón, explains this truth in his opening chapter of *Amiel*: If we visit a foreign country we are apt to look at maps, visit palaces, read histories and *Guides*, go to museums filled with art, see luxurious rooms and ancient ruins, but we haven't seen anything, he says, to speak for the country's soul. But then, as we pass down a street we may see a man dressing behind a window or a woman arranging furniture, and we recognize in these small scenes the real life of the country . . .

I can't think of a better way to describe the effect of *Los cruzados de la causa* on the reader. The pretender to the throne, Charles VII, is mentioned occasionally, Mendizábal and Isabel II are alluded to but not mentioned; for this is a novel of a miser, a nun, a feudal father, a sea captain, a girl, a *marinerito*, a superstitious servant and a provincial, fanatical society; moreover, great battles do not appear, only the effort to transport contraband rifles from one site to another. And if one reads this novel every five years or so, as I have, one realizes that the death of the little sailor, the miserliness of Ginero, and the young girl's desolation are unforgettable. The book leaves the reader with a series of small indelible impressions: Impressionism.

2. This thought will support the one above. When I studied at Columbia University in 1947, Professor Frank Tannenbaum spoke of his "philosophy of the little things," and he taught

History that way, for example he told us of his first visit to Peru, and at 14,000 feet he could scarcely breathe, whereas he saw an Indian hoeing the ground all day and then playing a fife while marching home. These highlands do not belong to the European or North American. Professor Tannenbaum added an example to his precept.

Valle's Carlist trilogy is rather like that, a series of small historical examples.

3. Valle's works achieve this historical quality through stellar vision, by selecting some thirty-odd bagatelles in thirty-two chapters, and devoting two to four pages to each one of them. Discounting all the blank spaces in *Los cruzados*, it has about a hundred pages. The reader comes upon traces, mainly autumnal, of the sonata, but they do not inundate his mind, attempting the musical miracle. They are sad, reflective, and apt to come at the end of a chapter as a means of closing it. They resemble the kind of ending Sean O'Faolain predicates of the short story, poetical or philosophical endings that prevent abrupt termination and give a sense of continuity; for example, in Chapter XXX the *mujerucas*, reciting exclamations as in a litany, bury the little sailor while his mother repeats her refrain: *¡Asesinos! ¡Asesinos!* (Murderers! Murderers!) . . . There is religious sentiment, and then:

> La mendiga seguía su rezo, sola, en medio del camino, mientras se perdía a lo lejos galopando el hermoso segundón.[2] Aquella vieja mendiga, temblorosa bajo el capuz del manteo parecía hecha de tierra, y el vuelo de los murciélagos, y el son de las campanas que tocaban a muerto, aumentaban la desolación de aquella sombra centenaria que caminaba trenqueante, apoyada en su palo, por el camino crepuscular. (*Cruzados de la causa*, pp. 136-137)

> The beggar woman continued praying, alone, in the middle of the road, while in the distance the handsome nobleman was lost sight of as he galloped away. That old beggar woman, shaking beneath the cowl of her robe, seemed made of earth, and the flying bats and sound of the bells tolling for the dead increased the gloom of that ghostly centenarian who hobbled, leaning on her staff, along the crepuscular road.

Temblorosa . . . vuelo de los murciélagos . . . sombra centenaria . . . camino crepuscular: These are sonatic, nostalgic words recalling the sonatas or yore, reminders yes, but they are only part of an historical, impressionist novel, not the stuff of the novel itself, as they are in *Primavera*. The four seasonal sonatas (Spring, Summer, Fall, Winter) are so cosmopolitan that the city of Ligura and other settings might be substitutible, whereas *Los cruzados de la causa* could only take place in "Las Españas," where you encounter verses like these:

¡La trincadura Almanzora
todo lo tiene de bueno,
el comandante rumboso
la gente mucho salero!

Verses sung to a guitar by an "atheistic" drunken sailor.

¡Isabel y Marfori,
Patrocinio y Claret,
para formar un banco
vaya unos cuatro pies!

¡Ave María Purisima!

The grand barge Almanzora
has everything good,
the captain very generous
the people very charming!

Isabel and Marfori,
Patrocinio and Claret,
to make a bench,[3]
there's four good feet for you!

Most Holy Mary!

"Las Españas": where, according to the Carlists, we have the tragedy of two kings, the good Christian Charles VII, and the other, the pagan one in Madrid, who has a hundred women.

No, in the sonatas one can devaluate old doctrines in any setting, be it Italian, Galician, Spanish or Mexican, and one can create celestial music anywhere, seeking the universal harmony; but the misers, caciques, and *mujerucas* of *Los cruzados de la causa* are full fledged Spaniards, Spanish "por los cuatro costados y todas las coyunturas."

4. Who are the greatest figures of nineteenth century literature? Surely the misers: Felix Grandet, Silas Marner, Nickleby's uncle, the vermin who sent Micawber to debtors' prison, the one Raskolnikov murdered, Torquemada, Juan Amarillo, Doña Perfecta (we forget she was an intimate friend of Torquemada), Mauro Requejo—they are legion. And how many pages did their creators write about them? Ten thousand? A hundred thousand? More? And yet in Valle-Inclán you will find

a miser who stands on the same infernal Parnassus as they, el señor Ginero. In *Los cruzados* his name is mentioned in Chapter VII and IX, a total of five pages. It is hard to believe. Let us look at this quintessential miser, and let us look from the stars. 5. In Chapter VI Bradomín decides to sell his ancestral home, his lands, everything for the Cause. This is a crusade and crusaders stop at nothing! He speaks with his mayordomo, Pedro de Vermo, an evil man who is hated by everyone. The mayordomo has been stealing money from the Marquis for years, and he has "a girl in every village"—the power of such men on the local scene is absolute. On a higher plane, Pedro's power and vision are limited, a sign of this being the wooden shoes he wears, but he knows a man of broader horizons, el señor Ginero, the only one who has enough wealth to meet Bradomín's request. Pedro's wife speaks:

> el gallego arcaico y cantarino de las montañesas . . .

> the archaic and sing-song language of the highland women from Galicia . . .

and her sing-song cadence adds to our presentiments; we might call this the musical score of usury. The mayordomo and el señor de Ginero are going to skin Bradomín alive, Bradomín being not merely himself but the archetype of old landholders in the nineteenth century; and Pedro de Vermo being not merely himself, but *the cacique* of his day, and el señor de Ginero the quintessential usurer. *Cacique* and *usurer* will destroy the ancient houses:

> ¡Son los usureros los acabadores de las casas! ¡Las comen por el pie!

> The usurers are the destroyers of the old houses! They'll eat the feet from under them!

The chapter ends:

> —Hablaríamos con el señor Ginero. Inda no hace mucho me preguntó si sabía de alguien con responsabilidades a quien prestarle.
> —De nuevo callaron marido y mujer. Pedro de Vermo fue por la vaca y la trajo al pesebre. El animal sacudió varias veces la cabeza y comenzó a mordisquear la yerba dando leves mugidos de satisfacción y de ansia.

—We ought to speak with el señor Ginero. Just recently he asked me if I knew someone in debt he might lend to.

Again husband and wife kept their silence. Pedro de Vermo went for the cow and brought her to the manger. The animal shook her head several times and began to nibble on the hay, emitting a soft lowing of anxious satisfaction.

Vermo and his wife kept quiet. They have a silent unholy agreement. They are like two barn animals in their wooden shoes, who will chew their cud, satisfied, for they are going to make a lot of money out of Bradomín; but they are somewhat anxious for they don't know exactly how much. That will depend on The Miser.

6. Chapter VII: El señor de Ginero, Miser of Misers, two pages and six lines, three or four details, and a brief description and conclusion. That is all. Quintessence. Stellar vision.

Every afternoon el señor de Ginero grabs his musket and goes for a walk, a wicker basket in hand. He peeps into houses as he goes by, and he may ask a question:

—Lagarteira, is your husband in?
—He's at sea.
—Tell him not to forget to pay me what he owes me. I wouldn't want to bring you to jail . . .
—Times are so hard!
—They're hard for all of us.

The miser continues on his way, to the "big orchard he had bought when they sold the lands of the monasteries." That must have been 1837 or so, when Mendizábal passed his laws freeing church lands from mortmain, and:

For some thirty years now, every afternoon el señor Ginero went to his orchard.

He gathers a few fruits there, depending on the season, and shoots some sparrows if he can, and all go into his basket. His supper:

Aquellos pájaros eran la cena del viejo ricachón que, al sentirlos crujir bajo los dientes, gustaba el placer de devorar a un enemigo.

Those birds were the dinner of the coarse rich old man who, on feeling them crunch beneath his teeth, enjoyed the pleasure of devouring an enemy.

He devours sparrows, and human beings, and likes the grinding sound in his jaws.
He meets a few of the local clergy:

> El señor Ginero, que era muy beato, se detenía siempre a saludarlos, pero aquella tarde llegó hasta levantar las hojas de higuera que cubrían el cestillo, y ofrecerles si querían merendar.

> El señor Ginero, who was very devout, always stopped to greet them, but that afternoon he even went so far as to raise the fig leaves covering the basket, and to offer them a snack.

There is only one descriptive phrase in this passage, namely, "que era muy beato," for everything else is action. A miser in action, "who was very devout." A hypocrite. He is about to acquire all the lands and estate of a reckless Marquis, so for once in his life, after thirty years, he offers a few pieces of fruit he has picked free in his orchard to his neighbors of a higher class, the clergy. Charity. And he then uses one diminutive, which underscores his fawning way:

> —¡El excelentísimo señor marqués tampoco quiere aceptar una ciruelita?

> —Wouldn't the most excellent Marquis like a little plum?

There follows a description:

> Era un viejo alto, seco, rasurado, con levitón color tabaco y las orejas cubiertas por un gorro negro que asomaba bajo el sombrero de copa. Se despidió con grandes zalemas. Desde la mañana sabía la llegada del caballero legitimista, y quedara convenido con el mayordomo Pedro de Vermo.

> He was a tall old man, lean and beardless, with a tobacco colored frock coat and his ears covered by a black skullcap which showed beneath his top hat. He took his leave, bowing obsequiously. Since early morning he had known about the arrival of the Marquis who supported the pretender to the throne, and he had an agreement with the mayordomo, Pedro de Vermo.

140

The Quintessential Miser: a cold lean hairless old man with cap-covered ears who grinds the poor in his teeth and obssequiously offers the powerful a little plum upon fleecing them. Two brief pages, that is all. Chapter VIII serves as a relief between VII and IX, for we meet Cara de Plata, the handsome *segundón* and opposite of The Miser. A feudal type like his father, Don Juan Manuel, he has thrashed the mayordomo:

> Pocos días hace tuve que ponerle los huesos en un
> haz a ese pillaván . . .
>
> That rascal, a few days ago I had to give his bones
> a going-over . . .

Then The Miser comes. In Chapter IX we find the formulaic verse, carried over from the sonatas, "entornando los párpados." His eyes half closed, el señor de Ginero is the consummate hypocrite. Bradomín and Cara de Plata disdain him, but he will get hold of everything they own:

> ¡Ese hombre será el heredero de nuestra casa!
>
> That man will be the heir of our house!

7. The art of this impressionistic novel is one of suggestion. Each chapter resembles a short story that begins abruptly, makes a comment on human nature, frequently a wry comment, and then ends, not abruptly, but with a statement or paragraph suggesting continuity. Suspension. Sometimes history or customs are substituted for human nature. Perhaps the major difference between this novel and the realist novels of a previous generation is this: Each chapter of *Los cruzados de la causa* can be read in isolation, by itself, as you might read a ballad, sonnet, or short story, or the chapters may be read in series. Each one evokes some phase of nineteenth century history, the cacique, the usurer, the quasi-feudal lord, the dandy, the *mujerucas*, fanaticism, a plan of war, political philosophy, irreverence, superstition, the horror of war, the abbess. It is an art of evocation, which we call impressionism.

8. An Aside: *Los cruzados* reminds me of Azorín's *Don Juan*, which has thirty-nine chapters and an epilogue, each of them two to four pages long. Azorin's *Don Juan* should really be called *Trasuntos de España* (the title of another book by him), because that's what *Don Juan* is, not a story of the contumelious lover but a series of forty models, types, ideas, impressions, (*trasuntos*) of

Spain; e.g. the small city, the old blind bishop, the Hieronymites, the saintly discalced nuns, the sensual nun, Doctor Quijano, the maestro and boys at school, the Guardia Civil, the family that's *afrancesada*, the *tía*, the goldsmith, the prisoners and so forth. Especially memorable is Azorín's "censo de población" (census), which reveals a surfeit of clergy and hidalgos and a lack of manufacturers and entrepreneurs. In this chapter on the census, in some two hundred and thirty words he shows the economic and political imbalance of Spain, which Jovellanos took a book-length essay to write about, and Galdós a score of novels. Valle's *Los cruzados* is a picture, the picture of Northern Spain; Azorín's *Don Juan* is the picture of Spain itself. Azorín most resembles Valle in Chapter XXXVII of *Don Juan*, where the saintly old bishop has seen The Enemy.[4]

9. Let us discuss now the figure of Bradomín's uncle, the crude, gruff, arrogant, selfish, self confident, courageous, grasping, violent Don Juan Manuel Montenegro. He is the quintessence of the manorial lords who had absolute power over those in their domain, and more than that, he is the archetype of unbridled masculinity.

When I read about Don Juan Manuel in the novel, I thought of Freud's *Moses And Monotheism*, where the father kept all the females to himself, and the brother horde rose up against him to slay him. Don Juan Manuel's concubine is his own son's *novia*, and the son, Cara de Plata, hates him for it and would kill him if he weren't going off to fight for the Cause. Crusader for the Cause of Carlos VII, Duque de Madrid!

> ¡Infame viejo! Si no me fuese de esta tierra, acabaría por matarlo.

> Vile old man! If I weren't leaving this land, I'd end up killing him.

Don Juan Manuel's voice is "violent and feudal":

> ¡Don Galán, trae un jarro del vino blanco de Arnela!

> Don Galán, bring a flask of the white wine from Arnela!

Don Galán is the hunch-backed, limping dwarf of a man who serves Don Juan Manuel and amuses him (*¡Jujú!*) as if he were a medieval monarch.

Don Juan Manuel Montenegro: the impression of a provincial authoritarian, an indelible impression left us in a half dozen pages.

10. Above all the impressions looms the death of the little sailor, the *marinerito*, caused by his mother's fanatical devotion to the Cause. The captain of the barge Almanzora comes to a convent looking for contraband arms; entering the cloister, he is irreverent and cynical, as is his squadron of four drunken sailors. One sailor, the *marinerito*, a draftee, has been left outside to stand guard. Then his mother comes up to him; she is queen of the fanatical old crones, the *mujerucas*, who follow him in a crowd. She starts to scream:

> ¡Ladrones! . . . ¡Enemigos malos! . . . Sacar a los mozos de la vera de sus padres para luego hacerlos ir contra la ley de Dios! ¡Arrenegados! ¡Más peores que arrenegados!

> Thieves! . . . Foul enemies! . . . To take young boys from the side of their parents, to make them go against the laws of God! Apostates! More worser than apostates!

She then castigates her son, screaming into his face:

> ¡Lástima de Inquisición! ¡Afuera de esa puerta, mal hijo! ¡He de hacerte bueno con unas disciplinas, mal cristiano! ¡Vergüenza de tu madre!

> Shame of the Inquisition! Get away from that door, bad son! I'll make you good with a sound thrashing, bad Christian! Shame of your mother!

She strikes him on both cheeks. He tersely replies:

> —It's orders!
> —You've forgotten your Christian religion!
> —It's orders!

She continues her wail:

> ¡Sé buen cristiano, rapaz. Si no eres buen cristiano, no podrás ajuntarte con tus padres, bajo las alas de los santos ángeles, cuando te llegue tu hora. ¡Ay, mi hijo, que la muerte no avisa y si agora llegase para ti, arderías en el infierno! ¡Ay, que tu carne de flor habría de ser quemada! ¡Ay, mi hijo, que cuando tu boca de manzana tuviese sede, plomo hirviente le habrían de dar! ¡Ay, mi hijo, que tus ojos de amanecer te los sacarían con garfios. ¡Vuélvelos a tu madre! Mira como va

arrastrada por los caminos para que Dios te perdone!

La vieja se había hincado de rodillas y andaba así sobre la tierra, los brazos abiertos y la cabeza bien tocada con la mantilla.

Be a good Christian, boy! If you aren't a good Christian, when your times comes you won't be able to join your father and mother beneath the wings of the holy angels. Ay, my son, death gives you no warning and if you died now you'd roast in hell's fire! Ay, your body that beautiful flower would have to burn! Ay, my son, when your beautiful mouth feels thirst, they'd give you boiling lead! Ay, My son, they'd gouge out your eyes with long hooks! Turn your eyes to your mother. See how she crawls through the streets so God will pardon you.

The old woman had fallen to her knees and walked on them over the earth, her arms wide open and her head well covered by her mantilla.

The old woman has thrown herself on her knees. The *marinerito* can't take any more. His eyes aflame, he shouts "¡Alzase mi madre!" (Get up, my mother!); he throws down his rifle and runs blindly toward the town. The squadron will finally catch up to him, shoot him, and his blood will flow in the cracks of the pavement, to be lapped up by a dog.

According to the Carlists, those opposing the legitimate king and supporting the other king, the atheist with his hundred concubines, are crucifying Christ Our Lord. Long live Charles VII! In the words of the mother:

No tenía otro hijo, pero mejor lo quiero aquí muerto, como lo vedes todos agora, que como yo lo vide esta tarde, crucificando a Dios Nuestro Señor.

I had no other son, but I prefer to see him here dead, as you all see him now, than the way I saw him this afternoon, crucifying God Our Lord.

Here is the pith of fanatical Carlism, imperishably preserved for us in a few impressions. The sidereal view.

11. The *marinerito* episode occupies the center of the novel, Chapters XIV-XVII, and as I see it, the historical center of Valle's scheme. We have: SONATAS—HISTORY—ESPERPENTOS. The *Cruzados de la causa* is not so much fiction

144

as fact, not what ought to have happened or might have happened but what indeed did happen. When Don Quixote gives his speech on the just war you are getting the synthesis of that doctrine as it was practised in the sixteenth century; you can read Vitoria and Aquinas if you want to, but you don't have to. Here it is in a nutshell, in the 1615 *Quixote*. Similarly, you can read the histories of Carlism if you want to, and the political philosophies, but it's unnecessary. Here it is, quintessentially preserved, medullarily preserved, with astral superiority. According to Valle's *Los cruzados*, Carlism is the system saying that those who oppose the legitimate Catholic King crucify Christ Our Lord; the King is God's vicar on earth. In a nutshell. This definition will account for the literary and political works of José María de Pereda, Manuel Tamayo y Baus, Francisco Navarro Villoslada and the Nocedals, Cándido and Ramón.

12. The *marinerito* episode reminded me of Federico García Lorca, or perhaps I should say Lorca reminds me of it, since I am assigning Valle the central position in modern literature. After the boy is shot, the sobbing *mujerucas*, covered in their black mantillas, kneel and begin their lamentation (*planto*):

     —¡Era el rey de los mozos!—
     —¡Era la flor de los marinos!—
     —¡Se lo robaron a su madre, para las escuadras!—
     —¡Otro amparo no tenía la madre!—
     —¡Ay, qué bien cantaba las coplas de la jota!—
     —¡Ay, qué bien cortaba castellano!—
     —¡Se lo robaron a su madre, y se lo tornan con los meollos partidos!—

     —He was the king of young lads!
     —He was the flower of sailors!
     —They stole him from his mother, for the Navy's crew!
     —He, his mother's only protection!
     —Ay, how he sang the verses of the jota!
     —Ay, how he spoke in Castilian!
     —They stole him from his mother, and return him all broken in two!

This is the same Greek chorus that Lorca employs in *Bodas de sangre*, and for all I know it may be its origin. I also thought of the *Llanto por Ignacio Sánchez Mejías*. Yes, I would even relate García Lorca to Valle, Don Benito el Garbancero on one side, and he on the other.

13. Valle was capable of writing a beautiful love story, and I, an admirer of love stories, wish he had written more episodes like the closing chapters of *Los cruzados de la causa*, where the

reader is so anxious over the fate of Míster Briand. In spite of a great storm, Míster Briand is sailing a frigate in the Bay of Biscay, because he has been summoned to pick up the contraband rifles. He has written a last letter to his *novia*, who sits in the window (*ventano*) watching, waiting. But the sea claims its own, Míster Briand and all hands disappearing beneath the waves. And in the last chapter the girl, widowed before her marriage, long before her time, discusses her fate with the abbess. This love, the lost love, the abbess's remorse, the futility of it all, are the most poignant scene in all of Valle's literature. There is no aesthetic deformation here. The futility of the Carlist War: Death. The last two lines present a proper frame to the war:

¡Cribos! ¡Cribos! . . . ¡Cedazos buenos! . . . Para harina de maíz, para harina de centeno.

Sieves! Sieves! . . . Large sieves you buy! For flour of corn! For flour of rye!

A return to the grotesque. The assonant rhyme (*buenos-centeno*) underscores the cry of the two esperpentic peddlers.

14. As I read about the storm and the sea claiming its own I thought of John Millington Synge and José María de Pereda (two disparate figures!), *Riders to the Sea* and *Sotileza*. Synge resembles Valle, his tragedy told in a few pages; whereas Pereda, carefully describing the *garbanzo* in long chapters, resembles his friend Galdós. Synge and Valle suggest, whereas Pereda recounts a long story: Quintessence versus profile, sidereal view versus the view of a man with a camera. Please don't misunderstand me, I like *garbanceros*, but we are not discussing them here, we are discussing the central poet of the post-Kantian era, Don Ramón María del Valle-Inclán y Montenegro.

15. One last word before leaving this marvelous volume: In *Los cruzados* the Carlists make several allusions to Mendizábal and mention him only once by name. He is the Antichrist, Attila the Hun, Attila's dog, the one who labored for Hell, the suppressor of the monasteries. They are allusions, that is, an impression here or there, but the reader does not forget Valle's impressions.

16. The student of historiography will want to read G.P. Gooch's *History And Historians In The Nineteenth Century*. Having discussed Ranke, Guizot, Hallam, Macualay, Froude and others, he comes to Spain and speaks of Benito Pérez Galdós:

No survey could ignore the historical novels of Pérez Galdós, the Walter Scott of Spain. His *National Episodes* relate the vicissitudes of the country from the Battle of Trafalgar in two score volumes, and offer a wonderfully living picture of the revolt against Napoleon, the despotism of Ferdinand VII, and the atrocities of the Carlist Wars. (Gooch, p. 409)

To place Galdós in the pantheon of modern historians is a tribute to his genius, for he was after all a writer of prose fiction. If you want a memorable love story read the ten novels about Gabriel Araceli, and if you want to understand Napoleonic Spain, read the same novels.

I would rank Valle-Inclán alongside Galdós in Gooch's pantheon. He has left a wonderfully living picture of the Carlist revolt against the republic of Spain.

17. Cervantes, they say, placed the novel between history and poetry, between what happened and what might have happened. I should say he did so with a certain bias towards history.

Valle I believe also placed the novel between history and poetry, with a certain bias towards poetry. It seems to me that Valle himself resembles Cervantes's great creation, Don Quixote, the extravagant figure who also leaned towards poetry:

Dichosa edad y siglos dichosos aquellos a quien los antiguos pusieron nombre de dorados . . .

Happy the age and happy those centuries to which the ancients gave the name of golden . . .

18. In a way Don Quixote resembles nineteenth century idealists, because he places the subjective over the objective. Valle-Inclán, in his search for the eternal moment, follows that same order; Things are what you the subject want them to be. Will the music of the sonata, and Nature will follow your will.

147

CANTO VII

El Resplandor de la Hoguera (The Bonfire's Glare)
(Volume II of the Carlist trilogy)

1. Let us follow Aristotle's pattern of *mythos* and *dianoia*. First we shall describe the plot and then tell what the novel is all about, and also the author's means of achieving this end.

The Plot
Cara de Plata is returning from France with his "barbarous and feudal laugh," to join the Carlist guerrilla forces fighting the republic, and accompanying him is his relative, the abbess, Madre Isabel. They meet Roquito, the sexton who disappears in *Los cruzados de la causa*. The priest Manuel Santa Cruz, the most famous of the guerrilla captains, has ordered the other captains to join him, but only Miquelo Egoscué seems disposed to do so although he has been warned of treachery. The Republican forces under General España are pursuing Santa Cruz, but there is a dilemma here: He is so atrocious and sanguinary he embarrasses Carlism in the eyes of all Europe, he hurts Carlism more than he helps it. A Republican rear guard is attacked but subsequently saved by the main force, which returns to its aid. The wily and crazed sexton Roquito burns down a barracks with all the Republican troops inside, and then at the novel's end he is the victim of unwitting justice; hidden in a chimney, he has his eyeballs seared when some Republican soldiers light a fire for warmth:

> —¡Nada veo! ¡Nada veo!
> La mendiga se acercó y dio un grito:
> —¡Tiene abrasado el cristal de los ojos!
> Con silencioso espanto, las mujeres juntan las cabezas en un racimo para comtemplar aquellos ojos ciegos y llagados.
> ¡Así termina *El resplandor de la hoguera*!

> —I can't see! I can't see!
> The beggar woman approached and gave a cry:
> —They've burned the whites of his eyes!
> With silent awe the women bunched their heads together to contemplate those blind and wounded eyes.
> Thus ends *The Bonfire's Glare!*

2. When describing the plot, one must remember that this is a short novel, one hundred and twenty pages or so, with twenty-four chapters, so that each chapter is very brief, about an

average of four pages. The main figures, Cara de Plata, Isabel the nun, the *cabecilla* Miquelo Egoscué, Roquito the sexton, the republican Ordax and General España briefly come and go, appearing in alternate chapters sometimes, or sometimes leaving the scene to appear again much later. There are no main characters in the sense that Villaamil is one in *Miau* or Fortunata in *Fortunata y Jacinta*. The presence of one man, Manuel Santa Cruz, brings the chapters together even though he doesn't appear in the book. He is the terrible bloody guerrilla chief, the *cabecilla*, who is on everyone's mind—Cara de Plata wants to join him, Miquelo Egoscué is summoned and betrayed by him, and the Republican generals plan their war around him. He personifies the words of the title, *el resplandor de la hoguera*, the bonfire's glare, the magnificence of the bonfire. He *is* the guerrilla, the little war, defender of ancient customs, civil war incarnate, and he will consume the country in flames if needs be, to preserve his quasi-mystical vision.

3. I find the final line of the novel, "¡Así termina el resplandor de la hoguera!", to be significant. As a frame it has the effect of freezing the scene, changing it and the entire novel before it into a tableau. The title of the tableau, *El resplandor de la hoguera*, the bonfire's magnificence, and the scene itself, a black house with a black leafless grapevine and black treetop, shade, a door open revealing a fire place and roaring fire ("Era una casa negra y sin hojas, tras una cerca asombrada por la copa negra de un nogal"), and an unseeing man covered with soot, surrounded by women staring at his glazed white eyeballs: All this is the bonfire's glare, the bonfire's glorious light, the magnificence of the Carlist civil war!

Were I to select one scene as the most memorable of all of Valle's literature, this scene of Roquito's vitreous eyeballs might be my choice, perhaps for its irony (though I must confess that coca green drooling Tirano Banderas framed in a doorway is a close rival). Perhaps there is a literary truth here: Valle is a master of painting tableaux. We have this scene of the scorched Roquito, Banderas the owl, the woman being stripped by dogs, Eulalia's drowning in the dark river, the little seaman, the miserly señor de Ginero . . . They are all immobilizations, tableaux, and as we have seen elsewhere, words suggesting *lo inmóvil* abound in Valle-Inclán.

4. Come to think of it, the last novel of the Carlist trilogy, *Gerifaltes de antaño*, also ends with the words "ASI TERMINA GERIFALTES DE ANTAÑO" (in capital letters). Let us discuss this tableau at the proper time.

5. In Chapter XVI of *El resplandor* the narrator writes:

Quedó pensativo, y lentamente alzó la cabeza
mirando a la cima de los pinos. Toldaba el cielo

una nube negra que parecía cerrar el raso como lo
cerraban el silencio y la sombra del pinar todo en
torno. *Límites de impresión y sugestión* (italics
mine). Pedro Guillén golpeaba los troncos con la
culata del fusil, y aplicaba el oído: —¡Zumban tal
que si tendrían una bala de cañón!

He grew pensive, and slowly he raised his head,
looking at the tops of the trees. A black cloud
covered the sky and it seemed to shut out the
open country just as the silence and shade of the
pine grove shut it out too. *The limits of
impression and suggestion.* Pedro Guillén struck
the tree trunks with the butt of his rifle, and then
applied his ear: —They buzz as if they had a
cannon ball!

In this scene the *forales* (enforcers)[1] come in two files, leading
five prisoners in a chain. They are the Republican counterpart of
the Carlist volunteers, "famed for their valor from the other
war" (1833-1839), and they know the land as well as the
guerrilleros themselves:

Aventureros en su tierra, tenían la alegre fiereza
de los soldados antiguos, y el amor de la sangre y
de la hoguera. ¡La hermosa tradición española! Las
partidas odiábanles como a gente renegada, y
todavía era mayor el odio en aquellos caseríos
patriarcales, donde entraban a saco sin respetar a
las mujeres ni al amo viejo, que ya no puede
moverse del sillón de enea. (*El resplandor de la
hoguera*, p. 88)

The beautiful Spanish tradition of Cain and Abel! In the other
war ("la otra guerra", p. 96) of 1833-1839,[2] don Pedro Mendía
killed twenty *cristinos* for the Cause, so then General Mina killed
forty Carlists for Her Majesty's Government. The bonfire's
splendorous light! The *forales* will now continue this glorious
tradition by killing four of their five prisoners, the fifth being
spared only because he is accompanied by a woman. Chivalrous
action!

Amidst this irony, however, the sergeant leading the
prisoners meditates. He thinks of the time after the war, when
every house will miss at least one man, and the women will be in
mourning, and he grows pensive. Slowly he elevates his eyes to
the pine tops, where the sky has hung a black cloud framing the
open country, just as the silence does and also the shadow of the
pine grove. Nature has a story to tell, or better said, to leave us

150

an impression of, to suggest to us for our rumination.

Nature does not put forth huge bonfires casting splendorous light, she has lights and shades, penumbras, containing great mysteries for those who seek them, and she also has silence, an eternal silence to be detected if we but listen for it behind the cacophony of war. Nature is *ultimately* gentle, sweet, harmonious, undisturbed, silent, and to know her is to experience an aesthetic illusion (a sort of beatific vision). But against this gentle background, there near the horizon!, we have bonfires, greed, selfishness, war (call them pride, avarice, lust, envy, anger), phenomena igniting the scene, destroying penumbral quietude. Even the sergeant Pedro Guillén, whose name evokes Pedro Grullo, can divine this truth, however briefly. Sky and pine grove, and also the narrator's art: These are the "límites de impresión y sugestión." But then noise breaks the mystical silence, when the butt of a rifle strikes a tree:

> Pedro Guillén golpeaba los troncos con la culata
> del fusil.

Other noises follow. The definition of war is NOISE, the contradictory of nature's rhythm and silence, and of the artist's sonata.

6. When Pedro Salinas made the formalist argument that.

> . . . verá la supremacia de una obra no derivada
> capitalmente del asunto o tema dado por la
> experiencia y sí del acierto de la operación
> subjetivante o poetizadora, fuente de la hermosura

> (He who believes this with me) will see the
> supreme quality of a work as being derived not so
> much from the matter or theme as from the skill
> of the subjective or poetizing operation, which is
> the source of beauty. (See Canto II above, End
> Note 4).

. . . when Salinas made this argument I gather he was thinking of extremely scandalous scenes in the sonatas, such as Bradomín's contumely towards a saintly girl, the Niña Chole's erotic abuse of a statue of Christ, Bradomín's adultery with a dying Magdalene and his incestuous temptation of a young girl in a convent. Perhaps he loved Valle's art so much he wanted to make an appeal for it to those millions of Spaniards who would be shocked by Bradomín's indecent actions, and to do so he had to strip form from meaning. Valle-Inclán himself makes a similar claim when he argues for the musical miracle of his works, and of life itself, rather than their "ideological meaning":

151

Hagamos de toda nuestra vida a modo de una
estrofa, donde el ritmo interior despierta las
sensaciones indefinibles aniquilando el sentido
ideológico de las palabras. (*Lámpara*, p. 29)

Let us conduct our entire life as a sort of strophe,
where the interior rhythm will awaken ineffable
sensations, annihilating the ideological meaning of
words. (The reader should remember that *strophe*
includes both poetry and the dance).

Fue obrado este ardiente milagro por la gracia
musical de las palabras, no por el sentido, que
acaso entendidas cabalmente hubieran sido menos
eficaces para mover los corazones, porque siempre
acontece que donde el intelecto discierne, arguye
la soberbia de Satanás. (*Lámpara*, p. 35)

This fervent miracle was achieved through the
musical grace of words, not through their
meaning, which, perhaps fully understood, would
have been less efficacious in moving human
hearts, because it always happens that where the
intellect operates, there reigns the pride of Satan.

I don't believe that such an argument need be made, or can be
made, for *El resplandor de la hoguera*, where the historical
interpretation, the message ("sentido ideológico") is extremely
clear. Chapter X reads:

¡Están de acuerdo para desacreditar a los carlistas!.
Las naciones nos hubieran concedido la
beligerancia sin las ferocidades de Santa Cruz! No
es afirmación gratuita. Son palabras del general
don Antonio Lizárraga.

They have agreed to discredit the Carlists! The
nations might have conceded us a state of true
belligerence if it weren't for the ferocities of
Santa Cruz! This is not a gratuitous statement.
They are the words of General Antonio Lizárraga.

Although Manuel Santa Cruz, *el cura*, never appears in *El
resplandor*, his presence is felt on every page. All the action
revolves around his actions, or better said, his fanaticism, and in
this sense he is the novel's main character. What will *el cura* do
next? The Republicans want to hunt him down as a Carlist

warrior, but the Carlists also want to destroy him because he has shamed their cause in the Courts of Europe. Were it not for his atrocities, France, England and Germany might have recognized the government of Charles VII, Duque de Madrid, granted it loans and trade, and recognized the Spanish conflict as a true belligerency between one government and another. The sanguinary Santa Cruz makes this impossible. At first both the Carlists and *guiris* (the liberals) want to stop him, but after a while it dawns on the liberals that he is an ally of sorts, embarrassing Carlism before all Europe. In the third novel of the trilogy (*Gerifaltes de antaño*) this knowledge will ripen into political cynicism, when the liberals let Santa Cruz escape after surrounding him, and when General España is relieved of his command for opposing such deviousness.

I believe that G.P. Gooch might have included Valle-Inclán as well as Galdós in his essay on historiography. Don Ramón María del Valle-Inclán, the Galician funambulist, also an authority on *garbanzos*. Not a *garbancero*, a mere describer, but a true scientist and botanist of the family *Leguminosae*, loments and legumes. If you doubt this truth, witness his interpretation of the Carlist civil war.

7. Speaking of *garbanceros* and botanists (*garbancistas* perhaps?) let us look to Plato. It is said that Plato was sitting before the Athenian Society of Social Engineers when someone raised the question: Why is Plato sitting? The engineers went into rumination. They finally voted unanimously that Plato is sitting because he is parallel to the ground from his heels to his toes, perpendicular from his ankles to his knees, from his knees to his hips horizontal, and from his hips to his head he is perpendicular, his buttocks resting on a solid object. ERGO, Plato is sitting. When apprised of the Social Engineers' decision, Plato replied: "I am sitting because I am tired."

Having no sense of finality and being glued to their senses, the social engineers describe. They take a snapshot of the man and say: "*This is* the man. This is the quiddity." They are *garbanceros*, vendors of garbanzo bean phenomena. Plato, on the other hand, looks for causes, reasons, finality. Unlike Social Engineers, he does not ruminate, he meditates. He wants to know *why*. Let us call him a *garbancista* rather than a *garbancero*. Don Ramón María del Valle-Inclán is a true disciple of Plato, a *garbancista*. Were he here and you told him that, he would probably reply: "Uzted ez un zopenco," but notwithstanding his buffoonery, he is a garbancist, an ironical, botanical garbancist. Author of the Galician *funambules*.

8. Some chapters of *El resplandor* are so essentially Spanish, so *castizo*, they will remind the reader of the *romances* (the ballads of Spain). Thus the novel becomes a sort of *romancero*, a series of songs celebrating a noble lord's deeds, or they may

153

contain a figure like Vellido Dolfos, Diego Ordóñez or the Mora Moraima. Take Chapter XI, for example, which presents the young *cabecilla* (guerrilla leader) Miquelo Egoscué. Miquelo and the other *cabecillas*—Pedro Mendía, el Manco and el Sangrador—have received a letter from Santa Cruz summoning them "to his court," so to speak. Although the others refuse to go, Egoscué will go as summoned. Then a loyal vassal, the miller from Arguiña, says:

—No me fío mucho, Miquelo.

—I wouldn't trust him, Miquelo.

The *cura* has disobeyed his king, Don Carlos VII, and cannot be trusted.

Here perhaps is another ballad scene: A feast is prepared for all the *mutiles* (translate as *mesnadas* or *warriors*) by a man

> con el torso desnudo y los brazos ensangrentados
> hasta el codo, que desollaba una cabra

> with his torso naked and his arms bloody up to
> the elbows; he was skinning a goat

The scene is feudal, and

> en la oquedad del roquedo, la voz de todos se
> juntó en un son oscuro, y despertó el eco que
> había repetido el rugir de los leones milenarios.

> in the hollow of the cave, the voice of everyone
> was joined into an obscure sound, and it evoked
> the echo which had repeated the roaring of
> millenary lions.

The chapters of *El resplandor* are millenary, ancient, like the ballads themselves; and like the ballads, their art is graphic.[3]

The chapters also hold some of the mystery of Conde Arnaldos, for they echo a reality from the Beyond:

> . . . un son oscuro . . . y despertó el eco que
> había repetido el rugir de los leones milenarios.

These chapters, moreover, repeat themselves in the fashion of the ballads: There is a noble lord, noble deeds, a letter, treachery, death . . . and there is even mention of Bernardo del Carpio and Count Roland (see *El resplandor*, p. 115)

These chapter-ballads, with their movement toward the

ancient, distant and unseen, hold the mystery of the *sonata*[4]; although these Carlist novels are histories, the spirit of the sonata is never entirely removed. The reader may recall the tripartite division of an earlier *pensée*:

SONATA	HISTORY	ESPERPENTO
Vols. I-IX	Vols. X-XII	XXI *El ruedo iberico*

From volume XIII to XX there is a coming and going (a *vaivén*) and stellar vision.

9. Chapter XI presents a singing contest between two *versolaris*[5], Martín Royal de Albéniz and Pedro Larralde de Astigar (the reader schooled in American tradition is reminded of Sarmiento's *gaucho cantaor*). The background displays the gnostic's love for creating the grotesque: There are a hundred red berets gathered around a bonfire in a rocky craggy place, a cave with one *versolari* stripped to the waist and covered with goat's blood, which was splattered on him while he prepared seven goats for roasting. There are seven bloody goat bells thrown in a sack, and seven goat heads placed in a row:

> . . . eran de aspecto brujesco bajo *el resplandor de la hoguera*, con sus ojos lívidos, y sus barbas sangrientas y sus cuernos infernales (italics mine).

> . . . the goats' heads had a witch-like appearance beneath the bonfire's glow, with their livid eyes, and their bloody beards and hellish horns.

The italicized words are the novel's title, suggesting that the Carlist civil war is bloody, wizardly, grotesque, diabolical, and at the same time aesthetic, beautiful, legendary, millenary:[6]

> . . . y en la oquedad del roquedo, la voz de todos se juntó en un son oscuro, y despertó el eco que había repetido el rugir de los leones milenarios. (*El resplandor*, p. 61)

This obscure sound and awkward echo are in keeping with the aesthetic gnosis of *La lámpara maravillosa*.

The bard (*versolari*) of Astigar rises to sing:

> Señora reina, rosa blanca,
> De la clara sangre real,
> Señora reina que hace hilas
> El panólico de cendal,
> Cuando del pecho me sacaban
> Una bala en el hospital,

Eran sus manos con anillos
A sostener mi cabezal.

Lady fair queen, white rose
of royal illustrious line,
Lady fair queen who converts to bandage
her kerchief of silk so fine,
When from my breast a bullet
they took in the hospital,
Your jeweled hands came
to support my headrest.

I have likened this chapter and others to a series of *romances* (ballads), and here we might expect a *romance viejo* or an approximation, a rustic poem sung by one of Miquelo Egoscué's warriors, but instead we get eneasyllables, a very rare verification in Spanish sung in consonant rhyme: One can hardly think of a more cultured scheme.[7] And the thought is so subtle as to be almost *conceptista*: A beautiful queen, a white rose, taking the silken threads of her tiny handkerchief to bandage a soldier with a bullet removed from his breast; she then goes to support his head with hands having rings on every finger. The rings must have seemed like other, benign, amoriferous bullets.

Then the other *versolari* rises to answer him in song:

Y entre el tumulto dorado de las llamas se destacó
la figura de un hombre, con el torso desnudo y los
brazos ensangrentados hasta el codo, que desollaba
una cabra, atada por la cuerna a un saliente de la
roca.

And amongst the golden flickering of the flames
there stood out the figure of a man, with his
naked torso and his arms bloody up to the elbows,
who was skinning a goat, which was tied by the
horns to a jutting rock.

The reader might also expect this strapping lad to reply with an assonant rustic song, but this is what he sings, in eneasyllables rhyming in consonance:

Blancas manos de la Señora,
Aun más que flor de limonero,
Más que bellón, más que farina,
Y el pedrisco del aguacero,
Más que la boina del rey Carlos
Y que la luna en el enero . . .
Blancas manos de señoría,

En cada un dedo su lucero.

> White hands of the Lady,
> whiter still than lemon blossoms,
> whiter than down, whiter than flour,
> and the hail of a shower,
> whiter than the beret of King Charles
> and of the moon in January . . .
> white hands of her ladyship,
> and on each finger a star.

On each finger a *lucero*, a shining star, a sparkling ring. This blood-covered warrior has glossed the other bard's verse "Eran sus manos con anillos" and turned it back on him, a gentle boomerang, so the first bard exclaims: "¡De la mano!" This verbal duelling reminds me of those literary contests (*certámenes*) of the seventeenth century, Baroque poetical fencing.

The greatest irony of this wonderful chapter lies in the narrator's words preceding the first poem:

> Cerró los ojos y empezó a cantar improvisando . . .

> He closed his eyes and began to sing, improvising . . .

Why these sylvan bards are improvising highly cultured verses! Shooting *guiris* (liberals), passing the *bota* (wineskin), and getting semared in goat's blood, they compose sophisticated eneasyllables all the time![8]

One hundred red berets (*boinas*), one white beret (the king's), a queen's moon-white hands, lemon blossoms, goats' heads, horns, bloody torsos: All this roars like a bonfire. The chapter ends:

> La luna caía sobre la nieve y entraba en la cueva
> el resplandor. El capitán dio orden de partir. Se
> alinearon fuera, bajo el azul nocturno, y las almas
> tenían el temblor misterioso y luminoso de las
> estrellas. En la bajada del monte, entre la masa
> fosca de un pinar, tiembla tambíen una luz. Allí es
> la venta del camino de Francia.

> The moon fell across the snow and its brilliance
> entered the cave. The captain gave the order to
> leave. They lined up outside, beneath the
> nocturnal blue, and their souls had the mysterious
> and luminous trembling of the stars. On the down

157

slope of the mountain, amidst the gloomy mass of a pine grove, a light also trembles. There is the inn on the road to France.

Although I have called Valle's *Guerra carlista* trilogy the most historic of his works and placed it at their center, as he himself did, the *sonata* and *esperpento* are never far removed. There, on the one hand, you always have the millenary, mysterious, tremulous, penumbral, luminous, stars and forest and moon, the horizon, call it the *masa fosca* (the gloomy, crepuscular atmosphere); and on the other hand, blood-smeared, infernal, horny, crazy, rocky goat-like beings, dancing and singing in caves, call them the esperpentic, *¡Jujurujú!*, head-lopped, distorted phenomena. I would also suggest that the final "road to France" is not to be taken only literally, but also as the road we must all travel one day to the horizon and beyond, beyond Pyrennean phenomena to the land of things-in-themselves, where dwells eternal Beauty. Aesthetic quietude.[9]

Gnosis

Hay dos maneras de conocer, que los místicos llaman Meditación y Contemplación. La Meditación es aquel enlace de razonamientos por donde se llega a una verdad, y la Contemplación es la misma verdad deducida cuando se hace sustancia nuestra, olvidado el camino que enlaza razones a razones, y pensamientos con pensamientos. La Contemplación es una manera absoluta de conocer, una intuición amable, deleitosa y quieta, por donde el alma goza la belleza del mundo, privada del discurso y en divina tiniebla: Es así como una exégesis mística de todo conocimiento, y la suprema manera de llegar a la comunión con el Todo. (*La lámpara*, p. 7)

There are two ways of knowing, which the mystics call Meditation and Contemplation. Meditation is that linking of reasonings by which one arrives at a truth, and Contemplation is the same truth deduced when it is made into our substance, when we forget the road that links reasons to reasons, and thoughts with thoughts. Contemplation is an absolute way of knowing, a loving intuition, delightful and quiet, a way where the soul enjoys the world's beauty, removed from discursive reasoning, and within divine darkness: Thus it is like a mystical exegesis of all knowledge, and the supreme way of arriving at communion with the All.

The "camino de Francia" is also Valle's other way of knowing, his other road, the one that forgets reasons and thoughts and phenomena, and leads to delightful intuition, to communion with the all. 10. We have spoken of stellar vision, sidereal vision and quintessential art. Quintessence, the fifth essence beyond earth, air, fire and water; quintessence, the vapor and dust of celestial bodies. Here is Miquelo Egoscué's speech from Chapter XVII of *El resplandor de la hoguera*. I should call it quintessential:

Al cabo, el viejo Pedro Mingo le interrumpió adusto:
—¡Hijo, lo que conviene tú lo verás, que para ello eres el capitán!
—¡Y usted de los mutiles que ahora se nos juntaron!
—Yo los encaminaba por aquello de ser más viejo, que a ésos no hay quien los mande. ¡Son lobos de Roncesvalles, de la ascendencia de los que devoraron al gran Carlomagno! ¡A ésos no hay quien los mande!
—Tío, que me hablen a mí.
—¡Pues ni que serías el gran Bernardo del Carpio!
—Soy Miquelo Egoscué.
Con los ojos brillantes y alzado sobre los estribos, avizoró el camino. Después, vuelto a su gente que se apretaba en un haz alegre y palpitante, habló con el calor ingenuo de un soldado antiguo, y era su voz un bronce sonoro:
—¡Muchachos, vamos a pelear por el rey don Carlos!
Si vencemos, a todos nos dará su mano por leales y por valientes, como hizo la vez pasada cuando lo de Aoiz. ¡Muchachos, vamos a pelear por el rey y por doña Margarita! Si hallamos la muerte, también hallamos la gloria como soldados y como cristianos. La gloria de la tierra y la gloria de luz que da Dios Nuestro Señor. ¡Ay, mutiles de Navarra, vamos también a pelear por nuestros niños los príncipes, que son tan pequeños que yo los vi estar al pecho de la reina!
Los soldados gritaron:
—¡Viva Dios! ¡Viva el rey!

Finally, the old soldier Pedro Mingo sternly

interrupted him:

—Son, You'll decide what's to be done, that's why you're captain!

—And you're captain of the warriors who just joined us!

—I guided them because I'm the oldest, because there's no one who can command them. They're the wolves of Roncesvalles, descended from those who devoured the great Charlemagne. There's no one who can command them!

—Uncle, let them speak to me.

—You couldn't, even if you were the Great Bernardo del Carpio.

—I am Miquelo Egoscué.

With his eyes shining and rising in his stirrups, he went to survey the road. Later, when he returned to his men who were crowded around a merry, flickering fire, he spoke with the ingenuous candor of an old soldier, and his voice was a sonorous bronze.

—Lads, we are going to fight for our king don Carlos! If we are victorious, he'll give us his hand, for we are loyal and brave, as he did last time during the action at Aoiz. Lads, we're going to fight for the king and queen Margarita! If we find death, we'll also find glory as soldiers and Christians. The glory of the earth and the glory of light given by God Our Lord. Ay, warriors of Navarra, we are also going to fight for the princes our children, who are so small that I saw them at our queen's breast!

The soldiers shouted:

—Long live God! Long live the king!

Dictionaries usually define traditionalism as the beliefs of those who oppose modernism and liberalism, or as the political system desiring to preserve ancient institutions for national rule. What bloodless definitions! What pedantic conglomerations of words! What skeletons! Here, in Miquelo Egoscué's speech, is traditionalism with flesh on it: lobos de Roncesvalles,[10] Bernardo del Carpio, ojos brillantes, calor ingenuo, muchachos, vamos a pelear, Dios Nuestro Señor, mutiles de Navarra, ¡Viva Dios!, ¡Viva el rey!. Miquelo speaks with Pero Mingo, an authentic grandson of Mingo Revulgo and Pero Grullo: this is pure, absolute, unadulterated Spanish truth.

Aesthetic truth. The Carlist Civil War. "Yo soy carlista por estética."

11. There is a kind of onomastic joy in Valle-Inclán that I

would call *sui generis*, and it sometimes results in an unusual concatenation, or so it seems to this reader. One volume of the *opera omnia* will recall another. Let me give an example from Chapter IX of *El resplandor de la hoguera.* General Enrique España establishes his military lodging in the palace of Redín, named for Captain General of the Armies Don Francisco de Redín y Espoz, marqués de los Arapiles. The old Countess of Redín has been living in the distant past, when her husband fought Napoleon's troops (sixty years before), but now she dresses up for General España's arrival. Still, there are ancient memories, the two battles of Arapiles, the first Carlist War (1833-1839), and then we see the Countess's granddaughter:

> Eulalia, si algún momento quedaba sin escolta, mirábase al espejo, se prendía una flor, y en el clavicordio de la abuela tocaba un vals, que había bailado mucho en otro tiempo, cuando sus padres daban fiestas en su palacio de Madrid.

> Eulalia, if for a moment she didn't have an escort, looked at herself in the mirror, pinned on a flower and played a waltz on her grandmother's clavichord, a waltz she had often danced in days gone by, when her parents gave parties in their palace in Madrid.

Eulalia, una flor, un vals, en otro tiempo: Hearing these words, who can forget Valle's sonatas of his very earliest years, especially, for example, the story "Eulalia," in *Corte de amor.* The name Eulalia evokes the sonatas, which in turn evoke the images from ancestral memory, sounds and images pointing beyond the horizon. The *Lámpara maravillosa* frequently speaks of evocations, and we may call Valle's literature primarily an art of evocations, and within his literature one word will constantly evoke another. In this sense, all his works are *Pipas de Kif, Claves líricas* and prodigious lamps: All of them are sonatas.

I should like to discuss briefly the story "Eulalia of *Corte de amor.* The book begins with a *Nota*:

> En este libro están recogidas aquellas novelas breves de mis albores literarios.

> In this book are collected those brief novels of my literary dawn.

Albores, dawn—the word seems prophetic. We are back at the dawn, when the light just starts to grow, when there is still twilight, and the forms of things are uncertain, when these forms must still be descried, adumbrated, intuited rather than fully seen. And that is how we must read the sonatic story of Eulalia and her link, if any, to the Carlist novels of later years. As I read *Corte de amor* and "Eulalia" I think of Joseph Bédier's version of Tristan and Isolde:

> My lords, if you would hear a high tale of love and death, then listen to the story of Tristan and Isolde . . .

And I also think of Denis de Rougemont's *Love In The West*, where he perceives the Manichaean passion for death, the yearning for this unknown state. Everything is sad, mysterious, tremulous, crepuscular in Valle's story as Eulalia takes the barque across the river to meet her lover: "¡Jacobo! ¡Jacobo!, ¡que te espero!" The afternoon is *azul* (blue), but then comes the twilight and mysterious light of the moon, and one sees the road from the river to the mill and beyond, the road to the moon where dead lovers go, the road so distant:

> . . . porque los ojos de Eulalia miran siempre a lo lejos

> . . . because Eulalia's eyes ever look at the far away

Eulalia speaks to Madre Cruces of her dead grandfather:

> ¡Pobre abuelo!

> Poor grandfather!

But Cruces replies:

> Mejor está que nosotros allá en el mundo de la verdad.

> He is better off than we are, out there in the world of truth.

That is where the road leads, to the world of truth, the world of things-in-themselves, of noumena. The adulterous Eulalia will agonize with her young lover over her daughters, her husband, the letters and "Will I see you again?":

> Permanecieron en la ventana con las manos unidas y las almas presas en la melancolía crepuscular.

They remained in the window with their hands clasped and their souls imprisoned in crepuscular melancholy.

They will anguish over her love letters, her children and husband, who will confine her:

> Aquella venganza indecisa y lejana transfiguraba
> su amor, dándole un encanto doloroso y
> poético . . .

> That vengeance so distant and vague transfigured
> her love, giving it a sorrowful, poetic charm . . .

But finally it is all resolved in the one supreme act everyone must make, pale, tremulous, afraid, on the lunar road and river, while nature stands by in a dim light, immobile:

> Las luciérnagas brillaban inmóviles . . .

> The fireflies were shining, immobile . . .

> La luz de la luna caía sobre sus manos cruzadas,
> inmóviles y blancas como las de una muerta, y
> más lejos temblaba sobre las aguas del río.

> The light of the moon fell on her crossed hands,
> immobile and white like those of a dead woman,
> and in the distance it trembled on the waters of a
> river.

Eulalia, she of Thanatos, goes forth to meet the moon on her river road:

> La luna marcaba un camino de luz sobre las aguas,
> y la cabellera de Eulalia, deschecha ya, apareció
> dos veces flotando. En el silencio, oíase cada vez
> más distante la voz de un mozo aldeano que
> cruzaba por la orilla, cantando en la noche para
> arredrar el miedo, y el camino por donde se
> alejaba aparecía blanco entre una siembra oscura.

> The moon drew a road of light above the waters,
> and Eulalia's hair, all undone, appeared twice,
> floating. In the silence could be heard, waning in
> the distance, the voice of a village boy who was
> singing to arrest his fear, and the road he was
> moving away on showed up white amidst the dark

163

seed beds.

Silence. Quietude. Like her grandfather before her, the sad woman, Eulalia, has gone to the world of truth, where things-are-in-themselves, where their form is not uncertain (*indecisa*). Eulalia, she of Thanatos, displays the Manichaean passion for death. After the silence, ("En el silencio . . ."), the boy's happy Galician song is an artistic frame to close the story. It enhances the quietude and reality of the world beyond. Whereas the boy sings to drive back fear, Eulalia no longer fears. She knows. Gnosis. LAUS DEO: At the end of his works, Valle used to write these Latin words and then place by them a gnostic eye and a rose.

(In this commentary I have deliberately not referred to Eulalia's death as a suicide, which is a phenomenal word of negative connotation. She slips out of the barque, to be sure, to her drowning, but her passage to the road beyond is crepuscular, vague, distant, moonlit, sorrowful, silent, musical, sonatic, aesthetic—in a word, gnostic. Her passage on "the road that mortals tread" is designed to cause delight and acceptance, not negation. She is liberated now from the jail of clay and monstrous attendant phenomena. LAUS DEO.)[11]

12. De Rougemont's thesis seems to be a valid starting place for interpreting *Corte de amor* and other sonatas, and also for interpreting the *Lámpara maravillosa*, which is decidedly Manichaean. There should be sufficient material here for a doctoral dissertation.

13. When I see the phenomenal Eulalia in *El resplandor de la hoguera*, granddaughter of Countess de Redín, I cannot help but think of something like her noumenal self, after her death, in *Corte de amor*, on the road beyond the river. And although the prose is less sonatic in *El resplandor*, it is not entirely dissimilar:

¡Oh, música ligera que el viejo clavicordio desgrana lleno de pesadumbre! Eulalia la tenía olvidada, y de pronto creyó oírla muy lejana, con vaguedad de sueño . . .

Oh, soft music that the old clavichord, filled with sorrow, unfolds! Eulalia had forgotten the music, and suddenly she thought she heard it very far away, with the vagueness of a dream . . . (*El resplandor*, p. 52)

Valle's evocative art is repetitious. Even in a more historical novel it keeps evoking itself, its sonatic self, as it evokes "the world of truth."

14. In *El resplandor de la hoguera* the reader encounters words and expressions such as these, *mutil, vaites, conia, pistolo, guiris, ventano, chacolí, mai, mulé, versolari, cantolari.* Valle's regional vocabulary belongs to the *costumbrismo* (local color) of the novel, which adds to its historicity. The *costumbrismo* is a means to an end.

15. GERIFALTES DE ANTAÑO

Although Manuel Santa Cruz, *el cura*, the most feared of all the guerrilla leaders, did not appear in *El resplandor*, his presence was felt throughout the novel. In this, the final novel of the Carlist trilogy, he appears from the very first line:

> Santa Cruz volvió a caer sobre Otaín.

> Santa Cruz again descended on Otaín.

. . . to the last line:

> Todos callan atemorizados, y en la oscuridad se oye sollozar al Cura de Hernialde.
> ASI TERMINA GERIFALTES DE ANTANO

> All keep silence, terrified, and in the darkness could be heard the Cura de Hernialde, sobbing.
> THUS ENDS GERIFALTES DE ANTANO.

This fanatic, who has raised bloodshed to a superior reality, a mystique, and looks upon himself as traditionalism incarnate, sobs as the liberals raise their siege, granting him salvation.

Like the other works of Valle-Inclán, the mood here is crepuscular:

> Santa Cruz volvió a caer sobre Otaín. Desde los hayedos del monte bajó como los lobos al ponerse el sol, y corriendo en silencio toda la noche, llegó a las puertas de la villa, cuando cantaban los gallos del alba.

> Santa Cruz was attacking Otain again. From the beech tree forests of the mountain he came down as wolves do at the setting of the sun, and running silently all night, he arrived at the gates of the town, when the cocks were crowing at dawn.

In *Gerifaltes*, the narrator recreates the gyrfalcon of yesteryear, the young Santa Cruz of the 1870's, and his art is so quintessential as to become transhistorical. It points to the horizon we have so frequently mentioned, and to the land beyond phenomena. Imperishable form.

16. In one scene (Chapter XII) the Duque de Ordax, Jorge, comes to see Eulalia after her venerable grandmother, the Marquesa de Redín has been honeyed and feathered and placed on a donkey by the mob. A middle-aged, handsomely bearded, affected man, he holds a deep attraction for Eulalia, who had a dream one day "a la caída de la tarde" ("at the end of day"). To her inquiries about his wife, he replies he knows nothing about her, not even the identity of her present lover. Eulalia blushes and begs his pardon, asking him not to say such things, and:

> Quedaron los dos silenciosos. En aquel gran salón de la abuela evocaban el aspecto amoroso y romántico de los héroes novelescos que en las litografías del año treinta se dicen sus ansias bajo una cornucopia, enlazados por las manos en el regazo del sofá, que tiene caído al pie un ramo de flores.

> The two remained silent. In that great drawing room of her grandmother they brought to mind (evoked) the amorous and romantic side of novelistic protagonists who, in the lithographs of the 1830's, told each other their longings beneath the cornucopia, lovers with their hands clasped in the depth of a couch, at the foot of which had fallen a bouquet of flowers.

The Romantic era had produced a series of novels with two lovers hampered by an impediment, e.g., the marriage of one of the lovers to a worthless spouse. Generations later, a quintessential artist reads the novels, extracts their pith, and then preserves it in a chapter of four pages, an evocation, as in a lithograph. This artist prepares his literary inks—the paleness and tearful eyes of a girl, a duke's strained smile, a girl's dream, a blush, an exchange of "pardon me's"—and runs off a stylized etching that arrests the lovers in their pose, just as they were in the 1830's. This quintessential artist, however, displays a touch of irony:

> . . . y sostuvo (Jorge Ordax) con afectación en los labios una sonrisa tirante . . .

> . . . and he kept, with an affectation on his lips, a strained smile.

> Ordax, con una expresión extraña, que cambió de ser dolorosa hasta ser cínica.

Ordax, with a strange expression, which changed from being sorrowful to being even cynical.

One senses a caricature here, as if the lithographer were aware of his picture's excessive sentiment and use of more ink than need be. In an esperpento the caricature would be harsher, but here it is gentler since *Gerifaltes de antaño* is not primarily esperpentic. The view is not phenomenally close, but sidereal.

In *Gerifaltes* the reader also encounters the perfect embodiment of dissolute youth. His name is Agila. In disgrace with his entire family, he lies to his sister and Ordax, pretends to be hungry, and hopes to reconcile himself with his grandmother, the honeyed-feathered Marquesa de Redín. But first he goes to see his grandaunt, Tía Rosalba, whom his grandfather sired by a servant girl. He talks to this venerable woman, who has always stood up for him, and:

—Antes nos llegaremos al Cristo del Gran Poder. Tengo que alumbrarle.

El Cristo del Gran Poder era una imagen antigua que había en una calle estrecha, cerca del palacio. La devoción de la vieja movió en el alma de Agila un despecho egoísta y frío. Hubiera querido que le llevase derechamente al lado de la abuela. Comenzaron a bajar la escalera en silencio. Agila miraba a la vieja y sentía la tentación de empujarla para que rodase. Era un pensamiento que le salía a los ojos, un deseo pueril y bárbaro de niño cruel. Le atraía la escalera larga, toda de piedra, un poco oscura, con el claro de la puerta abierto sobre el vasto zaguán, allá en lo hondo. Se quedó un poco atrás y empujó a la tía Rosalba. Al mismo tiempo sentía un gran frío en las mejillas y oprimido el corazón. Rodó la vieja con ruido mortecino, y a su lado la alcuza iba saltando hueca, metálica y clueca.

(Tía Rosalba)—First we'll go to Christ The King. I want to light a lamp.

Christ The King was an old statue there on a narrow street, near the palace. The old woman's devotion stirred in Agila's soul a self-centered cold resentment. He would have liked her to bring him directly to his grandmother. They began to descend the staircase in silence. Agila was looking at the old woman and then he felt the temptation of pushing her so she'd tumble down the stairs. It was a thought that sprang to his mind, a childish and barbarous thought of a cruel boy. He was fascinated by the long stairway, which was all stone and also dark, with the open doorway facing on the huge vestibule, there below. He drew back a little and pushed Aunt Rosalba. At the same time he felt his cheeks grow cold and his heart oppressed. The old lady rolled down the stairs with a deathly noise, and at her side the oil cruet came popping forth, empty, metallic, dilapidated.

Previously, the novel mentioned a lithograph, and here, at the start of the Agila episode (Chapter XIV) it speaks of daguerrotypes. Whereas Chapter XII was a lithograph, Chapter XIV is a daguerrotype, an obsolete, ancient pictorial process made with a dark camera, silently ("a bajar . . . en silencio"), penumbrally ("un poco oscura"), rather distantly ("allá en lo lejos"). In the twilight one descries a diminutive old lady tumbling down a long staircase that loses itself in the distance, and one hears a dancing (*saltando*) metal cruet clinking, clanking, clunking (*hueca, metálica y clueca*). And above all, near the top of the stairs one can pick out a spectral boy soldier in an ill-fitting uniform, his eyes aglow, his cheeks awry with glee, his hair on end, his feet on the verge of dancing, watching the old woman make her headlong descent. Agila, the pure and concentrated essence of a barbarous child, written large on an ancient plate: I would rank this scene with Roquito's burnt out eyeballs as being unforgettable.

17. A recapitulation: Quintessential art reaches its apex in the narrator's vision of Manuel Santa Cruz, *gerifalte*, falcon of gyrfalcons. He is called *El cura*, an irony augmenting his sanguinary being; of all the crusaders for the cause, he is the most *cruzado*; of all the bonfires (*hogueras*), his is the most resplendent; and of the gyrfalcons, he is falcon, wolf, cat, fox, buck. Indeed, he divides his warriors into these fauna:

> Para gobernarlos y valerse de ellos, los tenía en categorías: lobos, gatos, raposas, gamos.

> To govern them and make the best use of them, he put them into categories: wolves, cats, fox, bucks.

He himself cannot be categorized, he is all of these feral predators, *sui generis*, the archangel of guerrilla warfare. He calls one of his men, the *versolari*, a *ruiseñor* (nightingale), for he is to write the song of the new Cid, Manuel Santa Cruz Campeador:

Jamás hubo capitán que más reuniese el alma
colectiva de sus soldados en el alma suya. Era toda
la sangre de la raza, llenando el cáliz de aquel
cabecilla tonsurado.

There never was a captain who better represented
in his own soul the collective soul of his soldiers.
All the blood of the race was there, filling the
chalice of that tonsured head.

His head, his very being, is a chalice for the consummation of
the sacrifice, a bloody, unjust, cruel sacrifice (as opposed to the
unbloody sacrifice of the Mass), but a desirable sacrifice for all
that, its being in his mind a sacrifice of redemption.
Santa Cruz's conscience is clear and mystical. He can do no
wrong:

Las torturas, los incendios, las muertes eran males
de la guerra, no pecados del hombre. El había
salido de su iglesia puro y con las manos
inocentes. Jamás había tomado venganza de los
enemigos ni derramado sangre mientras fue pastor
que guiaba un rebaño de almas. Ahora sentía una
gran inquietud mística, y arrodillado en la sombra
de los nogales, rezaba con los brazos abiertos. En
aquella oración ardiente se fortalecía para sequir
en la guerra y hacer frente a todos los enemigos.
Salía mejor armado, con el alma fuerte y
resplandeciente, dispuesto a pasar entre las foces
enemigas como el acero de una hoz.

The tortures, the burnings, the deaths were evils
of war, not sins of the man. He had left his parish
church pure and with innocent hands. He had
never taken vengeance on his enemies or shed
blood while he was a pastor guiding the souls of
his flock. Now he felt a great mystical restiveness,
and kneeling beneath the shade of the walnut
trees, he prayed with open arms. During that
ardent prayer he fortified himself so he could
keep up the war and face his enemies. He came
forth spiritually better armed, with his soul
radiant and strong. He was prepared to pass
amongst the enemies' hosts like a steel sickle.

Our souls aflame, let us now mow down the enemy like the steel
blade of a sickle. San Manuel Batallador, Archetype Of
Belligerent Mystics, PRAY FOR US!

18. The art of *Gerifaltes de antaño* is crepuscular:

> Santa Cruz volvió a caer sobre Otaín. Desde los hayedos del monte bajó como los lobos al ponerse el sol, y corriendo en silencio toda la noche, llegó a las puertas de la villa, cuando cantaban los gallos del alba.

Quintessence: Ether, the fifth essence, can best be perceived not in broad day, not in the dark of midnight, but in the haze of twilight, when the shadows provide a background for the indistinct form of things, marked by dying or dawning rays. Lithographs, daguerrotypes, mystical poems, ballads, stories, reveal their ether at that time.

There are also revelatory murmurs and whispers. Audible penumbra. Synesthesia.

19. Since the novel ends with the words ASI TERMINA 'GERIFALTES DE ANTAÑO', I shall repeat the argument I used above: These words freeze the scene, transforming it into a tableau. The title for the trilogy might simply be ANTAÑO, painted by that stellar impressionist Don Ramón María del Valle-Inclán y Montenegro.

 **LAUS DEO**

20. The Austral edition of *Gerifaltes* carries a fragmentary prologue ("Fragmentos de una biografía inédita de Don Ramón del Valle-Inclán"), written by the author's son, Carlos Luis del Valle-Inclán Blanco. Perhaps this fragmentariness is felicitous, in keeping with the nature of the *opera omnia*, in which each work is conceived as a part of the whole. One phrase of Carlos Luis caught my attention:

> *Exagerado y embellecido* (italics mine), Valle-Inclán narrará a su vez lo que ha escuchado en las reuniones que el marqués de Besolla tiene en su casa de Pamplona, y todos le atendían con admiración y asombro, por la fidelidad con que ha captado tipos y ambientes de la Corte Carlista.

Exaggerating and embellishing, Valle-Inclán will narrate in turn what he has heard at the gatherings the marqués de Besolla held at his home, in Pamplona, and everyone would listen to him with astonishment and surprise, because of the fidelity with which he had captured the scenes and figures of the Carlist Court.

As we look and remember phenomena and human experience (let us call them *history*), we perceive them at one and the same time both distinctly and indistinctly; and perhaps, as memory serves them up to us, they are more distinct when we are young and less distinct when we are old. But in either case there is a sort of ether in the air, clouding at times and at other times unclouding the scene: This is the vaporous scene that Locke, Berkeley, Hume and Kant wrote about. Valle is an unusually gifted artist who perceives both history and ether, both the near and the far, the distinct and indistinct; and, exaggerating them and embellishing them, he tries to draw out their characteristic features, leaving us a strong impression. For example, a glorified picture of the Carlist War is false from anyone's point of view: Liberals push their aunts down stairs and release a sanguinary guerrilla leader for reasons of state, and Carlist reactionaries send young lovers and sea captains to their death, and bury rifles beneath the naves of churches. The Carlist Cause, which is ancient, distant, simple and ritual makes an excellent subject for an art of exaggeration and embellishment; consequently it is fine fare for the impressionist who delights in enlarging and adorning salient features, usually in short renditions. A non-impressionist, a *garbanzo* author, on the other hand, might easily espouse the cause of liberalism and write forty or more novels about it, creating an equally superior art by spelling everything out. But an impressionist can't write that way. He must be succinct; he must take a few phenomena, exaggerate them, embellish them, weave magical words around them and hope the reader will understand his creations (for *understand* read *intuit*).

If the author is an unusually talented impressionist, an artistic genius, a super-star as they say nowadays, he doesn't hope the reader will understand, he *knows* he will understand eventually, if he reads the works over and over again in the light of the lamp. Indeed, all the works of this artist are a gnostic *lámpara*. And such an artist would call himself Don Ramón María del Valle-Inclán y Montenegro, Cara de Plata, and if you praised him like this to his face he would look at you and say: ¡Abracadabra! ¡Pata de cabra! ¡Uzted ez un zopenco! Because stellar heights cause arrogance and inebriation. It isn't easy being a sidereal, astral stellar star.

CANTO VIII

A Prosaic Effort to Explain the Code

The present canto, number VIII, is not so much a canto, a lyrical attempt to reveal Valle's art, as a prosaic effort to explain his code in dispassionate, analytical language. Valle himself would not approve this effort, since analysis was not his way, but I have attempted to follow his spirit for two hundred pages and feel I have earned some liberty. I shall now turn deliberately to the dispassion and, I hope, clarity of discursive reasoning.

For some twenty years now I have been teaching honors seminars and using F.C. Happold's Pelican edition of *Mysticism: A Study And An Anthology.* The argument of Happold's long introduction will suitably interpret the aesthetic code of Valle-Inclán; in other words, I am saying that Valle's gnosis is allegedly a mysticism.[1]

Happold himself is a Christian who claims to have had four mystical experiences (see pp. 133-135 of his book), which he includes in his anthology. Nevertheless, he says, he will earnestly try not to assume the truth of mysticism, nor will he attempt to give his book a Christian bias but will include *The Upanishads,* the *Tao Te Ching,* the *Bhagavad Gita,* Buddhism, Plato, Plotinus, the Sufi Path of Love and many revelations of a private, unique character, as well as the mysticism of a dozen or more Christians (following T.S. Eliot, he calls private revelations "The Timeless Moment"). Happold disqualifies himself from writing on Jewish mysticism, not for want of enthusiasm but for want of knowledge. Indeed, he hopes this deficiency will be filled in a future volume, just as he added *"theosis,* the deification of the creature," from the Eastern Orthodox Church to later editions of his anthology.

What Happold is looking for in his argument is a common denominator, a statement that will apply to all mysticisms, be they private experience, Buddhist, Hindu, Catholic, Protestant, Moslem, Eastern Orthodox or of any other kind. He believes he has found one that will stand the test of reason. It may not fully satisfy every reader, Happold argues, but it will serve as a classification for the genus *mysticism.* Specific mysticisms, Buddhist Nirvana, Catholic Contemplation[2], Orthodox Theosis will require an added taxonomy. In short, Happold is looking for a simple statement to cut across all lines.

As I read Happold's one hundred and fifteen page Study, I couldn't help but notice the repetition of the word *phenomenon,* which occurs more than two score times. The word thing-in-itself also occurs at least once:

There is first, what may be called the 'Ultimately

172

Real', the thing-as-it-is-in-itself. This may prove to be unknowable in its completeness. (p. 24)

Kant is mentioned at least three times, and the words *noumenon* and *phenomenon* appear in italics, contrasted on page 30 under the section called "The Problem Of Knowledge." F.C. Happold has chosen the vocabulary of Immanuel Kant for an insight into the common denominator of all mysticism.[3] This does not of itself make him a Kantian, but rather a discerning scholar who will use the dichotomy of Kant for an illustration. And what is more important for the thesis of the present volume, Happold's illustration will include the Galician hierophant, don Ramón María del Valle-Inclán.

The main passage concerning Kant is explicit:

Minds are conditioned by such factors as heredity, history, and environment, and, further, are of varying quality. So the clear but undifferentiated and formless vision, seen at the Primary level of awareness, as it passes through the medium of mind, is distorted and coloured. The result is, therefore, that we find different schools of thought, different theological and philosophical systems, different value-judgments, and different art forms. What may be the same vision seen at the level of Primary awareness may be given a variety of forms as it is interpreted by differently conditioned minds.

The eighteenth-century philosopher, Immanuel Kant, maintained that, constituted as we are, we only know the world outside ourselves as a mental construction; things as they really are are unknown to us; we live in a world of appearances. The thing as it appears and is known to us Kant called the *phenomenon*, that which is unknown, perhaps unknowable, the *noumenon*. Further, he argued that through self-consciousness, nothing can be known about a noumenal world or a noumenal self, that is, a self as it really is in its essential nature, but only about a phenomenal world and a phenomenal self which is as much a part of the phenomenal world as anything else within our experience. Though he qualified his main thesis by allowing that through moral experience direct contact with a noumenal world was established, Kant's main argument was that the world we know is not the world as it really is but only a mental construction of it.

173

Kant is not the only philosopher who has argued that we cannot know things as they really are, that the world we think we know so well is a construction of our minds. For Bertrand Russell, the fundamental stuff of the physical universe is something he calls *sense data*. These sense data, impinging on our sense organs, give rise to the impression of shape, sound, colour, etc., which make up our world. Our world is, therefore, a *logical construction* from these sense data. What sense data are in themselves is unknowable; they cannot be examined or analyzed; it is only possible to postulate their existence at all by their effects in our experience.

The deeper we delve, the more it becomes evident that the universe may not be what it seems to be. What we know is the particular picture of it possible within the range of human perception and capable of being interpreted by human reason. (F.C. Happold, pp. 29-30)

There is in the Kantian division no *forma indecisa de las cosas*, no *lejanía*, no crepuscule, no penumbra, no *esdrújulos*, so to speak. The dichotomy is perfectly clear. On the one hand, we have the *phenomenon*, the thing as it appears to be and is known to us; on the other, we have the *noumenon*, the thing-as-it-is-in-itself, which is unknown and perhaps unknowable. But, IT IS NOT UNKNOWABLE TO THE MYSTIC. The mystic is the one who pierces the veil, who breaks through, who spans the bridge, who arrives at Ultimate Reality; in short, the mystic is the one who *knows*. This statement can be predicated of a Buddhist, a Hindu, a Catholic, a Protestant, a Moslem, or anyone else who has been there, who has sensed, who has felt, who has known The Presence. Here are several examples taken from personal experiences, which are described in the section of Happold's anthology called "The Timeless Moment":

The words of the 23rd Psalm came into my head and I began repeating them: He maketh me to lie down in green pastures; He leadeth me beside the still waters. Soon it faded and I was alone in the meadow with the baby and the brook and the sweet-smelling lime trees. But though it passed and only the earthly beauty remained, I was filled with great gladness. I had seen the 'far distances'. (Margaret Isherwood, *The Root of the Matter*, quoted by Happold, p. 130)

The 'far distances' of Margaret Isherwood call to mind the aesthetic geography of Valle-Inclán.

> Then and there came on me the hour of revelation, when, though savagely hungry, I forgot about breakfast. Scents, sights and sounds blended into a harmony so perfect that it transcended human expression, even human thought. It was like a glimpse of the peace of eternity. (John Buchan, *Memory Hold-the-Door*, quoted by Happold, p. 131)

Scents, sights and sounds blending together call to mind Valle's synesthesia. The peace of eternity resembles his aesthetic quietism. The hour of revelation would be his eternal moment.

> It flashed up lightning-wise during a performance of Beethoven's Seventh Symphony at the Queen's Hall, in the triumphant fast movement when 'the morning stars sang together and all the sons of God shouted for joy.' The swiftly flowing continuity of the music was not interrupted, so that what T.S. Eliot calls 'the intersection of the timeless moment' must have slipped between two demi-semi-quavers. (Warner Allen, *The Timeless Moment*, quoted by Happold, p. 132)

As far as Valle's *Lámpara maravillosa* is concerned, the thought that music leads to gnosis requires no further explanation. It goes without saying.

> It was a time of mingled feeling and dawning thought. In the coalescence of new and old Experience inchoate phrases were beginning to shape themselves. A dim impression of the condition of the objective self might be given by a jumble of incoherent sentences. 'Something has happened to me—I am utterly amazed—can this be that? (*That* being the answer to the riddle of life) . . . (From Warner Allen, *The Timeless Moment*, quoted by Happold, pp. 132-133)

Inchoate phrases, a dim impression, incoherent sentences: Here are Valle's *forma incierta de las cosas* and *balbuceo*.

> I came to a point where time and motion ceased . . . The peace that passes all understanding and the pulsating energy of creation are one in the

centre in the midst of conditions where all opposites are reconciled. (From Warner Allen, *The Timeless Moment*, quoted in Happold, p. 133)

The cessation of time and motion is Valle's *inmovilización*. The pulsating energy of creation, as in a dance, moves rhythmically through all the sonatas. The reconciliation of all opposites is the aim of aesthetic gnosis, or better said, its issue.

And over all was a deep sense of peace and security and certainty. (This was Happold's own experience; see p. 134)

Gaston de Etchegoyen has spoken of the mystical *confiance* in Saint Teresa de Avila and other mystics: They are absolutely certain of their Beloved and show no doubt. Although I would halt at comparing Valle's *Lámpara* with her *confiance* and Contemplation, he does display artistic and aesthetic certitude.

One need only read pages 129-142 of Happold's prologue, "The Timeless Moment," to find other experiences resembling Valle's aphorisms in the *Lámpara maravillosa*.[4]

I repeat: According to Happold, the noumenal world is not unknowable to the mystic, who has been there, who has sensed, who has felt The Presence. This statement will include the Poet with his aesthetic gnosis. Thus we may define the Valleinclanesque Poet as "the one who by his musical miracle has pierced the veil between phenomenon and noumenon, or the horizon of knowledge, who has broken through (or rhythmically penetrated) the shadows and indecise forms surrounding us, who has arrived at Ultimate Reality in a Timeless Moment." To achieve this, the Poet may have to distort proximate reality, write, nay, sing, strange tales, create a bizarre atmosphere, engage in *poética manquedad, cecear*, stammer, in a word, do anything, apparently foolish or not, as long as his Word reaches those capable of receiving it; they will sense its music through the stammer.

This, then, is the code of Valle-Inclán: distance (*lejanía*), millenary chronology, aesthetic deformation, music, dance, synesthesia, instead of *sentido ideológico*, in order to pass from *phenomena* to *noumena*. In order to capture Novalis's blue flower.[5]

2. The code of Valle-Inclán may be summed up in a few words. In 1970, in a students' edition of Pío Baroja's *El árbol de la ciencia*, I wrote:

Azorín (José Martínez Ruiz, 1873-1967) elude el perfil de las cosas, es decir, pasa por alto su descripción realista, y sugiriendo o susurrando un detalle aquí y allá espera que el lector trascienda el mundo de los fenómenos para llegar al mundo de las cosas en sí mismas (el mundo de los noúmenos de Kant). El impresionismo azoriniano se encuentra muy cerca del de Valle-Inclán.

Azorín eludes the profiles of things, that is, he skips their realist description, and suggesting or whispering a detail here and there he hopes that the reader will transcend the world of phenomena to arrive at the world of things-in-themselves (the noumenal world of Kant). Azorinian impressionism is very close to the impressionism of Valle-Inclán.

The point of reference of course is always Valle-Inclán, the central figure of modern Spanish literature.*

*Unamuno's *intrahistoria* is also noumenal. Baroja is the opposite of Valle-Inclán, Unamuno and Azorín. He scoffs at metaphysics and any thought of a Beyond, of a *lejanía ideal*. Rather than being an idealist, he professes to be a scientific materialist of a humanistically pragmatic bent.

APPENDIX I

Some Ideas for Future Students. Unamuno.

Dear Reader,

The thesis of my book is finished, namely, the Halloween art of Valle-Inclán, the night the veil between the two worlds thins, the gnostic attempt through art to arrive at the world of things-as-they-are-in-themselves. If my thesis has any validity, it is now concluded.

At the end of my manuscript, I find I have written down some twenty pages of notes. I shall put these here in appendices for future doctoral students. The notes are, as I have indicated, part of a workbook. If they are fruitful, I hope students will use them; if not, they can do no harm. Some of these notes are inchoate, but then Valle's sonatas, which cope with invisible reality, also, necessarily, have a sort of inchoate nature. In any case, I am unable at the moment to flesh these notes out.

To the graduate student: I wish you well!

* * *

The purpose of the present appendix is to set forth some ideas that may be helpful to future students.

It seems to me that Spanish criticism has abused the idea of *Generation*, and this has had the effect of pigeon-holing various forms of literature. Thus one might speak of a Generation of 1850, Generation of 1868, Generation of 1898, Generation of 1910, Half Generation of 1923, Generation of 1927, Generation of 1936, and so forth. And one might even divide Latin American literature into blocks of fifteen or thirty years, each to be assigned a generational unity. One sets up a series of pigeon holes, as in a mail room where postal workers cast letters, and then stuffs authors and novels and poems into the various boxes. What is amiss here is that critics ought to read novels and poems and plays first, and then, *after* a profound reading, come up with metaphors to describe a certain kind of literature; they should not create critical categories and then stuff the literature into them. (Otis Green called this "textual control of the imagination.")

In assigning critical metaphors (Baroque, Neo-Classicism, Romanticism, Realism, Naturalism), however, I believe that the Generation of 1898 and Modernism do have validity, and I believe this validity stems from the vision of Valle's penumbral, crepuscular, distant (*a lo lejos*), indistinct, (*la forma incierta de las cosas*), whispering (*murmurar, susurrar*) art. There is a noumenal world and a phenomenal world with a veil, a horizon, in between. I should place Valle, Unamuno and Azorín on one side of the veil, and Baroja on the other, although Baroja's Andrés Hurtado and Fernando Ossorio display a noumenal longing. I should place Antonio Machado nearer the border with proclivities toward Valle; at a later date, Pedro Salinas and his extreme formalism also lie with Valle. Paradoxically, I would place orthodox figures like Marcelino Menéndez Pelayo, Manuel Tamayo y Baus and José María Pereda alongside Baroja, because the skepticism raised by the Kantian inability to know noumena causes them no problem. People who believe in the Mystical Body of Christ and Communion of Saints are not bothered by horizons and the piercing of veils to arrive at Ultimate Reality. Their *gnosis* is of a different sort: they *know* that given a good life they will one day rest with Jesus and His Blessed Mother. And they know this with *confiance*, beyond peradventure of a doubt. Perhaps one can say that the literature of Menéndez y Pelayo, Tamayo, Pereda and others is phenomenal because it is concerned with what one can see, touch, smell, hear and taste. These men are *garbanceros.*[1]

Let us turn now to Unamuno. In his seminal work, *En torno al casticismo*, he writes:

En nuestro mundo mental flotan grandes nebulosas, sistemas planetarios de ideas entre ellas, con sus soles y sus planetas y satélites y aerolitos y cometas erráticos también; hay en él mundos en formación y en disolución otros, todo ello en un inmenso mar etéreo, de donde brotan los mundos y a donde al cabo vuelven. El conjunto de todos estos mundos, el universo mental, forma la conciencia, de cuyas entrañas arranca el rumor de la continuidad; el hondo sentimiento de nuestra personalidad. En lo hondo, el reino del silencio vivo, la entraña de la conciencia; en lo alto, la resultante en formación, el *yo* conciente, la idea que tenemos de nosotros mismos. (*En torno al casticismo*, p. 61)

It seems to me that this paragraph is in keeping with the idealism of Kant . . .

. . . forman en torno de aquellos un nimbo, una vaga penumbra. (*En torno al casticismo*, p. 62) . . .

El universo todo es un tejido de hechos en el mar de lo indistinto e indeterminado, mar etéreo y eterno e infinito, un mar que se refleja en el cielo inmenso de nuestra mente, cuyo fondo es la ignorancia.

Again, I perceive the influence of Kantian philosophy here. "El mar de lo indistinto" resembles "la forma incierta de las cosas" de Valle-Inclán; the forms are *indistintas* in Valle-Inclán. (I suggest the students read pp. 61-64 of the Austral edition of *En torno al casticismo*, 2a. ed., 1945)

In *Niebla* Unamuno writes: (I have various passages underlined in the copy I have at home, with notes in the margin) . . .

And in *Tía Tula* he writes: . . .

Then examine Azorín, *Don Juan.*

And then examine Baroja. The Fourth Part of *El árbol de la ciencia* is all about Kant and Schopenhauer. Baroja's essays, Volume V of his *Obras completas*, are very suggestive. His bah humbug attitude towards religion and metaphysics will show that his principal concern is palpable reality, which is why he shows respect for the natural sciences. For Baroja, impalpable reality is a subject for *farsantes* . . .

* * *

The *hombre de carne y hueso* of Unamuno obviously is not what we ordinarily would call "a man of flesh and blood." The latter is our neighbor next door, be he good or bad, or a fictitious character like Villaamil in Galdós's *Miau*, or David Copperfield or Effie Briest or George Apley or Huck Finn. These are people of flesh and blood. Unamuno's Alejandro Gómez in *Nada más que todo un hombre* or Abel Sánchez hardly resembles them. They and Tía Tula and San Manuel and El hermano Juan and Raquel and the others are all cut of the same cloth, they are metaphysical figures representing Unamuno's peculiar, contradictory, "indefinitionist", anguished ontology of *querer serse, querer serlo todo, no querer serse, no querer serlo todo* (the *congoja*). Their dialogues, or monologues, recited over and over and over are corollaries of the alleged metaphysical contradiction in man. Unamuno's characters (better to say, figures) are *examples* of his philosophy, so that his works, all of them, are repetitious, exemplary novels trying to throw light on a deep, obscure truth; thus they are a sort of *lámpara*. And they are uniquely impressionist; whereas Valle's impressionism was based on musical sound and distance and crepuscular shadows and penumbras, Unamuno's impressionism is devoid of *garbancero* descriptions and is based on words, words, words (dialogue), and more words, all of them anguished, confused, paradoxical:

—¿Y hay psicología? ¿Descripciones?
—Lo que hay es diálogo; sobre todo diálogo. La

180

cosa es que los personajes hablen, que hablen mucho, aunque no digan nada.

—Esto te lo habrá insinuado Elena, ¿eh?

—¿Por qué?

—Porque una vez que me pidió una novela para matar el tiempo, recuerdo que me dijo que tuviese mucho diálogo, y muy cortado.

—Sí, cuando en una que lee se encuentra con largas descripciones, sermones o relatos, los salta diciendo ¡paja! ¡paja! ¡paja! Para ella solo el diálogo no es paja. Y ya ves tú, puede muy bien repartirse un sermón en un diálogo . . .

—¿Y por qué será esto?

—Pues porque a la gente le gusta la conversación por la conversación misma, aunque no diga nada. Hay quien no resiste un discurso de media hora y se está tres horas charlando en un café. Es el encanto de la conversación, de hablar por hablar, de hablar roto e interrumpido.

And just as Valle-Inclán called his impressionist tales *sonatas*, so Unamuno calls his *nivolas*:

—Pues acabará no siendo novela.

—No, será . . . será . . . *nivola*.

—Y ¿qué es eso, qué es *nivola*?

—Pues le he oído contar a Manuel Machado, el poeta, el hermano de Antonio, que una vez le llevó a don Eduardo Benot, para leérselo, un soneto que estaba en alejandrinos o en no sé qué otra forma hterodoxa. Se lo leyó y don Eduardo le dijo: "Pero ¡eso no es soneto! . . ." "No, señor—le contestó Machado—, no es soneto, es *sonite*." Pues así es como mi novela no va a ser novela, sino . . . ¿cómo dije?, *navilo* . . . *nebulo*, no, no, *nivola*, eso, ¡*nivola*! Así nadie tendrá derecho a decir que deroga las leyes de su género . . . Invento el género, e inventar un género no es más que darle un nombre nuevo, y le doy las leyes que me place. ¡Y mucho diálogo!

The word *nivola* means "an impressionist novel based on dialogue," or perhaps "a novel based on impressionistic dialogue." The form is heterodox, and so, by the way, is the content (*fondo*).

Unamuno refers to himself as a word-battler:

"este logómaco de don Miguel" (*Niebla*, Prólogo,

p. 10)

I suppose in a way Valle is a *logómaco* also, a musical word-battler, whereas Unamuno is dialogic and philosophical. Unamuno is an indefinitionist and confusionist, a Socratic gadfly:

"lo mío es indefinir, confundir." (*Niebla*, p. 12)

. . . and so in a way is Valle. Apparently when one struggles with *phenomena* in order to arrive at the Reality beyond, the *intrahistoria* of Unamuno or Eternal Rhythm of Valle, one must struggle with, nay, fight with words. And why wouldn't this be so? Words after all are based on phenomenal reality: one not only battles against others with words, one battles with the words themselves. Confusion and indefinition are inevitable.

I would suggest to future doctoral candidates that Unamuno's *hombre de carne y hueso* "no lo es" in the ordinary sense of the phrase. When we ordinary readers use the term "man of flesh and blood" we mean Villaamil, Copperfield or the man who cuts his hand and bleeds next door, whereas for Unamuno, Villaamil and the others are merely phenomenal persons. When he says "hombre de carne y hueso" he is looking toward The Thing-As-It-Is-In-Itself, towards *noumena*, towards Man as he might appear in Plato's Form, could we see it. Villaamil is but a shadow in Plato's cave whereas Tía Tula and Abel Sánchez are suggestions of the Form of Man outside it, in the land of total understanding. There is confusion and identification here resembling Valle's "forma indecisa de las cosas", but in any case Unamuno's appetite for the noumenal world, the Great Beyond, is the same as Valle's. This is what Unamuno means by the thirst for the immortality of the soul.

This argument will explain the statement in *Niebla* about *entes de ficción* and *entes de sueño*:

—Sí, dicen que nadie conoce su voz . . .
—Ni su cara. Yo por lo menos sé decirte de mí que una de las cosas que me da más pavor es quedarme mirándome al espejo, a solas, cuando nadie me ve. Acabo por dudar de mi propia existencia e imaginarme, viéndome como otro, que soy un sueño, un ente de ficción . . . (*Niebla*, p. 114)

It also explains the following paragraph:

Todo este mi mundo de Pedro Antonio y Josefa Ignacia, de don Avito Carrascal y Marina, de Augusto Pérez, Eugenia Domingo y Rosarito, de

Alejandro Gómez, "nada menos que todo un hombre", y Julia, de Joaquín Montenegro, Abel Sánchez y Elena, de la tía Tula, su hermana y su cuñado y sus sobrinos, de San Manuel Bueno y Angela Carballino—una ángela—,y de don Sandalio, y de Emeterio Alfonso y Celedonio Ibáñez, y de Ricardo y Liduvina; todo este mundo, que me es más real que el de Cánovas y Sagasta, de Alfonso XIII, de Primo de Rivera, de Galdós, Pereda, Menéndez y Pelayo y todos aquellos a quienes conocí o conozco vivos, y a algunos de ellos los traté o los trato. En aquel mundo me realizaré, si es que me realizo, aun más que en este otro.

Y bajo estos dos mundos, sosteniéndolos, está otro mundo, un mundo sustancial y eterno, en que me sueño a mí mismo y a los que han sido —muchos lo son todavía—carne de mi espíritu y espíritu de mi carne, mundo de la conciencia sin espacio ni tiempo, en la que vive, como ola en el mar, la conciencia de mi cuerpo. (*Niebla*, p. 23)

The world of Cánovas and Sagasta, Alfonso XIII and Menéndez y Pelayo (Unamuno's own professor!) is less real because it is completely phenomenal; it is in truth Plato's shadows on the wall; it is, so to speak, a world of *entes de ficción*. On the other hand, the world of Augusto Pérez and Tía Tula, of San Manuel Bueno and Unamuno's nebulous *nivola*, strives to reach beyond Plato's cave and points to the noumenal world beyond, of *serlo todo*; or more humbly stated, it is an artist's dialogic attempt to indicate the world of Man-As-He-Is-In-Himself, noumenal man, the man of *carne y hueso*. The *nivola* is based on words, words, words, or if you will the artist's Word, which Unamuno called the Word made flesh, incarnate.[2]

Thus Unamuno sees three worlds: (1) the world of King Alfonso XIII, which, though apparently real, is in truth a world of fictitious, unsubstantial beings, phenomena. Here everything is shadowy and proximate. At best it is like the waves on the surface of the ocean, which reveal nothing of what transpires down below. (2) The world of novelistic (nivolistic!) characters like Augusto Pérez, who, though apparently fictitious, have a certain substance, a real reality so to speak, because they are aware of and face the third, noumenal world. This world of *Niebla* is penultimate. (3) The third world is substantial and eternal and sustains the other two. Here the corporal wave on the surface of the sea (*conciencia de mi cuerpo*) is accounted for by the world of consciousness in the depths, where there is neither time nor space nor corporality as we know it. Unamuno's imagery conforms to Kant's transcendental idealism, where the phenomenal world of human understanding opposes a world of things-in-themselves.

I hope some dedicated graduate student will learn German and study Kant, Fichte, Schelling, Krause and Hegel, and Plato and Berkeley, and apply his studies to Valle-Inclán. It seems to me that this is the key issue in Spanish *modernismo* and Generation of 1898, which are one.

* * *

Conclusion

Valle-Inclán points to the world beyond the phenomenal horizon, and so in his unique way does Unamuno, speaking of an unquenchable thirst for immortality. I myself see Valle as the central figure of the authors of 1898, whereas others will prefer Unamuno. I myself belong to the phenomenal world, which is why I like Galdós's *National Episodes* and Valle's Carlist trilogy. But then, in spite of his suppressing descriptions and in spite of the mist and indefinition, Unamuno presents the phenomenal world rather well in *Niebla* (where Augusto Pérez pursues a woman enamored of ne'er-do-well, Mauricio—the plot is phenomenally acceptable). Why then do I place Valle in the center, as first author you might say? Because Valle brought me to an understanding of Unamuno, Unamuno did not bring me to Valle.

"Valle is the central figure of modern Spanish literature": An invidious statement, but perhaps it will evoke a deeper scholarship, deeper, dear reader, than the one you now have before you.

(A note to myself: now write up Azorín and Baroja).

APPENDIX II

Azorín

I have read in some article or other that Azorín is an author of the second category, which means I suppose that he does not belong up there with the others, on some Parnassus. I cannot agree with this disesteem. At home I have his *Obras completas* and have read a good share of them, but I should base my case for Azorín's inclusion amongst the Elect on one short novel alone, *Don Juan*. I do not imply that his other works are wanting, I merely believe this one work will explain his *opera*.

Perhaps Azorín's being considered second rate by some observers stems from his lack of dogmatism, for no matter what the intellectuals say, they like a firm statement, be it Valle's *Lámpara*, Unamuno's rhetoric of assertion, Cartesianism, Voltairean negativity, Kantianism, Liberalism, or doctrines from the Political Right. People like to be told. And Azorín is not like that; his *lejanía ideal* is always what is says it is, distant, soft, gentle, hushed, diminutive, old, even subdued. His narrators are like that, and, who knows, even he himself might have been too; after all, don Pío Baroja, He Of The Harsh Judgment, has in his essays some kind words for Azorín, calling him a good friend (he certainly has no such words for Unamuno). Be that as it may, we are only interested in *Don Juan* and his narrator. (His Don Juan of course is not Don Juan, the contumelious presumer of Seville, but more a penitent of Gonzalo de Berceo, a new St. Francis Assisi.)

This novel of Azorín is the perfect impressionist picture of Spain, and Don Juan is the compleat Spaniard. Menéndez Pidal has said that if you want to know Spain you need only read *Don Quixote* and the *Romancero*: I should add, and Azorín's very brief *Don Juan*, if you want to know Spain both ancient and modern. Spain is the theme of the book, although there is a hushed hint, a slight gesture, a tiny finesse toward the *lejanía ideal*, which I gather is not phenomenal but the vision of Novalis's blue flower.

Don Juan might be renamed *Trasuntos de España*, which is the title of another book by Azorín.

APPENDIX III

A Millenarian Tale: The Hymn of Pipa Kif
(With Apologies to *The Hymn of the Pearl*)

Behold I was born of a Great King and when I was young in my Father's house all was peaceful and quiet. There was joy in the land. But then one day some robbers came and stole me from my couch and took me to a horizon where they stripped me of my garments, clothed me in some beggars' rags and left me to my fate. I took up with a band of vagabonds who brought me to a desert place with many caves by a great sea near a giant rock, and I grew up there surrounded by thieves and hypocrites, with bulbous eyes and facial tics and physical distortion. Friars and statesmen came and pursuers of gain, liars and cheats and counterfeiters. I forgot my noble birth and where I came from, a palace in a land of peace and quiet.

I stayed within my cave and never ventured forth and grew accustomed to the dim light and shadows on the wall. My eyes too grew dim and when people spoke I saw their form but indistinctly as from afar, and if they moved about I could barely distinguish them from dogs and horses. At last I kept to myself and paid attention to no one. I found myself all alone.

One day a strange man came at eventide and in the twilight I thought he was a goat or monkey. He did a cabriole, a pirouette, he stood on his head and attracted my attention. I could see he was strangely garbed, with a turban and robe and yard-long beard and one of his arms was missing. He was lopsided. His ring flashed, an unwonted sight in the dimness of the cave and he began to stammer, such gibberish I have never heard. Still his stuttering stirred a faint memory, I couldn't tell what, a faint, vague, distant hint, like a memory, not a thought exactly but a slow, interior movement. And then . . . he took out a pipe and began to play a tune I had never heard and do a dance I had never seen, a weird, uncanny rhythm. I don't know how, I can't explain, my mind had grown so torpid, but the rhythm swelled and took me beyond my cave to the sea and rock and further to the mountains and there beyond the horizon I could see a plain and my father's house, the light, the peace and quiet.

The one-armed loon is gone now, I shall never see him again, and I shall be going too on a distant timeless journey. I can still hear the music and he left behind a chapbook with notes which I can play if I want to. But that hardly seems necessary. I shall leave my cave and wander to the sea and mountains and plain, where I shall find the horizon. And beyond I shall find my father's palace, I am going home.

 **LAUS DEO**

The Celtic New Year: This is the night when the veil between the two worlds thins . . .

APPENDIX IV

Opinion

I believe my thesis will support the following argument:
Until the year 1800 or so people knew there were two worlds, this everyday world we live in, where people are born, eat food, make love, have children and die, and the next world, where they go after death to be happy. Call this next world the Bosom of Abraham, the Communion of Saints, the Mystical Body or simply Heaven, it was very real. There was a veil between the two worlds, which thinned for simple folk on the Eve of All Saints; since there were pagan remnants and superstition, on this Halloween hobgoblins, witches, brooms, teensie weensies or lighted pumpkins decorated the scene. The veil thinned for the literate in books like Dante's *Commedia*, Calderon's *Vida es sueño*, Augustine's *Civitas Dei* or the lessons of St. Francis de Sales, all of which artistically demonstrated the *reality* of the two worlds. There were some skeptics to be sure who either doubted or ignored the world beyond the veil, but a formidable opponent, Blaise Pascal, peerless scientist and writer of prose, held the ground: There were two worlds, and a veil, a frightening abyss, and one had to make a choice, a wager, there was no getting away from it.

But then a series of philosophers entered the scene and began to question the nature of *metaphysics*, the very term suggesting that there are two worlds, the physical world and the *meta* world beyond, a world resembling the forms outside Plato's cave. Finally the greatest modern philosopher of all came and divided the two worlds, calling them *phenomena* and *noumena*. There was no longer to be a veil but a wall, so high there was no peering over it. The one world, *phenomena*, could be known, but the other world, *noumena*, could not be known; the metaphysical world, or the next world as it is sometimes called, could not be known. This problem caused the German Pietist, Immanuel Kant, no problem because given his early religious training he *simply knew* there was another, invisible world; he could always exercise his practical reason and MORALIZE, and arrive at a sense of duty that told him it was there: Yes, there is another world, there are *noumena*. Why? Because why that's why, because. *Porque sí.*

But how about those thinkers who weren't raised as Pietists or in any other faith following the Good Book, those who had no world of universals to draw on? Suppose their pure reason told them that noumena were perhaps unknowable, and they had no practical moralizing reason to tell them that, "yes, noumena exist, your sense of duty should tell you that." Might these faith-less thinkers not argue: "Well, pure reason tells us we can't know noumena; then, how do we know they exist? Perhaps there is no

188

world of noumena, perhaps there is nothing beyond the veil, perhaps there is no veil for the simple reason there is nothing to veil. Nothing to hide. Look about you, the *it* there, see it, touch it, smell it, feel it, hear it: That is all we've got. There is no other world."

This intellectual story might take place after 1788, between 1800 perhaps and 1850. The way would be opened for a new materialism, a positivism that would hail the reality of this palpable world, converting it into a religion, and of a naturalism that would eliminate noumenal activity like free will. Translated into literary art, this might mean an emphasis on quantity, on palpable action, on a minute description of the profile of things. In the hands of a great artist, a *garbancero* so to speak but nonetheless great, this material emphasis might be wholesome, even welcome, but in the hands of lesser authors surely it would be disastrous, especially in the theater, where prosaic prose would be substituted for lyrical poetry, and the trivia of a so-called well-made play, a totally soul-less artificial construction, a glass of tepid water, would be substituted for authentic themes, dramatic poetry, choreography, and intelligent spectacle and diction.

And in politics, was the situation not like art? True the monstrous Church had received its comeuppance, but after the suppression of the monasteries in 1837, had the political and economic scene really improved? Instead of counterfeit, stealthy friars, wasn't the stage now filled with inflated hypocritical buffoons, avaricious *haute bourgeoisie*, pompous men of selfish rhetoric?

A few men tried to fill the void, *krausistas* they called themselves, but though their motives were pure and their actions good, they were an artless crew. Just read Francisco Giner de los Ríos's twenty volumes, well intentioned to be sure, but uninspiring reading. Big fat tomes of materialist prose, positivist really. One can hardly find this exciting.

That's it, that's the key: Materialist prose. Materialism is stolid but prose should be art, the two just don't go together. Yes, there is a reality, another reality, the only one that counts. Art will tell you that:—the Lay of the Cid, the ballads, ancient cathedrals, Santillana, Manrique, Galician singsong, an *auto sacramental*, legends of yore, a Basque *versolari*, St. Bernard of Clairvaux, Tristan and Isolde, a guerrillero, a superstitious old woman—they all belong to another existence really, they're not like those *fantoches* in the Cortes or that hypocrite in his cassock ostentatiously telling his beads. They're different, they move you. They're above money and greed and power, they don't care about these things. They're . . . beautiful. You can love them.[1] They're beyond, or they point beyond "the uncertain form of things," beyond the grotesque monsters before us, beyond time and the

189

here and now—they're eternal. Yes, that's it, eternal, and an art must be created to capture them, to arrest them, to immobilize them in the stream of life, to preserve them for eternity, the eternal moment. My heart tells me this, my feeling . . . my very *being*. That's the way things are. (This is the *Lámpara*; this is the *Critique of Aesthetic Reason*, or better said, *Critique of Aesthetic Divination*.)[2]

This, then, is my thesis. There are two worlds, the visible and the invisible. The Kantian revolution split the two worlds, making the invisible one inaccessible; more than that, the latter simply wasn't there. But as every man who tills the soil knows, every Galician peasant, everyone in communion with Nature, there are indeed two worlds, yes there are!, but a veil lies between them. And on Halloween, when hobgoblins roam, the Galician peasant gets an insight into the invisible world, and the veil between the two worlds thins. But there is another way of piercing the veil, or transcending it, the Halloween art of Don Ramón María del Valle-Inclán y Montenegro. There it is. Just listen. Hear it.

APPENDIX V

Thoughts I'd Rather Not Leave in the Inkwell

I suppose I might call this appendix "Thoughts I'd Rather Not Leave In The Inkwell," thoughts I'd like to include in this workbook. Perhaps the students can use them.

(1) It's odd how a great artist will affect many of your thoughts and almost everything you read. Whenever I read of war in the newspapers I think of the Carlist trilogy, or when I see a homicide like Noriega or Hussein I think of Tirano Banderas. In literature, when I chance upon the uncanny, the weird, the archaic, the mystic, or aesthetic deformation, I naturally think of Valle-Inclán. I shall now give two unexpected examples, which are typical.

During my sabbatical year of 1992-1993 I planned to go to Germany, so I decided to read Gordon Craig's book *The Germans*. I had read many of his articles in the *New York Review Of Books*, his textbook on European History and his lectures on Bismarck so I knew his study would be worthwhile.

Chapter IX of Craig's book is called "Romantics," where he quotes from Tieck's novel *Franz Sternbald's Wanderings*, and speaks of archaism and *Schwärmerei*, forces of terror and violence, *Sehnsucht*, a poetical world of fancy and wonder, a sinister wood, Twilight, the chtonic, irrational forces, a curiosity about the supernatural, fundamental pessimism, transfiguration, the world of dream and myth, the spell of music, the refinements of decay, the sultry combination of eroticism and religiosity, the lost world of childhood, dream elements, the last elements of nature against an artificial world, the will, the longing, a form of primitivism, myth, the Blue Flower—when I read all these expressions, and others, I immediately thought of Valle-Inclán. Craig's discussion of the Romantics seems to apply to Valle. This Galician pied piper, then, is a Romantic or perhaps better said, a Manichaean neo-Romantic, and Craig's *malaise allemand* is converted in him into the *malaise espagnol*. I conclude that Valle should be read above all in the light of German Romanticism and metaphysics.

(2) The other author that made me think of Valle is the psychiatrist, Karl Stern, whose autobiography appeared in 1951. Later Stern wrote a book on the feminine question ("the rejection of the feminine") called *The Flight From Woman*. His arguments concerning the *mysterium tremendum*, the vast time universe, *bios*, the polarity of the sexes, the chtonic, Jung's *Animus* and *Anima*, archaic imagery, a pre-rational world, discursive reason and intuition, and decadence—his arguments will, I believe, throw light on the female figures (figures, not characters) in the four seasonal sonatas, and in a sonata like

"Eulalia." I believe one can say that Eulalia's "outlines blend mysteriously with the chtonic," and that she, like an infant, inhabits "a vast time universe." I conclude that Valle should be read in the light of archaic imagery, the world of childhood and the chtonic.

(3) I shall leave it to Valle's biographers to write a detailed *Life*, but here is a stellar vision of its quintessence, a *finesse*:

Two men are born into a land of ancient tradition, known as *casticismo*. It is a Catholic, Latin land, in the South the country of Ave María Purísima, in the North of Castilian fortitude in the face of Moors and infidels. It can boast of Pelayo, San Fernando, Isabel I, Manrique, Garcilaso, Lope, Cervantes, and its greatest writers are saints, Teresa and Juan. But this *casticismo*, this golden age, has come to an age of iron. The generals are no Pelayo, the clergy no San Juan de la Cruz, in a nutshell, the court of Isabel II is not the court of Isabel I. The regnant vice is hypocrisy.

One of the men born into this land is the gentle priest, Fernando de Castro, chaplain of the Queen. He has been likened to Saint Francis Assisi, but this is not the thirteenth century, and he is so scandalized by the *furor erótico* of his court and country and the inattention to Christ's poor, he abandons his orthodoxy to become a heterodox *krausista*. He will not suffer hypocrisy. His action is frightening in the nineteenth century, but he places his faith in his Risen Savior. He strives irenically for the education of Spain. He is praised by the humble Concepción Arenal.

The second man is Ramón . . . to be renamed Don Ramón del Valle-Inclán y Montenegro. He has seen the hypocrisy Castro has seen, but he has never been likened to Saint Francis Assisi. In talent he has few peers (I should argue no peers in his day), and his pride and hurt are equal to his talent. His peers are Juvenal and Quevedo, and he will spare nothing to right the wrong, neither himself, his country nor his family. He will live in great pain. Down with *casticismo*, down with Santos Banderas, who is as Spanish as he is American. Valle is far too bright to be a positivist, to be restrained by the fetters of matter, and far too dedicated, too incisive to shrug it all off with a frown. He reads incessantly, books from the East, books from the West, Manichaeanism, Valentinianism, Zoroastrianism, the little flowers of Saint Francis, the sermons of Saint Bernard, theosophy, spiritism, idealism, and arrives at, or is thrust upon a strange conclusion: There is indeed something out there, or Something, call it the *Alma Mundo*, call it the Form beyond Plato's cave, call it Nature, call it what you will, because no matter what you will it, the name will not suffice; it is there though and demands a kind of Communion or Eucharist or Holy Word, yes, the *Verbo*, the priest's *Verbo*, no, the poet's *verbo*, the rhythm of poetry and sex and dance; yes, the poet, the idealist poet can do that, he is the spirit, the truth, the way and light, a sort of Christus whose sonatas will be bound as prayer books. To the uninitiated, the shopkeepers, the philistine professors, this stellar vision of reality might seem like balderdash, mere abracadabra, and should be rejected out of hand, except for one thing: Its author is the greatest artist of his day and must be taken seriously.

(4) Perhaps a psychoanalyst should study Valle-Inclán, not as a clinical case of course, but for his literary symbols, his markers, his clues, his *claves líricas*. Denis de Rougemont once said that myths are to society what dreams are to one of us, to you, dear reader and me, separately. Perhaps Valle's decadence belongs proximately to the dream world and ultimately to myth, for example, Eulalia's drowning in a darkened river, taking her own life. The chtonic.

(5) Valle's code will lead to self anagnorisis. That's what descrying the noumena is, or means: We will see ourselves-as-we-are-in-ourselves. We are a transcendent, Manichaean, aesthetic soul (better said, spark), in tune with the Grand Harmony: Salvation.

(6) I don't think Valle would call his way a code or even a system. Gnostics like him don't have codes or systems, they *simply know*. It is better to say *lamp* than *code*. Nevertheless, if the critic speaks of a code he can reduce it to nine or seventeen words: (1) Musical art pierces the veil between phenomena and noumena, or, (2) Musical art pierces the veil between phenomena and the world of things-as-they-are-in-themselves.

(7) In the *New York Times Book Review* of May 30, 1993, an article appeared concerning Antoine de Saint-Exupéry's *The Little Prince*. One sentence of the article reads:

> It is altogether appropriate that the book's most quoted line—'What is essential is invisible to the eye'—should be spoken by the fox. (*New York Times Book Review*, p. 15).

This sentence may be predicated of the sonatas of Valle-Inclán, which, according to him, are aimed at essentials, and essentials are invisible. Valle is an old fox.

APPENDIX VI

Octavio Paz: Las Trampas de la Crítica

SOR JUANA INÉS DE LA CRUZ:
LAS TRAMPAS DE LA CRITICA

Gerard Flynn
University of Wisconsin, Milwaukee

In 1982 Octavio Paz published his remarkable book *Sor Juana Inés de la Cruz o Las trampas de la fe*[1], to which he added subsequent editions in 1983 and a reprinting in 1985, the copy I have used for the present study. It is important to note these subsequent editions because they include, in an Appendix, a letter from Sor Juana to her confessor Padre Antonio Núñez. This letter, a new discovery not published until 1981 by Padre Aureliano Tapia Méndez, seems to bear out some of the conjectures made by Octavio Paz many years before.

I have called Paz's long volume remarkable because it is one of those books you live with for a while rather than read in passing. I myself read it over the winter vacation of 1986-1987, perhaps forty pages a day, which I reflected on every night. This paper is a result of those reflections.

The reader can only admire this new book. Into it a poet, who writes a limpid prose, puts some fifty years of his thoughts on Latin American colonial history, Mexican history, European history, neo-Platonic philosophy, mysticism, biography, Peninsular literature, European literature, notably the English and the French with some Italian, jurisprudence, psychology, and subjects like prosody, metrics and literary criticism. In a word, the tome is encyclopedic, though not at the expense of profundity. You might consult, for example, his chapters on the *Neptuno alegórico* and the *villancicos*, two areas of literature many modern critics tend to neglect. And his studies of authors like Atanasio Kircher and Marsilio Ficino, whom he relates to Sor Juana, are truly a labor of love. I gather that Octavio Paz has poured his heart and soul into his book, *Sor Juana Inés de la Cruz*, and that were we to inquire he might tell us it is his *hijo predilecto*; he might just reply that *Sor Juana Inés de la Cruz* is a poem, his best poem, a new genre, a lyrical essay.

I should like now to examine two parts of Paz's book, pages 11-18, where he explains what I will call his "epistemology of literary criticism" and pages 469-507, his estimate of the *Primero Sueño*, a patently epistemological poem. The two parts I have just mentioned are inseparable and contain the key to the entire volume. Paz begins by saying (p. 13):

Hay algo que está en la obra y que
no está en la vida del autor, ese
algo es lo que se llama creación o
invención artística y literaria.
El poeta, el escritor, es el olmo
que sí da peras.

He correctly advises us here against the autobiographical fallacy, suggesting that literary *opera* are not limited to being the record of an author's life; and so he correctly chides Padre Calleja, Sor Juana's contemporary, for interpreting everything Sor Juana writes as an ascent to sanctity; in the opposite corner, he also chides Ludwig Pfandl for examining Sor Juana's literature psychoanalytically, as a "fixation on the paternal image, leading her to narcissism."

As for the expression "El poeta . . . es el olmo que sí da peras", this may be the most striking verse ever written by Octavio Paz, because poets and poetry certainly bear unexpected fruit, perfections and grotesques not to be observed elsewhere in nature. I would add a *caveat* here, however, by saying that poetry and literary criticism are not one and the same thing, nor is a literary critic *qua* critic a poet. He does not enjoy poetic license. Although a critic may have great poetical insight, he cannot be an elm tree bearing pears but only elm seeds or elm shoots or elm leaves, whatever it is that elm trees grow. I would draw here on a phrase from the late Professor Otis Green, who in his study *Spain and the Western Tradition*, volume I, p. vi, speaks of "textual control of the imagination", which he sees as the core of literary criticism; you might say it is Green's definition of literary criticism[2]. Literary

195

critics may let their imagination roam freely providing they rein it in from time to time with the text at hand, for if this is not done criticism becomes a kind of gab session, an open panel where a gaggle of voluntarists say whatever they please. No, the critic may read the text and on it erect as many imaginative superstructures, categories, as he descries, but he should not create categories beforehand, pigeon holes (or pear holes if you will) and then stuff the author's text into them. There must be textual control.

Perhaps the preceding paragraph may be stated differently: The imagination is poetic, it is poetry, and textual control is scientific, it is science. Thus literary criticism lies between science and poetry, and as science it cannot be an elm tree producing exotic fruit.

Let us turn to another thought. On page 14 Paz writes:

> Las obras no responden a las
> preguntas del autor sino a las del
> lector. Entre la obra y el autor
> se interpone un elemento que los
> separa: el lector. Una vez
> escrita, la obra tiene una vida
> distinta a la del autor; la que
> le otorgan sus lectores sucesivos.

In this passage Paz seems to argue against the intentional fallacy, which has received so much attention these last four decades, and he draws from his literary theory an allegedly apodictic reader-response clause. The *lectores sucesivos*—let us call them the Lectorial Succession—must practise good bookmanship because given the limited understanding of all authors, who may create in their poems forms and ideas they never intended, the readers alone with their right of succession can impart life to them. This argument to be sure is epistemological and one might even say ontological. I myself should call Paz's opinion a critical idealism[3], for just as Bishop Berkeley argued that there is no existence of matter independent of perception, or Fichte, that the individual ego is the source of experience, so, according to Paz, literary texts enjoy no formal existence unless we read them (left to themselves

196

they are inchoate prime matter), and no meaning unless we read the preferences of our individual egos into them[4]. It seems to me that Paz's critical idealism will lead to literary chaos and that an author like Sor Juana will become whatever readers will her to be: orthodox, pantheist, irreligious, intellectual, protestant, medieval, mystical, Renaissance, Baroque, modern, nationalist, Marxist. Why not? Under the Lectorial Succession critics become poetical elm trees freely exercising their imaginations and often yielding pears. I myself prefer a middle ground emphasizing both the dignity of the reader and of the text. The reader's intentions have a certain rectitude and so do the author's; and the text, the book at hand, is the common ground for assembly[5]. Although the book is out of the author's hands the reader will respect the author and his work of art by exercising textual control of his own inspiration.

Having placed literary works in the hands of readers (Las obras no responden a las preguntas del autor sino a las del lector), Paz speaks of another kind of reader, the *lectores terribles*, by which he means the censors of the seventeenth century and the censors we have today, that is to say, the Tertullian ecclesiastics of Baroque Spain amd the orthodox Marxists of our present scene. These censors create codes of what you and I may or may not write ("el código de lo decible"), some of which are explicit and some implicit, the latter being more profound. Consequently, we must pay attention to those things Sor Juana does not say, to those subjects she passes over, for they tell a great story; indeed, silence is an eloquent raconteur. I would agree with Paz that we must read between the lines, in all authors, but I would add that before reading between the lines we must first examine the lines themselves, for otherwise there is no silence to be observed. This means once again "textual control of the imagination"; the reader cannot create the lines subjectively through critical idealism and then read between them; he must first establish the lines (the text), as Alfonso Méndez Plancarte did thirty-five years ago, and then establish their meaning, as most of the older critics, Abreu Gómez in the van, did not do thirty-five and more years ago; having made this establishment he can then observe the silence. This is the way the critic should approach all of Sor Juana's texts, especially the epistemological *Primero Sueño.* After discussing the *lectores terribles* (Alas!, aren't we all at times *lectores terribles?*) Paz closes his prologue:

La obra sobrevive a sus lectores;
al cabo de cien o doscientos años
es leída por otros lectores que
le imponen otros sistemas de
lectura e interpretación.

I should answer yes and no. The early Don Quixote may have been a figure of fun and his book a funny book[6], whereas after the Romantic criticism of the year 1800 he has become the dreamer of impossible dreams and paradigm of all humanity, but is the Quixote always in a state of becoming?; is it always and everywhere relative to the age in which it is read? Is this novel written only for nominalists and relativists? Is there nothing we can take as given, nothing we can seize and hold and say "this is ours?", nothing corresponding to Platonic forms? Consider the phrase again:

Las obras no responden a las
preguntas del autor sino a las
del lector . . . la que le
otorgan sus lectores sucesivos.

Can this opinion be predicated of the beautiful Marcela who disdains temporal pleasure as she seeks her first abode, or of the braying ass aldermen in the 1615 book who abuse the doctrine of just war, or of Anselmo who destroys his wife, his friend and himself by testing that which absolutely cannot be tested, absolutely, that which no subjective state can alter, the love of one human being for another, especially of a man for his wife? The Lectorial Succession may uncover truths in the text hitherto not detected but they do not radically alter the text unless they are misguided, or, like Fernández de Avellaneda, he of the false *Quixote,* choose deliberately to be mistaken.

We come now to Octavio Paz's chapter on the *Primero Sueño* (pp. 469-507) and here more than elsewhere I must part ways with his critical idealism for he lets his great poetical faculty, his imagination, *la loca de la casa*, go astray. These forty pages are a work of art, a lyrical essay, but they issue from the author's heartfelt desires, from his advocacy, rather than from the lines of Sor Juana's text or the silence between them. Here Octavio Paz has created a series of pigeon holes and stuffed *El Primero Sueño* into them. Although few readers can match his diligence, zeal and poetry, any attentive reader may question his science.

First of all, Paz considers the *Primero Sueño* to be a confession, an autobiographical dream in which Sor Juana, like Saint Augustine before her and Rousseau after her, makes a formal avowal and revelation of her innermost thoughts and aspirations. She is like Phaeton, like Isis and the priestess of Apollo at Delphi. She is hermetic, neo-Platonic, a woman acquainted with the lore of Atanasio Kircher and Marsilio Ficino; she has an insatiable thirst to know more and not to know less, and so, given the rigid bureaucratic society of her day, with its *lectores terribles*, its Inquisitors ("no quiero ruido con la Inquisición") and purblind fanatical prelates like Archbishop Aguiar y Seixas, she describes a dream in which her rebel soul scales the highest mountain and, another Phaeton, rises to the stars to drive the chariot of the sun, the illumination of intellectual understanding, only to be struck down by Zeus (a *lector terrible*) for scorching the earth on its descent. The key word in this portrait is the *rebeldía* of Sor Juana, the thought that although she may have been outwardly orthodox and Scholastic, deep down within, in her heart of hearts, where the true self is, where the silence is, she was an intellectual who resisted and defied ecclesiastical and civil strait jackets. I ought to add that this interpretation of the *Sueño* is not abrupt; in an earlier chapter of the *Neptuno Alegórico* Octavio Paz built up a case for Sor Juana's Neo-Platonism and her vinculum with Isis and ancient Egypt.

I want to say it is not my purpose in this paper to argue with Paz's portrait of Sor Juana as a rebellious woman for that is not the question at hand, and it is such an interesting portrait it could easily become a red herring. No, the question boils down to this: Do the 975 verses of the *Primero Sueño* reveal her to be a Phaeton driving the chariot of the sun so high and then so close to the earth as to risk divine (ecclesiastical) retribution? Does the *Sueño* show her to be Neo-Platonic and hermetic, a daughter of Isis, as Octavio Paz pictures her? External evidence—her society, the history of Mexico, her criticism of Antonio Vieyra—are secondary here; only the internal evidence of the *Sueño* is primary. Textual control of the imagination.

In reading the Primero Sueño we should distinguish between the story it tells (*mythos*) and the meaning of the story (*dianoia*).

The narration itself is quite simple, although it is not told in a simple style. Night rises up from the earth to rule the atmosphere, and all sorts of life go to sleep—the birds, the beasts, the fish, nocturnal robbers, lovers, everything. There is total silence. The body sleeps a death-like sleep so that the soul no longer need govern it. The liberated soul senses its freedom and ascends a summit so high that Mt. Atlas and Mt. Olympus do not approach its slopes. Even the eagle who soars to the sun cannot reach this mountain top. The soul is alone, above the world, contemplating all of creation. Proudly it attempts to intuit its own being and the being of the entire universe but finds itself unequal to the task, for just as the eye, whose proper object is light, cannot look directly at the Sun without being blinded, so the soul cannot contemplate all of being without losing its sight (vv. 412-539). In trying to see everything it will see nothing; it is simply stupefied by so many species. This is the defeat, the total rout, of cosmic intuition.

What then happens to the soul? In verses 540-638 Sor Juana changes her metaphor from the eye blinded by light to a ship battered at sea. In these verses the soul flees intuition and universal being for more modest ground, namely the evidence of the senses and individual, separate being. Like the ship with broken mast and shattered rudder, it seeks the mental shore. It will kiss each grain of sand, it will look at one thing at a time, it will use

Aristotle's ten categories of being—substance, quantity, quality, relation, place, time, situation, action, passion and possession—since it cannot know all of creation in one intuitive act. It will follow the scale of being, it will examine the mineral, vegetable and animal worlds.

In the remaining verses the *Sueño* says that the soul cannot understand the simple things of this world, a fountain, a lily, a rose. How then can it ever hope to understand by one intuitive glance the cosmos and all of Nature? There was indeed a youth who tried to drive the chariot of the Sun, Phaeton (v. 786), but his example is not to be followed. At dream's end the body starts to wake up, the eyes open, the senses recover and the brain is free of oniric phantasms. The sun arrives, the world is lighted and "I am awake." What is the philosophic meaning behind this narrative?

Sor Juana's dream is an Aristotelian —Thomistic explanation of the nature of human knowledge. Man is higher than the other animals, whose knowledge is restricted to the evidence of the senses, and lower than the angels, those pure spirits who by their nature intuit the reality of things or enjoy infused knowledge. Man is a "triple composition" (v. 655) since in addition to his own rational nature he possesses the natures of plants and animals; but man's animal condition is a "haughty baseness" (v. 694) for through his intellect he can rise above all visible creation. Thus he is the hinge linking the material and spiritual worlds (v. 659) and the seat of that "amorous union" (v. 699) by which the Word, Christ, became flesh.

If man has a low estate, like the plants and animals, he also has a dignity comparable to that of the angels. He must not, however, look upon himself as an angel, for that is an act of pride characteristic of a Phaeton, who attempted to steer the sun. Any human being who tries to intuit the spheres as if he were an angel (vv. 297-302) will find that he must rush down from his high mountain and return to the mental shore (v. 566). What is that mental shore? It is the evidence of the senses and discursive reasoning. Man abstracts his ideas from sense evidence for "there is nothing in the intellect that was not first in the senses." Man cannot intuit everything at once, his intellect is not equal to the charge, nor can he simply know things, one fountain, one lily, one rose. Individual objects escape his definition. But he is able to consider phenomena one at a time, abstract universal ideas (v. 588) from his sense data, and so have a glimpse into the essence of things. He can use the ten categories of Aristotle (v. 582). In a word, he can reason discursively (v. 579) as indeed he must for it is his nature to do so.

In keeping with her Scholastic training, Sor Juana held the idea of God The First Cause, Nature the secondary cause (v. 623) and a natural law uninterrupted by God in its operation. Her poem tells us that man has to be true to his own nature for if he attempts to act beyond it he will suffer metaphysical inundations holding him to his natural state.

Thus I cannot agree with Octavio Paz that Sor Juana resembles Phaeton, offspring of the god Helios, who drove his chariot so near the earth he nearly scorched it and had to be stopped by Zeus's thunderbolt, a figure of pride and rebellion. Rather I see her as a courageous intellectual who stood up and spoke her mind when someone had to stand up to be counted. She seems to have paid a price for her fortitude, as Paz suggests, but she paid it for the sake of an ancient devotion to truth rather than for some modern hubristic individualism. I must say that in January of 1987 I lay down Octavio Paz's great book with a sense of sadness. It might have been a polestar for all of us to follow, perhaps an *Anatomy of Latin American Criticism*, but owing to its author's subjectivity and critical idealism, his penchant for yielding hermetic pears where the fruit of the elm is called for, it has fallen short of that distinction.[7]

NOTES
[1] See Octavio Paz, *Sor Juana Inés de la Cruz o las trampas de la fe*, 3a. edición (México: Fondo de Cultura Económica, 1885).
[2] See Otis Green, *Spain and the Western Tradition* (Madison: University of Wisconsin Press, 1968), Vol. I, p. vi.
[3] Alfred North Whitehead has said that all philosophy is a footnote to Plato, and following his lead Lionel Trilling has written: "It can be said that all prose fiction is a variation on the theme of

Don Quixote. Cervantes set for the novel the problem of appearance and reality . . ." Trilling, *The Kenyon Review*, Winter 1948, as quoted in Miguel de Cervantes, *Don Quixote*, translated by Samuel B. Putnam (New York: Random House—Modern Library, 1948), p. 469. One might continue in this vein by saying that all literary criticism is a footnote to philosophy, and so Paz's reader-response position is a footnote to Idealism. It would be interesting to examine the literary positions of recent years as footnotes, for example, formalism, structuralism, semiotics.

[4] Shades of Unamuno, who displays the preferences of his ego in *Vida de Don Quixote y Sancho!*

[5] The intentional fallacy, as it has been called, applies to the reader as well as the author. The reader's intentions are far less important than Paz seems to think, so that reader-response positions such as his should always carry a *caveat.*

[6] See P.E. Russell, *"Don Quixote as a Funny Book,"* in *Modern Language Review*, vol. LXIV (1969), pp. 312-326.

[7] During the discussion following this *ponencia* two ideas were introduced throwing light on "las trampas de la crítica". First, in 1925 Américo Castro published his *Pensamiento de Cervantes*, where he argues that in *Don Quixote* Cervantes was writing with tongue in cheek. Some time after that Ermilo Abreu Gómez read Castro's opinion and applied it to Sor Juana; thus in his prologue to the *Poesías* of Sor Juana he writes: "Ya Américo Castro ha mostrado las reservas mentales con que, en materias de fe y política, se expresaba Cervantes". And also: "Es necesario rastrearlo (el pensamiento vivo de Sor Juana) en el acervo de su obra llena de disimulos y reservas". (Sor Juana, *Poesías*, Edición de Ermilo Abreu Gómez (México: Ed. Botas, 1940), pp. 17, 85). Thus began the criticism of the Abreu Gómez school (Anita Arroyo, Clara Campoamor, Elizabeth Wallace). Octavio Paz's book falls within this tradition, although it stands head and shoulders over the others. My own reaction to the Abreu Gómez School is similar to that of Samuel B. Putnam towards Américo Castro: "After reading and rereading *Don Quixote* many times and studying every line and word, as a translator must, I remain

unconvinced by Professor Castro's theory to the effect that Cervantes wrote with tongue in cheek and dissimulated his real views in order to evade the censures of the Holy Office. The argument is an ingenious one, based largely upon textual control and linguistic interpretations, but it may be met with an equal degree of ingenuity, as Aubrey Bell and Father Rubio have shown". Putnam also mentions the arguments of Helmuth Hatzfeld and Joaquín Casalduero. See Cervantes, *Don Quixote* (New York: Penguin Books, The Viking Portable Library, 1976), pp. 29-30. Second, in the earlier chapters of his book Octavio Paz frequently employs expressions like "No es difícil que . . .", "No es imposible que . . .", "Es fácil que . . .", all of them followed by subjunctives of conjecture. In literary criticism, it is better not to base arguments on subjunctives of conjecture, especially when they argue for "las trampas de la fe". A critic like Paz has the privilege of not accepting the religious faith and institutions of seventeenth century Spain, but he should not predicate his own bias of seventeenth century authors unless he finds internal evidence in the text for doing so.

This article is taken from *Sor Juana Inés de la Cruz: Selected Studies*, edited by Luis Cortest (Asunción: Colección de Estudios Humanísticos y Sociales, 1989), pp. 44-52.

I shall close my appendices here and with them my book. In closing, I want to reiterate the following ideas: (1) This is the code of Valle-Inclán: distance (*lejanía*), millenary chronology, aesthetic deformation, music, dance, synesthesia, instead of *sentido ideológico*, in order to pass from *phenomena* to *noumena*, in order to capture Novalis's blue flower, and (2) The Halloween Art of Valle-Inclán, the night the veil between the two worlds thins, is the gnostic attempt to arrive at the world of things-as-they-are-in-themselves.

I have enjoyed writing this book and hope that my readers find it delightful and instructive, or, in the words of Cervantes:

". . . y, finalmente, (la poesía) deleita y enseña a cuantos con ella comunican." (*La gitanilla*)

". . . and, finally, poetry delights and instructs those who commune with her."[1]

END NOTES

Prologue

[1] Desmond MacCarthy was quoted in the *London Review of Books* in 1990 or 1991.
[2] The references are to Marcel Bataillon's *Erasme et Espagne*, a study of Renaissance Spain, and Dámaso Alonso's famous 1927 dissertation, *La lengua poética de Góngora*, which solved the riddle of the baroque Prince of Darkness.

First Proem

There are no notes.

Second Proem

[1] Given the subjectivity of recent critical theory and its consequent relativism, I am not sure everyone will construe the word *code* as I do. As I say, I am following Webster: You keep repeating certain words and phrases over and over again, as Valle does, because you wish to point to something else. In his case, that something is hidden and ultimate, or I should say, Ultimate. As for Valle himself, I don't believe he would talk of a code. Gnostics don't have codes, they *simply know*: they might, however, write a *Lámpara maravillosa*.
[2] I deliberately write *events* rather than *phenomena*, so as to avoid confusion with my use of *phenomenon* later on.
[3] Azorín (José Martínez Ruiz), *Don Juan* (Madrid: Espasa-Calpe, 1968), p. 42.
[4] The episode of the Niña Chole—her action before the statue of the Christ Child—lies far below Valle's talent, so far below it passes belief. One can only surmise that even great geniuses slip at times into the role of smart alecs.
[5] See my article on Octavio Paz, "Las trampas de la crítica," which I have placed in an appendix. It is saddening to read Paz's essay, where trendy criticism has destroyed what might have been the pearl of Latin American criticism.
[6] When I speak of form, I am thinking of Plato's Ideas and Aristotle's hylomorphism. Please remember that this paper is an essay, an attempt to open a door. I make no claim for the final word. Indeed, I believe the compleat *valleinclanista* should verse himself in German and German metaphysics, ancient Gnosticism, the Cathari and Albigensian Crusade, Symbolism, Yeats and Madame Blavatsky, Expressionism, Impressionism, Greek Philosophy, Spanish History, Translation (just try translating *El ruedo ibérico!*), *krausismo*, the Modernism of Loisy and Tyrrell and Modernism of Rubén Darío, orthodox and heterodox

mysticism, the *alumbrados*, Miguel de Molinos, and a host of other subjects. The compleat *valleinclanista* will require the erudition of Menéndez Pelayo and gracious insight of Dámaso Alonso. I make no such boast, I merely attempt to open a door. The criticism of Valle-Inclán must be a cumulative effort.

Proem III

[1] See Ramón Gómez de la Serna, *Don Ramón María del Valle-Inclán* (Buenos Aires: Espasa-Calpe, 1944). Gómez de la Serna sings a joyous paean to the memory of Valle-Inclán. His biography agrees wholeheartedly with the aesthetic gnosticism of Valle and is filled with sentences like these: "Ya está en la nirvántica posición más envidiable del proverbio indio: ¡Que el Gran Silencio le consuele." (p. 215) . . . and . . ."Como convalecencia de su operación radical don Ramón comenzó a predicar por los cafés el quietismo, inspirado quizás por su mano quieta en el fondo de la fosa común, dormida en el nirvana de los brazos muertos." (p. 52) . . . and . . . "Adiós, mi querido y admirado don Ramón rey sin corona y sin un cobre, tu melena debía de campar aun entre nosotros . . ." (p. 216).

Gómez de la Serna approves Valle's insults and anti-social actions: "Un día tiró la colilla de su cigarro a la cara de un joven pintor . . ." (p. 88) . . ."Entraba en su filosofía el improperio liberado en la obra y en el café, porque lo que tiene que saber el escritor escritor—no el bodoque—es mucho de ascética." (p. 88). This attitude of Valle and of Serna brings up the question of the artist's responsibility, or irresponsibility. Serna writes: "Valle era el artista irresponsable que vivía entre sus grandes paradojas y su sobremadurada desesperación bohemia." (p. 120)

The question of the artist's responsibility or irresponsibility appears elsewhere in Spanish literature, e.g., in the criticism of the much more traditional don Juan Valera:

> Dice Enrique Heine, y tiene razón, si se despoja lo que dice del encarecimiento y de la imagen, propios de la poesía, y si se pone en estilo pedestre, que el poeta, rey del pensamiento por derecho divino, en virtud de la *gracia*, es irresponsable ante los hombres, los cuales podrán matarle, pero no juzgarle. En efecto la *gracia* limpia y justifica muchas cosas; el entusiasmo del poeta le hace en cierto modo y hasta cierto punto irresponsable. Además de ser rey por esta *gracia*, el poeta es rey por sufragio universal; rey de su público, cuyas opiniones repite con bella resonancia. Tiene, pues, el poeta todas las legitimidades modernas y antiguas, y no debemos

juzgarle en nombre de determinada creencia, opinión o secta." (Valera, *Apuntes sobre el nuevo arte de escribir novelas*, Capítulo VIII, in *Obras completas*, Tomo II, p. 679)

Doctoral students may want to study this question, which is philosophical and ethical rather than literary. Where does the artist's special *grace*, and irresponsibility as Valera and Heine call it, leave off, and his duties as a responsible citizen begin? Does the artist's privileged position permit his throwing cigarette butts in another man's face, or his engaging in insults (*improperios*, which sound very much like contumely). In other words, is libertine gnosticism an admissible system?

Canto I

[1] From the sonnet by Francisco de Quevedo.
[2] See Pedro Salinas, *Literatura española Siglo XX*, 2a. ed. (México: Antigua Librería Robredo, 1949). I shall quote from this book in the course of my study.
[3] Joan Maragall, *Elogios* (Buenos Aires: Espasa-Calpe, Col. Austral, 1950), p. 124:

> Y asimismo, paralelamente, en la danza encontramos el principio y el fin de todas las artes: desde la danza caótica de las olas en el mar y de toda multitud confusa y primitiva, hasta aquélla absolutamente individualizada y más pura que podemos imaginar, y que sentimos latir ya en el fondo de nuestros amores, de una Unica atrayendo a un Unico a confundirse con ella para siempre en amor en la suprema cima de la Belleza inmortal.

[4] Valle-Inclán, *La lámpara maravillosa* (Madrid: Espasa-Calpe, 1974), p. 54: "El baile es la más alta expresión estética, porque es la única que transporta a los ojos los números y las cesuras musicales."
[5] Read the *Lámpara*, pp. 76-78: ". . . las formas son logos de multiplicación, vasos fecundos de la imagen eterna." . . . "El erotismo anima como un numen las normas de aquel momento estético donde la voz del sexo es la voz del futuro." . . . "La primera rosa estética florece del concepto teológico del Logos Espermático."
[6] See the *Lámpara*; p. 70: "El espíritu de los gnósticos descubre una emoción estética en el absurdo de las formas, en la creación de monstruos, en el acabamiento de la vida . . ."
[7] I have translated *entraña* as *will*, but it might also be rendered

as *force*, or *power*, or even as *entrails*, given Valle's erotic vision of ultimate reality. I also translate *quieto* as *quiet*, whereas I might have used, *peaceful, tranquil, silent*, or *still*, because I am thinking of quietism and Miguel de Molinos, whom Valle mentions elsewhere.

[8] The student of Valle-Inclán would do well to read Johan Huizinga's *Homo Ludens*. I recall that Huizinga, following the lead of the German theologian Romano Guardini, suggests that even in the Mass there is an element of play.

[9] For the sake of brevity, I have coined two words for this study, *sonatic* and *esperpentic*, adjectives referring to Valle's *sonatas* and *esperpentos*. I have also coined the word *garbanzatic*, once humorously, and the second time as an adjective referring to the garbanzo bean or realist attitude towards literature.

[10] I have not used words like *signifier* and *signified*. Wherever possible, I shall use the language of common sense rather than the special language of science.

[11] *Écrasez l'infâme*: The phrase comes from Voltaire and means in effect "Crush the infamous beast," the beast being the Church and by extension the *ancien régime*.

[12] See Johan Huizinga, *Homo Ludens*.

[13] See Pedro Salinas, *Reality and the Poet*.

Canto II

[1] See Hans Jonas, *The Gnostic Religion*, p. 69.

[2] This paragraph will account for the extreme formalism of Pedro Salinas.

[3] See H. Cornélis, O.P. and A. Léonard, O.P., *La gnosis eterna* (Andorra: Editorial Casal I Vall, 1961).

[4] See Pedro Salinas, *Literatura Española Siglo XX*, Segunda edición *aumentada* (México: Antigua Librería Robredo, 1949), 101. Salinas's thoughts are a restatement of Valle's *Lámpara*: "Para los gnósticos la belleza de las imágenes no está en ellas, sino en el acto creador . . ." (*Lámpara*, p. 71).

[5] Speaking of *garbanzos*, perhaps a page from science and philosophy will help us here. Let us take the example of three persons, the scientist Piaget, a mother and a poet. Nobody knows more about children than the great Piaget, who has studied their every motion. His knowledge is unsurpassable. But a mother knows better than he, not more, but better, and when the child cries (even a child not her own) she can take him to her breast and console him, which Piaget cannot do. The two sorts of knowledge are different. Piaget is an eminent *garbancero* whereas the mother rather resembles a poet. Her wisdom used to be called knowledge by connaturality, a mode wherein she and the child become one, sharing as it were the same nature. One might also call this knowledge intuition.

208

The poet Rubén Darío resembled the mother when he wrote, intuitively, "A Margarita Debayle." He and the little girl in their psychology, nay, in their psyche, become one. Again, I would say that Galdós was far more than a *garbancero*, although he was that also. Rubén, on the other hand, couldn't change a baby's diaper: He wouldn't know where to look for the pin. Perhaps the genius of great novelists is that they are both, both Piaget and the mother.

[6] See my book *Luis Coloma* (Boston: G.K. Hall, 1987), pp. 11-13 for the remarks on Fernán Caballero, and pp. 53-55 for those relating to Coloma.

Canto III

[1] For deciphering the code of Valle-Inclán, no passage will equal the night of the garden in *Primavera* (pp. 41-42), where Bradomín says: ". . . y poco a poco mis ojos columbraron la forma incierta de las cosas." The images we perceive with our senses, the phenomena (shall we call them the alleged form of things?), hide the true form of things and make it uncertain. But the true form is the noumenon, plural *noumena*, which pertain to the world of things-in-themselves. This world is the aim of the poet's music and of his code. We shall discuss this later, when we study *Primavera*. But as I say, I can think of no more striking phrase in Valle than "poco a poco mis ojos columbraron la forma incierta de las cosas."

[2] There is an addition to *La Media Noche* called *En La Luz del Día*, which is appended to the former in the Espasa-Calpe, Colección Austral edition. For the passages cited see pp. 170 and 174 of this edition.

[3] In the Royal Academy's eighteenth edition of its *Diccionario* we read under *potencia://5*. Por antonomasia, cualquiera de las tres facultades del alma, de conocer, querer y acordarse, que son entendimiento, voluntad y memoria. In the dictionary of María Moliner, we read under *potencia del alma*: "En el catecismo se llaman 'potencias del alma' a la 'inteligencia, memoria y voluntad.' "

[4] The phrase calls to mind "un no sé qué quimérica ilusión" in the *Sonata de primavera*. Leathered pilots as scientific monsters are chimera or chimerical illusions. One of Valle's books will always evoke another. Some phrase, some image, some allusion will evoke another.

[5] I have translated *mancha* as *blur*; it could be a spot, stain, patch or blur. Azorín frequently uses this word. Just as in an impressionist painting, a fluff of cotton in a lady's hand becomes a lap dog as the viewer moves away from the portrait, so in impressionist writing, a blur in the scene (or a spot or stain or patch, that is to say, something indistinct) can become a herd of

cattle. Whereas I have also translated *confusamente* as *indistinctly*, it could also be construed as *hazily*. Such a word, along with *crepúsculo, penumbra, ráfaga, a lo lejos, vaho* and others is part of the code. One is dealing with something vague, hazy, indistinct. Phenomena like garbanzo beans have distinct profiles; they are so many millimeters long, they are red, yellow or blue on the chromatic scale, they are in the foreground or in the background on a designated spot, and so forth. But the code seeks to go beyond phenomena, which are a veil obscuring the true reality behind them, beyond them. And so the poet creates a haze, penumbras, gusts, twilight, in a word, *manchas*, beyond which is ultimate reality.

Canto IV

[1] In *La media noche* we also encounter the word *revoloteando*: "Las hojas de los árboles caen revoloteando" (p. 174). Falling, fluttering leaves should be considered part of the dance.
[2] Aristotle's criticism is discussed in Northrup Frye, *Anatomy of Criticism*.
[3] I cannot agree with Valle. I think that the plot is, as Aristotle suggests, the soul of a story, especially in books like the Carlist trilogy and *Tirano Banderas*. Valle is a great plot weaver in spite of himself.
[4] Strictly speaking, a criollo is the offspring of Spanish parents who is born in the Indies.
[5] This monadic structure is in keeping with the art of cubism, which the narrator associates with the novel. In *Tirano Banderas*, see the "Visión cubista del Circo Harris," in Libro Segundo, Segunda Parte (pp. 30-32), and also Libro III of the Quinta Parte: "Sentíanse alejados en una orilla remota, y la luz triangulada del calabozo realzaba en un módulo moderno y cubista la actitud macilenta de las figuras." (p. 95)
[6] By the way, I have left out the word *mojiganga*, which appears twice in the novel. *Mojigangas* were the farces in which the actors wore *botargas*. *Tirano Banderas* is among other things a *mojiganga*.
[7] I am troubled by one detail, the name of the honorable effeminate Minister of the Madre Patria, Don Mariano Isabel Cristino Queralt y Roca de Togores, the most ridiculous clown of the farce. In the nineteenth century, Mariano Roca de Togores (1812-1889) was the name of the Marqués de Molíns, friend of Larra, Vega, Pezuela, Escosura and Bretón de los Herreros, and Bretón's distinguished biographer. I find it difficult to believe that Valle is writing a *novela de clave*, with excessive individualization, which might detract from the art he so adored. A *clave* might reveal the hand of the puppeteer.

Curiously, P. Luis Coloma was accused of singling out Molíns for ridicule in his thesis novel, *Pequeñeces* (1891), where the character Butrón, like Molíns, is beetle-browed. In any case, I leave this issue to Valle's biographer.

[8] The bird of prey is indispensable here, since Santos Banderas also feeds on living and dead flesh.

[9] *Huevón* is an Americanism meaning stupid, lazy, sluggish, torpid, but in my translation I have chosen to retain the metaphor of eggs. The image is less figurative, stronger.

[10] The *facón* is a large knife that was used by the *gauchos*, and so it comes from Argentina rather than from equatorial Indians. This is one more proof of the novel's composite nature: It represents all Latin America.

[11] The passage suggest that the *vieja de rebocillo* is a *celestina*, a procuress.

[12] See also E.K. Rand, *The Founders Of The Middle Ages*. Rand is very fond of the founders of the Middle Ages, but not of Pope Gregory I, who spent years in Byznatium and never learned Greek. I daresay Gregory was interested in the evangels of the Church, which translate here as the good and the true, but not in beauty.

[13] Those interested in this idea might read Jacques Maritain's essay on Descartes in his *Trois Réformateurs*.

[14] Descartes, to be sure, excoriates Raymond Lull.

[15] I remember reading in *Time* magazine several years back of the closing of the Gran Guignol. The word *guiñolada* seems to be a neologism, and if by analogy we compare it with *canalla-canallada*, then a *guiñolada* would be the action of winking. Thus the characters in *Libro Tercero* of *Tirano Banderas* are trapped like puppets in a tableau, exchanging rigid winks, coarse remarks and chucks under the chin ("El Señor Inspector atravesó la estancia cambiando con unos y otros guiños, mamolas y leperadas en voz baja."—*Leperadas* is a Mexican expression.)

[16] As an admirer of Valle-Inclán's art (I should place him first among modern Spaniards), I abhor using words like *liberals, reactionaries* and *political reality*. But perhaps I can justify my using them: Whereas an historian or political scientist might write a thousand pages on liberals, reactionaries, government, Indians, mestizos, and so forth, Valle in two hundred pages provides an unforgettable experience and the reader is far the wiser. He has experienced (seen, felt, heard) the political reality.

[17] The triangle also happens to be Gnostic. See, e.g., the *Lámpara maravillosa*, p. 99: "Para el ojo que se abre en el gnóstico triángulo, todas las flechas que dispara el sagitario están quietas." Amidst the "ráfaga de violencias", amidst the phenomenal movement and sterile satan of Time, the gnosis will lead to the quietude of the eternal moment.

I may not place a great gnostic emphasis on Valle's triangles here since there is always room for an element of play, artistic play (see Huizinga, *Homo Ludens*). On the other hand, see the *Sonata de primavera*, where there are three doors, three *viejas*, three *aldabadas*, and "he blessed himself three times." Julio Casares, moreover, speaks of Valle's constant use of three adjectives. Then there is in *Tirano Banderas* the theosophical calabozo #3: *Libro Segundo* of the *Quinta Parte* is called *El número tres*. There are references to theosophy, the cabala, the occult and Alexandrine philosophy. There is also a Colonel Irineo Castañón: "Por hacerles a los políticos más atribulada la cárcel, les befaba con estas compañías, el de la pata de palo, coronel Irineo Castañín." The wryness of Valle's humor will not be lost on his reader. Saint Irenaeus (130-202) was the formidable opponent of the ancient Gnostics, and his book *Against The Heresies*, was, until the discovery of the Chenoboskion library in 1945, a main source for the doctrines of Gnosticism.

[18] See Gaston Etchegoyen's book on Santa Teresa de Avila.

[19] Pío Baroja of course despised cubism, an attitude I believe in keeping with his vaunted *probidad* and *estilo de reportaje*. In his essays *Rapsodias* he writes:

> Nuestros revolucionarios son como los cubistas: quieren hacer pasar cuatro tonterías manoseadas que ruedan por el mundo como genialidades de gran porvenir. (*Obras completas*, V, p. 925)

> Our revolutionaries are like the cubists: They want a few outworn stupidities floating about the world to pass as clever ideas with a bright future.

> La tal sexología es algo como el cubismo aunque no tan petulante ni tan necio ni tan absurdo como este sistema pictórico. (*Obras completas*, V, p. 926)

> The sexology I have mentioned is rather like cubism, although it's not as impertinent or as idiotic or as absurd as this pictorial system.

More will be said about Baroja at the end of this book.

Canto V

[1] Ugly, Catholic and sentimental, three adjectives: Remember also that Julio Casares speaks of a trifold adjectivization.
[2] The specific sin of the hermit Paolo in Tirso's *El condenado por desconfiado* is the opposite offense against Hope, namely,

despair. Don Juan and Paolo represent reverse sides of the same coin.

[3] "You have to choose," you have no choice not to. On writing these words I naturally thought of Pascal's *Pensées*; and in paragraph 7 I write: "You must make the wager."
I believe that the Montaigne-Pascal contrast is valid. If, like Montaigne, criticism holds back and engages in subtleties, it will not comprehend the ruthless system of Valle-Inclán. It must wager like Pascal, the Frenchman who disdained Montaigne.

[4] See above. I have already translated and quoted this passage from Pedro Salinas.

[5] At least I believe it's anonymous. I saw those verses in a red-colored intermediate textbook, back in 1956.

[6] I use the word *things* advisedly. Ordinarily it might be a dull word, too general, too easily come by, but I think in Valle it has a special meaning; Valle, who often speaks of "la forma indistinta de las cosas." A thing, or in a proximate sense the form of a thing, is a phenomenon, but as it draws away in time and space (e.g., cipreses milenarios, lejanos) it becomes indistinct, and the gnostic can descry the thing-as-it-is-in-itself, beyond phenomenal appearances. Thus Valle's use of *thing* is Kantian.

[7] The graveyards of churches are bordered by cypress trees; the branches of cypress trees are used as symbols of mourning.

[8] I would remind the reader that the word *strophe* not only means strophe, stanza or verse. It also means "the moment of the classical Greek chorus while turning from one side to the other of the orchestra;" and "the part of a Greek choral ode sung during the strophe of the dance." Thus *strophe* suggests poetry, music and dance, which lead to the gnosis.

[9] Valle's contemporary Azorín always uses *destacarse, enhestarse, levantarse* in a novel like *Don Juan*, instead of *estar* or *encontrarse*. Trees and monasteries, for example, always loom or rise up or come forth instead of merely being there. I shall discuss Azorín and his *lejanía ideal* in the last canto.

[10] See Julio Casares, *Crítica profana* (Buenos Aires: Espasa-Calpe, 1944). I believe that doctoral candidates should make a close study of Pythagoras, the Kabala, Jung's archetypes and other works dealing with numerology.

[11] The number five also stands out in the sonatas. The Princess Gaetani has five daughters, and in *Flor de santidad*, which reads like a rosary, there are five decades. Within orthodoxy, there are five first Saturdays dedicated to Mary the Mother of God. Valle is always apt to play with orthodoxy.

[12] Valle's adversaries, if they argued the same way he does, would scoff at his faith and call it self-deception.

[13] One might quote many similar lines, e.g.: "Al oír el canto de madrugueros gallos y el murmullo bullente de un arroyo que parecía despertarse con el sol . . . A lo lejos almenados muros se

213

destacaban, negros y sombríos . . . &c." *Madrugueros*: it is dawn, twilight, and a brook is dancing as it is awakened by the sun. Penumbral music, the sonata, the dance.

[14] The model of all sonatic women in Valle-Inclán is Eulalia, she of *Corte de amor*. Her adultery, melancholy and longing for death remind me of Denis de Rougemont's Manichaean thesis in *Love In The West*. This is not surprising, for Valle's *Lámpara maravillosa* is manifestly written in the spirit of Maní.

[15] I hesitate to use the word *value* here because of its association with anthropological relativism. I don't mean it in that way, I mean *doctrine* or perhaps *worth*. I say *value* here because I thought it made a nice contrast with *face value*, which has no relativist connotation. Elsewhere, I write *doctrine* instead of *value*. In any case, Valle was no relativist.

[16] The "something special" is a miracle, like a woman, a sonata or a dance. A musical miracle. One might here compare Don Quixote's Golden Age speech with the sonatas, and also look into the archetypes and unconscious of C.G. Jung. Don Quixote's speech strikes one as a sort of sonata.

[17] *Congal*, m.—in Mexico, a bordello or whorehouse. Valle feminizes the word, *congala*, in *Tirano Banderas*. (He also changes *cachizo* into *cachiza*.)

[18] To establish or to institute in the *Lámpara*. Just as Calvin wrote the *Institutes of the Christian Religion*, so we might call the *Lámpara* the *Institutes of Aesthetic Gnosis*.

[19]I am tempted to call Bradomín, and his Galician creator, a Quaker, Shaker, Ranter or Barker. Perhaps the title Shaking Druid will do. See Norman Cohn's book, *The Pursuit of the Millennium*.

[20] Formulaic verses are the sign of the code.

[21] See the section on *admiratio* in E.C. Riley's *Cervantes's Theory Of The Novel* (Oxford: Clarendon Press, 1962). Unamuno's novels and plays are also *exempla* of his philosophy. Perhaps this is a major characteristic of the authors of 1898, exemplariness.

[22] *Things* may seem to be a prosaic word, but Kant uses it, the Thing-in-itself, and Valle employs it frequently in the *Lámpara*. Even in the *Sonata de primavera* Bradomín says: ". . . mis ojos columbraron la forma incierta de las cosas" ("my eyes could descry the uncertain form of things.) This is a most sonatic sentence, with vague forms being seen from afar and surmised. The evidence is scanty in this phenomenal world; one must intuit (that is to say, *columbrar*).

Here is a passage from the *Lámpara* in which Valle uses the word *things* in the philosophical sense I speak of: "En este amanecer de mi vocación literaria hallé una extrema dificulted para expresar el secreto de las cosas, para fijar en palabras su sentido esotérico, aquel recuerdo borroso de algo que fueron, y aquella aspiración inconcreta de algo que quieren ser. Yo sentía la emoción del mundo místicamente, con la boca sellada por los siete sellos herméticos, y mi alma en la cárcel de barro temblaba con la angustia de ser muda." "During this dawn of my literary vocation I found it extremely difficult to express the secret of things, to put into words their esoteric meaning, that cloudy memory of what they were, and that indistinct aspiration of something they want to be. I felt the emotion of the world mystically, with my mouth sealed by the seven hermetic seals, and my soul in its jail of clay trembled with the anguish of being speechless." In this passage "the secret of things" is their noumena, they-as-they-are-in-themselves: and their "esoteric meaning" consists of our apprehension of the noumena. We have a dim sense ("a recuerdo borroso") of the noumena's existence, but this can only be approached mystically (in Valle "mystically" means "through art", which has eucharistic grace). Our souls are in a jail of clay, that is to say, in a phenomenal body with five senses, which can never comprehend the noumena, "the secret of things."

[23] See Manuel Machado's poem "La Primavera." in *Poesía, Opera Omnia Lyrica* (City not indicated: Editora Nacional, 1942), p. 56.

[24] For a study such as the present one on Valle-Inclán, I particularly like one dictionary definition of *teleology*: "A doctrine explaining phenomena by final causes." The final causes are not phenomenal.

[25] One might put it this way: The shadows in Plato's cave are apparently real, in all their profiles, and yet they are but phantoms. On the other hand, the Forms of things are not at all clear to us in the cave, they may even seem illusory, as seen in twilight, and yet they are substantial; they are what is real.

[26] Perhaps I should write "the cypresses" instead of "even the cypresses." For a gnostic who seeks the Light, Death is the great Liberator, so the cypresses would naturally be calm and ethereal. See the thesis of Denis de Rougemont.

[27] A diaphanous Sacred Host: I should remind the reader that the word *diaphanous* suggests extreme delicacy of form, or an ethereal, vague, insubstantial quality. María's hands point beyond the phenomenal world; I should say her feminine hands, for sex is the one thing we all have that is patently not merely phenomenal.

[28] It seems to me that criticism has tended to indulge in Menéndez Pelayo bashing, as if that most learned of men were a bagatelle. Perhaps this disdain is owing to his youthful attack on the *krausistas*, his belonging to an earlier stage of more literal, factual criticism, or his orthodoxy. But I believe the opinions of such a scholar deserve more attention. In his *Discurso Preliminar* of the *Heterodoxos*, Menéndez shows little esteem for the Reformation in Spain, and then writes: "En casi todos los heterodoxos españoles de cuenta y de alguna originalidad es fácil

descubrir el germen *panteísta*." Valle and Unamuno are certainly "heterodoxos de cuenta." It might be fruitful to study them in the light of the great polymath's opinion. See Marcelino Menéndez Pelayo, *Historia de los heterodoxos* (Madrid: BAC, 1956), p. 51.

[29] The word *órbita* might be translated as *sphere, orbit* or *field of action*. I have chosen the last because Bradomín's field of action is violent. *Sphere* and *orbit* would make fine translations, however, since they are in keeping with the thought of gnostic circles. Perhaps the best rendition would be "sphere of action," which captures both ideas.

[30] Since the *Lámpara* alludes to Miguel de Molinos (p. 105) and devotes a whole section to aesthetic quietism, I believe the following two statements are in order. (1) On the one hand, quietism is a devaluation. Valle purposely appeals to Molinos because he is heterodox, and his doctrine was condemned by the Church. (2) One should look to Molinos for guidance when studying Valle, because aesthetic quietism is the major theme of the *Lámpara* and hence of the sonatas. The chain of thought runs like this: phenomena, the uncertain form of things (see *Primavera*, pp. 42, 73), the poet's musical miracle, the eternal instant, immobility, immutability, apprehension of Beauty, quietude in union with the Alma Creadora, the Alma Mundo.

[31] See pages 42 and 73 of *Primavera*, where the uncertain form of things is mentioned; "y poco a poco mis ojos columbraron la forma incierta de las cosas," and "apenas si se distinguía la forma de las cosas." Ordinarily an artist like Valle would not employ a word like *cosas*, but here it has a Kantian meaning. In the agitated world of phenomena the form of things is not discernible, not even vaguely, whereas in a penumbral artistic setting they are discernible, though barely. With the help of the sonata, they can be grasped by the gnostic who is prepared to receive them. (The form of things can also be stated in Platonic terms: see End Note 25).

[32] Infused knowledge: this term comes from orthodoxy. Valle-Inclán's system often strikes me as a parody of orthodoxy.

Canto VI

[1] I have avoided extensive use of the phrase "Generation of 1898" because I feel the Generation metaphor has been abused in Spanish criticism (I even read once, somewhere, about a "Half Generation.") In the case of 1898 and 1927, however, I feel it can be helpful. On the negative side, the authors of 1898 criticized the old *casticismo*; on the positive side, there is somewhat less unity, although I believe Azorín, Unamuno and Valle had a *lejanía ideal*. Baroja of course despised metaphysics, ideal or otherwise.

Perhaps I shall use "Generation of '98" at times as a pronoun for Azorín, Unamuno, Antonio Machado, Baroja and Valle-Inclán.
[2] I am translating *segundón* as *nobleman*, whereas it is said of Cara de Plata, who is not the firstborn of his family but a lesser son. In other words, he is not the *mayorazgo*, who under the laws of primogeniture inherits everything. *Segundones* were apt to be adventuresome.
[3] Isabel II, the scandalous queen of Spain, had to flee the country in 1868. Carlos Marfori was her favorite during the last part of her reign and is noted for his persecution of the liberals. Sor Patrocinio was the *milagrera*, the miracle-making nun who had a large influence at court, and Padre Claret was a priest who also influenced the court. There is an apparent play on words here; *banco* means *pew* or *bank* as well as *bench*, and in one country at least, Chile, *pie* means not only *foot* or *foundation* but also a *down payment*.
[4] THE ENEMY of course means the devil, and in this passage he is Ernest Renan, whom the old bishop had seen once in Paris. In his *Life Of Jesus*, published in 1863, Renan had denied the divinity of Jesus Christ.

Canto VII

[1] *Foral* comes from *fuero*, which means the old code of laws, usually with special exemptions for a jurisdiction or province. *Foral* itself is an adjective meaning *statutory*. I interpret *forales* here to mean special forces representing or enforcing some old laws and customs: I didn't want to call them special forces because of the twentieth century connotation. The main point is that they knew the land as well as the guerrilleros and could be equally ruthless.
[2] The dates of the first Carlist War are 1833-1839. The dates of the second Carlist Civil War, which is the subject of *El resplandor de la hoguera*, are 1872-1876.
[3] Recall the graphic art of the *Poema de mío Cid: del cobdo destellando sangre*—"his elbow dripping blood"; and *nos arranca los ojos de la cara*—"he will pluck the eyes from the face."
[4] I wonder if one dare call the *Romance del Conde Arnaldos* a kind of sonata, pointing to the reality beyond the sea.
[5] The word *versolari* comes from Basque: (voz vascuence) m. Folk. improvisados versos en las reuniones o romerías de las provincias vascongadas. (Folklore. improvised verses at the gatherings of pilgrimages in the Basque provinces.) Valle-Inclán is calling the minstrels who sing the improvised verses *versolaris*.
[6] War is bloody, wizardly, grotesque, diabolical, and at the same time, aesthetic, beautiful, legendary, millenary: This sentence will account for Valle's statement that "Yo soy carlista por estética."

We have a similar sentiment in the United States, where the old South is an aesthetic favorite even though seven hundred thousand men died in the bloody Civil War.
[7] According to the *Diccionario de literatura*, edited by Germán Bleiberg, the *eneasílabo* is the verse of nine syllables: "No es muy corriente en la versificación española." And in the *Enciclopedia Universal Ilustrada*, under the article "Verso," we read: "*Eneasílabo* . . . Sea lo que fuere, su cadencia se desliza tan inadecuada al oído español, que yace, cuatro siglos ha, desterrado del Parnaso, omitido en muchas poéticas y apenas recordado por algún antojadizo escritor o prosaico fabulista. Casi no se aplica más que a los versos cantables, y en este caso lleva los acentos en la cuarta y en la octava sílabas. Los celtófilos, para apoyar su afirmación de que el eneasílabo procede de la poesía irlandesa, se fundan en un texto que, según parece, es una imitación de un manuscrito francés del siglo XIV." Perhaps the Galician Valle-Inclán employed the eneasyllable because he was a Celtophil who liked to amaze his readers.
[8] Doctoral students might investigate the versification known as *gaita gallega*, although these verses are usually decasyllables or hendecasyllables. See Pedro Henríquez Ureña, *La versificación española irregular*, 2a. ed. (Madrid: Centro de Estudios Históricos, 1933).
[9] I remember some verses I once saw, in Callao, Peru, in the British Cemetery:

> She is not dead,
> but on some road that mortals tread,
> gone some few trifling steps ahead.

The "camino de Francia" is not only the road to France, it is also the road that mortals tread.
[10] At the battle of Roncesvalles in 789, the rear guard of Charlemagne's warriors was wiped out. In the French *Song of Roland* this action is attributed to the Moslems, but it was really the deed of the Basques.

Bernardo del Carpio, the legendary hero of the *romancero*, defied Alfonso el Casto, who held his father prisoner.

Miquelo Egoscué's speech appeals to some of the oldest legends of Spanish history.
[11] One should note that when Valle writes "the light of the moon fell," he uses the imperfect tense, *caía*; the moon trembled, *temblaba*; the village boy *cruzaba, se alejaba*, and so forth. As I have noted in a previous chapter, the imperfect is more in the background, more distant, more vague . . . in a word, it is imperfect, less clearly defined.

218

Canto VIII

[1] One learns from Happold that William Butler Yeats translated *The Upanishads* (see Happold, p. 12). Perhaps there are some insights here for the *valleinclanista*. Yeats was also attracted to Madame Blavatsky, whose theosophy reveals kinship with Neoplatonism and the mysticism of Johannes Eckhart and Jakob Bohme. Her teachings may also throw light on Valle's *Lámpara*.

[2] A mystic like Raymond Lull of course, with his deep concentration on the Incarnate Savior, would oppose (I should say vehemently oppose) all impersonal talk about noumena, phenomena, primary awareness, the two realities etc. For him there is only one reality, a person, *El Amado*, and he is very annoyed that so many people have forgotten his *Amado*.

[3] As I say in the text, Happold's use of Kant's philosophy does not of itself make him a Kantian. Indeed, I gather he is not one. He also uses Bertrand Bussell's philosophy as an illustration of his argument although he is not a disciple of Russell.

[4] The book of William James, *Varieties of Religious Experience*, may throw some light on these mystical, or allegedly mystical, experiences. Indeed, some of Happold's examples are taken from James.

[5] The present canto, VIII, says quite briefly what all the other cantos say put together; nevertheless the other cantos seem necessary for a proper understanding. Valle's method is to write thirty rhythmic volumes rather than a syllogism, however correct and concise that syllogism might be.

Appendix I

[1] I believe the prejudice against authors like Menéndez and Pereda is not merely anti-Catholic but also comes from another source. For modern taste, these two are not skeptical enough, they are too sure of themselves and the joys of the next world. Tamayo of course is a lesser figure.

Fernán Caballero resembles Menéndez and Pereda, although in one chapter of *La gaviota* she displays noumenal tendencies.

[2] This is also a play on the Second Person of the Blessed Trinity, the Word of God. See Unamuno's *Cartas a Clarín*, where he frequently plays with theological language.

Appendix IV

[1] According to Plato, Beauty is all that in an object which excites us to love it. Perhaps this statement can be predicated of Valle Inclán's aesthetics. Even in a sanguinary guerrillero, in his *visionism*, Valle can find something lovable, something to attract us.

[2] Valle has his own *porque sí*. He knows that eternal reality exists because his heart tells him so, on aesthetic grounds, not on grounds of duty or moralization. Why? How? Because why, that's why, because. SPECIAL NOTE: I believe that E.M. Forster's article "Art For Art's Sake" will throw light on the position of Valle-Inclán. Forster argues that art is a world of its own and has an Order evolved from within. He rejects the claim of an ultimate Order in the social, political and astronomical categories. He allows for Order in the religious category on the evidence of the mystics. In the aesthetic category, which he clearly prefers, he admits the claim for Order on the evidence of various works of art. He concludes: "I do believe in Art for Art's Sake."

Valle's position is similar to Forster's. He scathes religious hypocrisy but seems to admire St. Bernard, St. Ignatius and the mysticism of ancient cathedrals and pilgrims. And he believes in Art for Art's Sake, the Order being apprehended in the "eternal moment." (See E.M. Forster, "Art for Art's Sake," *Harper's Magazine*, 1949, pp. 31-34.)

Appendix VI

[1] In the course of this essay I have used the words *garbancero, garbancista, garbancismo,* and *garbanceroísmo.* Perhaps they will need some modification. A purblind *garbancero* is a social engineer, a hylic, a Comtean positivist, who will merely describe Plato's recumbent position, whereas a gifted *garbancero* may be a great novelist, a Galdós. A *garbancista* would have a greater sense of finality than a purblind *garbancero.* These words will always have a certain jocular air owing to Max Estrella's use of *garbancero.*

BIBLIOGRAPHY I

In the present series of thoughts I have concentrated on the following works by don Ramón María del Valle-Inclán:

Aguila de blasón (Madrid: Espasa-Calpe, 1946).

Corte de amor (Buenos Aires: Espasa-Calpe, 1954). The story "Eulalia."

Claves líricas (Madrid: Espasa-Calpe, 1964).

Los cruzados de la causa (Buenos Aires: Espasa-Calpe, 1954). This is the first of the three novels known as the Carlist trilogy.

Flor de santidad (Madrid: Espasa-Calpe, 1978).

Gerifaltes de antaño (Madrid: Espasa-Calpe, 1960). This is the second novel of the Carlist trilogy.

La lámpara maravillosa (Buenos Aires: Espasa-Calpe, 1948).

Luces de Bohemia (Madrid: Espasa-Calpe, 1982).

La media noche. Visión estelar de un momento de guerra (Madrid: Espasa-Calpe, 1978).

Pipa de Kif. This is part of *Claves líricas*, ut supra.

El resplandor de la guerra (Buenos Aires: Espasa-Calpe, 1954). This is the third novel of the Carlist trilogy.

Sonata de primavera. Sonata de estío. (Madrid: Espasa-Calpe, 1975).

Sonata de otoño. Sonata de invierno. (Madrid: Espasa-Calpe, 1963).

Tirano Banderas (México: Editorial Porrúa, 1980).

Special note: Valle-Inclán, Ramón del. *Publicaciones periodísticas de don Ramón del Valle-Inclán anteriores a 1895* (México: Colegio de México, 1952). Edition and prologue of William L. Fichter.

221

BIBLIOGRAPHY II

The following works have been quoted or referred to in my thoughts on Valle-Inclán:

Abentofail, Abucháfar. *El filósofo autodidacto* (Buenos Aires: Espasa-Calpe, 1954).

Adams, Henry. *The Education of Henry Adams* (New York: Modern Library, 1931).

Alas, Adolfo. *Epistolario a Clarín* (Madrid: Ediciones Escorial, 1941). Includes the letters of Unamuno to Leopoldo Alas (Clarín), which are cited in the text.

Alonso, Dámaso. *La lengua poética de Góngora*, 3a. ed. (Madrid: CSIC, 1961).

_____. *La poesía de San Juan de la Cruz* (Madrid: Aguilar, 1958).

Augustine, Saint. *Confessions* (London: Penguin Books, 1975).

Azorín (José Martinez Ruiz). *Don Juan* (*Madrid: Espasa-Calpe, 1968*).

Baroja, Pío. *El árbol de la ciencia*, edition of Gerard Flynn (New York: Appleton-Century-Crofts, 1970).

_____. *Camino de perfección* Las Américas, 1952).

Bataillon, Marcel. *Érasme et l'Espagne* (Paris: E. Droz, 1937).

Baudelaire, Charles. *The Essense Of Laughter And Other Essays*. Edited by Peter Quennell (New York: Meridian Books, 1956).

Bédier, Joseph. (*The Romance Of Tristan And Iseult As Retold By Joseph Bédier* (Garden City: Doubleday Anchor Books, no date.) Copyright by Pantheon Books, 1945.

Benavente, Jacinto. *Los intereses creados* (Madrid: Espasa-Calpe, 1956).

Bergson, Henri. *La risa* (Buenos Aires: Editorial Losada, 3a. ed., 1953).

_____. *Le rire* (Paris: Presses Universitaires de France, 1958).

Caballero, Fernán (Cecilia Böhl de Faber). *La gaviota* (Buenos Aires: Espasa-Calpe, 1951).

Casanova, Jacques. *The Memoirs Of Casanova* (New York: Modern Library, 1929).

Casares, Julio. *Crítica profana* (Buenos-Aires: Espasa-Calpe 1944).

Cervantes, Miguel de. *La gitanilla*, in Cervantes's *Novelas ejemplares* (México: Porrúa, 1983).

Cohn, Norman. *The Pursuit Of The Millennium* (New York: Harper Torchbooks, 1961).

Coloma, Luis. *Lecturas recreativas* and *Pequeñeces*, in *Obras completas* (Madrid: Razón y Fe, 1960).

Cornélis H. and Léonard, A. *La gnosis eterna* (Andorra: Editorial Casal I Vall, 1961).

Craig, Gordon. *The Germans* (New York: Meridian Books, 1983). See Chapter 9, "Romantics."

D'Arcy, Martin C. *The Mind And Heart Of Love* (New York: Meridian Books, 1956).

Darío, Rubén. "A Margarita Debayle," in *Poemas de otoño* (Buenos Aires: Espasa-Calpe, 1951).

De Rougemont, Denis. *Love In The Western World* (Garden City: Doubleday Anchor Book, 1957).

Eco, Umberto. *The Name Of The Rose* (New York: Warner Books, 1984).

Etchegoyen, Gaston. *L'amour divin: essai sur les sources de Sainte Thérèse* (Bordeaux: Feret et fils, 1923).

Fichter, William L. *Publicaciones periodísticas de don Ramón del Valle-Inclán anteriores a 1985* (México: Colegio de México, 1952).

Flynn, Gerard. *Luis Coloma* (Boston: G.K. Hall, 1987).

_____. "Sor Juana Inés de la Cruz: Las trampas de la crítica," in *Sor Juana Inés de la Cruz; Selected Studies*, Luis Cortest, editor (Asunción: CEDES, 1989).

Forster, E.M. "Art For Art's Sake," *Harper's Magazine* (1949), pp 31-34.

Freud, Sigmund. *Moses And Monotheism* (London: Hogarth Press, 1951).

Frye, Northrup. *Anatomy Of Criticism* (Princeton: University Of Princeton Press, 1957).

García Lorca, Federico. *Bodas de sangre* (Buenos Aires: Editorial Losada, 1957).

Gobineau, Joseph Arthur, comte de. *Essai sur l'inégalité des races humaines.* Deuxième edition (Paris: Firmin-Didot, 1884).

Goethe, Johann Wolfgang von. *Las cuitas de Werther* (México: Espasa-Calpe, 1954).

Goldoni, Carlo. *The Liar.* (London: Heineman Editorial Books, 1963).

Gómez de la Serna, Ramón. *Don Ramón María del Valle-Inclán* (Buenos Aires: Espasa-Calpe, 1944).

Gooch, George Peabody. *History And Historians In The Nineteenth Century* (Boston: Beacon Press, 1968).

Green, Otis H. *Spain And The Western Tradition*, Volume I (Madison: University of Wisconsin Press, 1963).

Griffin, John Howard. *Black Like Me* (Boston: Houghton Mifflin, 1961).

Happold, F.C. *Mysticism, A Study And An Anthology* (Middlesex: Penguin Books, 1981).

Henríquez Ureña, Pedro. *La versificación española irregular*, 2a. ed. (Madrid: Centro De Estudios Históricos, 1933).

Huizinga, Johan. *Homo Ludens* (New York: Harper and Row, 1970).

James, William. *The Varieties Of Religious Experience* (New York: Mentor Books, 1958).

Jovellanos, Gaspar Melchor de. *Informe . . . en el expediente de Ley Agraria*, in *Obras escogidas*, volume I (Madrid: Espasa-Calpe, 1945).

Juan de la Cruz, San. *Vida y obras de San Juan de la Cruz* (Madrid: Biblioteca de Autores Cristianos, 1950).

Las Casas, Bartolomé de. *Brevísima relación de la destrucción de las Indias* (Buenos Aires: Mar Océano, 1953).

Llull, Ramón. *Del libro del Amigo y del Amado*, within his novel *Evast y Blanquerna*, in *Obras literarias* (Madrid: Biblioteca De Autores Cristianos, 1948).

MacCarthy, Desmond. Referred to in the *London Review of Books*, 1990-1991.

Machado, Antonio. *La tierra de Alvargonzález*, in *Poesías completas* (Madrid: Espasa-Calpe, 1969).

Machado, Manuel. "La Primavera," in *Poesía, Opera Omnia Lyrica* (City not indicated: Editora Nacional, 1942).

Maragall, Juan. *Elogios* (Buenos Aires: Espasa-Calpe, 1950).

Marañón, Gregorio. *Amiel* (Buenos Aires: Espasa-Calpe, 1955).

Maritain, Jacques. *Trois Réformateurs* (Paris: Librairie Plon, 1925).

Marti-Ibáñez, Félix. In the text I refer to a private letter he wrote me.

Maugham, Somerset. *Of Human Bondage* (New York: Modern Library, 1915).

_____. *The Summing Up* (New York: Pocket Books, 1967).

Menéndez Pidal, Ramón. *Flor nueva de romances viejos* (Buenos Aires: Espasa-Calpe, 1963). Read the "Romance del Infante Arnaldos."

Menéndez y Pelayo, Marcelino. *Historia de los Heterodoxos españoles*, Dos tomos (Madrid: Biblioteca de Autores Cristianos, 1956).

Montaigne, Michel de. *Selected Essays* (New York: Modern Library, 1949).

Newman, John Henry. *Grammar Of Assent* (Garden City: Doubleday Image Books, 1955).

Novalis (Friedrich von Hardenberg). *Enrique de Ofterdingen* Translation of Germán Bleiberg (Buenos Aires: Espasa-Calpe, 1951).

O'Faolain, Sean. *The Short Story* (New York: Devin-Adair, 1951).

Pascal, Blaise. *Pensées* (New York: Modern Library, 1941).

Pereda, José María de. *Sotileza* (Buenos Aires: Editorial Sopena, 1943).

Pérez Galdós, Benito. *Bailén*, in *Obras completas*, Tomo I (Madrid: Aguilar, 1950).

_____. *Zumalacárregui*, in *Obras completas*, Tomo II (Madrid: Aguilar, 1963).

Picard, Max. *The World Of Silence* (Chicago: H. Regnery, 1952).

Pirsig, Robert. *Zen And The Art Of Motorcycle Maintenance* (New York: Bantam Books, 1976).

Quevedo, Francisco de. *La vida del buscón*, in *Obras completas, Prosa* (Madrid: Aguilar, 1945).

Rand, Edward Kennard. *Founders Of The Middle Ages* (Cambridge: Harvard University Press, 1941).

Renan, Ernest. *The Life Of Jesus* (New York: Modern Library, 1927).

Riley, E.C. *Cervantes's Theory Of The Novel* (Oxford: The Clarendon Press, 1962).

Ripalda, Gerónimo de. *Cathecismo* (Madrid: D. Antonio de Sancha, 1783).

Salinas, Pedro. *Literatura española Siglo XX*, 2a. ed. (México: Antigua Librería Robredo, 1949).

Santillana, Marqués de. *Canciones y decires* (Madrid: Espasa-Calpe, 1954),

Sarmiento, Edward. His review of François Meyer, *L'Ontologie de Miguel de Unamuno*, in *Bulletin Of Hispanic Studies* 1957 (Vol. XXXIV), 54-56).

Schopenhauer, Arthur. *Parerga And Paralipomena* (Oxford: The Clarendon Press, 1974). The essay on "Suicide."

Spitzer, Leo. "On The Significance Of Don Quixote," *Modern Language Notes* (1962), pp. 113-129.

Stern, Karl. *The Flight From Woman* (New York: Paragon House, 1985).

Synge, John Millington *Riders To The Sea* (London: Heinemann, 1961).

Tirso de Molina. *El burlador de Sevilla*, in *Diez comedias del Siglo de Oro*, 2a. ed., edited by José Martel and Hyman Alpern (New York: Harper and Row, 1968).

_____. *El condenado por desconfiado* (Buenos Aires: Espasa-Calpe, 1943).

Unamuno, Miguel de. *En torno al casticismo* (Buenos Aires: Espasa-Calpe, 1945).

_____. *Niebla. Abel Sánchez. Tres novelas ejemplares* (México: Porrúa 1989).

_____. *Tía Tula* (Madrid: Espasa-Calpe, 1968).

_____. See also the entry under Adolfo Alas, above, which contains Unamuno's letters to Clarín.

Vega, Lope de. *Arte nuevo de hacer comedias* (Madrid: Espasa-Calpe, 1973).

Villiers de L'Isle-Adam, Conde de. *Cuentos crueles* (Madrid: Espasa-Calpe, 1948).

Waugh, Evelyn. *Brideshead Revisited* (Boston: Little Brown, 1946).

_____. *Brideshead Revisited*, A Revised Edition (London: Chapman and Hall, 1964). The author says: "I have modified the grosser passages."

INDEX

230

233

About the Author

In 1956 Professor Gerard Flynn began teaching Spanish at Rutgers University, New Brunswick, New Jersey, where in a 215 course he taught the four *sonatas* of don Ramón del Valle-Inclán. He became interested in these stories with Valle's mellifluous language and wrote a series of articles for *Hispanic Review*: "The Adversary: Bradomín," (1961); "Casanova and Bradomín," (1962); "The *Bagatela* of Ramón del Valle-Inclán," (1964). For the Vanderbuilt University Press he also wrote an article on "*Psiquismo*: The Principle of the *Sonata*," (1966). During the last thirty years Gerard Flynn has written books and articles on several authors and finds that Valle's gnostic art holds a key to all of them.

Flynn's favorite works of Valle-Inclán are the civil war trilogy, *La guerra carlista*, and the inimitable *Tirano Banderas*, which contains the elements of a tragically significant *commedia dell' arte*. As Flynn looks out over Random Lake, where he lives, thirty-five miles north of Milwaukee, he can visualize the valleinclanesque figures in the distance, on the opposite shore, the little *marinerito*, Miquelo Egoscué, the bloodthirsty *cura* Santa Cruz, el coronelito de la Gándara, Zacarías el Cruzado, and of course, the president of the republic, Santos Banderas. Visualization and evocation. Valle-Inclán's art, says Flynn, is one of evocation.

Books published by Gerard Flynn: *Sor Juana Inés de la Cruz, Manuel Tamayo y Baus, Manuel Bretón de los Herreros, Luis Coloma*, Students' Edition of Pío Baroja, *El árbol de la ciencia, The Bronx Boy* (novel).